HUMAN DIGNITY

Practices, Discourses, and Transformations

HUMAN DIGNITY

Practices, Discourses, and Transformations

Essays on Dignity Studies in
Honor of Evelin G. Lindner

Editors

Chipamong Chowdhury

Michael Britton

Linda Hartling

Dignity Press
World Dignity University Press

For inquiries about author interviews, in person or via the Internet, by Chipamong Chowdhury or Michael Britton, please contact Chipamong Chowdhury: chidhamma@gmail.com.

Published by Dignity Press
16 Northview Ct.
Lake Oswego, OR 97035
www.dignitypress.org

Cover design by Linda Hartling
Cover image: Microsoft Office Powerpoint Template

Book website: http://www.dignitypress.org/human-dignity

ISBN 978-1-937570-92-7
ePub edition: ISBN 978-1-937570-93-4
Kindle edition: ISBN 978-1-937570-94-1

Written as a loving tribute to
Evelin G. Lindner

Publisher's Note

This book embodies the spirit of *unity in diversity*, a fundamental principle that has shaped the life and work of Evelin Lindner. The contributors come from a wide variety of backgrounds and experiences, both professionally and personally. Rather than seeking uniformity, the chapters are presented in the writing style selected by each author. Though modestly edited to accommodate the design of the book, no effort was made to standardize this text. Every effort was made to remain consistent with each author's original manuscript.

Contents

Preface and Acknowledgements

Chipamong Chowdhury

With respect, admiration, and affection, we dedicate this volume of essays on "dignity" as our tribute and appreciation to our dearest Dr. Evelin Gerda Lindner for her dedication, devotion, and contribution to the study of dignity and humiliation. This volume in her honor is a small token of our deep gratitude and esteem. Her invaluable service in leading us to a deeper understanding of the relationship between humiliation and dignity in the context of social and political history and toward the goal of global peace, security, and a more egalized world for more than three decades have brought us together to honor someone who is worthy of honor by virtue of her life and deeds. All contributors in this volume, and in the field of dignity and humiliation studies in general, are profoundly indebted to Evelin in numerous ways. As a friend, colleague, admirer, and well-wisher, we all are directly or indirectly influenced and inspired by Evelin's abiding love, compassion and active kindness, but most importantly by the scale and substance of her work on human dignity. Michael's paper on the fond memories we share with Evelin is a keen testimony to this.

The area of dignity and humiliation has long attracted the interest of scholars, policy makers, and practitioners alike; however, our understanding of the nature and practice of dignity across diverse cultures and history still remains a focus for further exploration. With a tribute to Evelin, this book offers a multifaceted discussion of dignity from social, cultural, religious, legal, educational, psychological, and political perspectives.

Like every ambitious project, this project was stimulated by an idea. It began at the conclusion of the 28th Annual HumanDHS Conference, the twelfth in a series on Transforming Humiliation and Violent Conflict at Columbia University, New York, in 2016. Three members of the HumanDHS network, Gabriela R. Saab, Mariana Araujo, and I, were discussing a way to celebrate Evelin's sixty-third birthday. The idea of a commemorative volume began circulating between Gaby and me through enthusiastic text messages, phone calls and email exchanges. To materialize the project, we first shared the proposal with Michael Britton, Janet Gerson, and Judit Revesz of the network in January at the first meeting of a new dignity group in New York City, initiated by Michael, which we now call "DignityNowNYC." With their support, I next talked with Linda Hartling, Philip Brown, and Zuzana Luckay Mihalcinová and solicited their editorial supports, advice, and logistical guidance. They all have responded with great encouragement and offers of assistance.

This volume would not have been possible without the tireless efforts made by everyone involved in this project. I wish to say "thank you" to all contributors for their excellent and interesting essays: your articles made this volume what it is. My special thanks and appreciation to Michael Britton and Linda Hartling, who have been with me since the beginning of this project, helping me in every possible way to make it happen in a timely way. Most of the contributors' essays are proofread and edited by Michael Britton. I also wish to express my deep appreciation to Linda Hartling, Dignity Press Director, Uli Spalthoff, Dignity Press Director of Operations, and Zuzana Luckay Mihalcinová who took on the responsibility of publishing, imputing, typesetting and printing the work in this volume on a short notice.

I am grateful to Philip Brown, Tony Gaskew, and Michael Perlin who were always ready to help me. Some of the contributors' essays are also proofread, edited, and corrected by them. Finally, I am thankful to the academics, nonacademics and practitioner–members of the Human Dignity and Humiliation Studies network for helping me in numerous ways to make this volume celebrating Evelin Lindner's work a reality.

With palm joined
Chipamong Chowdhury/Marma

Foreword

Linda M. Hartling

This book is a celebration! It is an intellectual surprise party for Evelin Lindner in honor of her birthday. It celebrates the wisdom, compassion, and connected collaboration that flourishes in her evergreen, ever-growing sphere of love and dignity. It is a tribute to — and an appreciation of — Evelin's lifelong dedication to awakening and strengthening mutual understanding in the world. Evelin's life work offers us a river of renewable energy that flows from nurturing relationships that cultivate the dignity of all people and the planet.

By reading this book, we learn that Evelin is the rarest of visionary leaders. She is a global social scientist, a Da Vinci of academic inquiry, transformative thought, and collaborative activism. You will not meet a researcher or a leader who has had a similar life design. Her path has led her beyond the tragedy of her family's forced displacement during WWII to the highest levels of scholarship. All the while, her journey has been profoundly enriched by her capacity to form deep connections with countless individuals and communities throughout the world.

One might describe Evelin Lindner as a "resonant leader," as Mariana Vergara depicts in her chapter. Evelin's resonance is rooted in listening. She plants seeds of dignity by listening others into voice and creative action. She listens to the rising crescendos of social degradation, violent conflict, and environmental destruction that move human existence closer to sociocide, ecocide, and genocide. Her incandescent resonance and uncompromising courage define her as a dignileader who walks her talk with the highest integrity. Evelin Lindner has spent more than four decades leading people away from the toxic logic and reasoning that perpetuate the social ills of domination, disconnection, and oppression. She helps us understand the limits of Western individualism, dualism, materialism, economism, and patriarchy. She is listening for and leading us to new ideas for a new world, a world that provides for the equal dignity and participation of all people.

One way to know Evelin best is by knowing the community of connection that surrounds her, the Human Dignity and Humiliation Studies family of friends who share her journey. Each chapter of this book is a small sample of the garden of ideas and actions that have grown as a result of this community. Each chapter illustrates a new path for realizing humanity's need for dignity. Michael Britton's words remind us that Evelin "holds the world in her heart" as she shows us ways to transform cycles of humiliation with love, humility, and mutual dignity. Claudia Cohen prompts us to see the power of everyday dignity that can affirm the lives of all those around us. David Yamada delves into the qualities of the HumanDHS community as an organizational role model of deeply humane collaboration. Judit Réveze describes her personal story of Evelin's presence and support that brought light into her life, illustrating how Evelin is building a dignifamily of humanity one invitation at a time.

This book offers practical inspiration to all who strive to turn dignifying ideas into global action. Michael Perlin puts dignity at the core of therapeutic jurisprudence, offering a prescription for dignity energized by the music of Bob Dylan. Mariana Vergara reminds us of the transformative learning that can be found when we listen to the wisdom of indigenous cultures, wisdom that may save the world. Philip Brown teaches us that schools fostering mutual empathy and fairness build strong and healthy children, families, and communities for generations. Zaynab El Bernoussi challenges us to recognize the complexity of human rights and human dignity in a post-colonial world. Janet Gerson examines the potential that grows when we practice justice as global citizens in an interconnected world. Kebadu Gebremariam explores how respect for human dignity is a powerful restraint on human cruelty, when we have enough moral courage. Tony Gaskew challenges us to unearth the systemic humiliation imbedded in our criminal justice system, which can only be transformed by the light of truth and accountability. This book, as illustrated in Noriko Ishihara's chapter, explores the power of language, which provides the necessary foundation for communicating the message of dignity, perhaps the most important message of our time.

With the deepest gratitude, all of the contributors to this book recognize Chipamong Chowdhury as the sturdy human oak tree who provided the essential root of inspiration and motivation that made this book possible. He initiated and cultivated a mini "digni-community" that tenderly conspired to celebrate Evelin's birthday with this special tribute. Importantly, Chipamong understands that Evelin would never want to be idealized or put on a pedestal. In this book, he honors Evelin's superpowers of love and compassion and also honors our power to practice these superpowers. Chipamong Chowdhury applied and personified these powers in every step that led to the development of this book.

Finally, this book is a love letter written to Evelin and to future generations. Evelin Lindner teaches us that we have the capacity to save people and our only planet if we can accept our universal responsibility to become the heroes we wish to see in the world. She lovingly reminds us:

> Please know that your ability to think and reflect, and your ability to do this lovingly, is worth more than all gold and all diamonds of this world. Your wisdom and innovative creativity, your talent to lovingly envision different futures, all this is of unparalleled value. Your ability to see nuances, to turn around and look at all situations from many perspectives, is brilliant. Your willingness to extend your loving reflectiveness to all beings of this world is priceless. Your capability to seed our world with seedlings of loving care is wonderful. You are precisely the kind of thinker, the kind of responsible intellectual, the caring nurturer and gardener of humanity that we are in dire need of in these times of global challenges and crises![1]

1. From an "Invitation to a Future that Dignifies People and the Planet: New Definitions of Heroism" by Evelin Lindner, on Behalf of Humankind, August 12, 2017.

Chapter One

Introduction

Michael Britton

I have been asked to introduce you to Evelin Lindner, the person this book was created to honor. I can't think of a better first thing to tell you about her than this: Several years ago she invited me to join the Human Dignity and Humiliation Studies (HumanDHS) network and in the process changed my life, not just my thinking but my sense of what life is about and how to live — just as she has changed so many lives, always for the better. This is what she does. What she *aspires* to do is unleash the best in all of us, unleash our thinking, our imagining of our global future and our deepest longings for what it might be, so that together we change the life *of our whole world* to be much better.

Evelin scans the horizon of global possibilities for pathways to a better shared life. She is a path-finder and also a path-changer, actively working to get us off our present course onto one that will lead us to create historical times we'll actually like living in. In introducing you to this compassionate and generous visionary, I decided there could be no better way to make that introduction than to share her message with you in her own words as much as possible, and that's what I've done.

~

Evelin Lindner wants the more than seven billion of us on this

1

planet to see each other differently, treat each other differently, and become happier together. The key to this resides, she tells us, in living together without humiliating each other. Life is better when we tend to each other's dignity. She wants us to discover that we can feel at home with each other and at home sharing life together on this planet. She knows that feeling at home is no small achievement. It was not a feeling she grew up with in her own home.

Evelin was born in 1954 in Hameln, Germany, to a mother and father who had themselves grown up in different parts of Silesia. As a young man her father was drafted into World War II, lost an arm in the war, lost his brothers, and then lost the farm he expected to inherit. He and the woman he would later marry were among more than one million people of German descent who were forcibly relocated at the end of the war, losing the only homes they'd known, the only homes they ever loved. Evelin has written..

> I was born into a displaced family...and I grew up, not so much in my actual geographical and cultural environment, but in my father's imagination and stories of the farm that he had lost (which is now in Poland). I grew up with the deep-felt identity of displacement of "here, where we are, we are unwelcome guests, we are not at home, and there is no home to go back to." Most of my early years were characterized by the feeling of a lack, lack of belonging, lack of roots.

This was not a happy beginning to a life, and yet you can see in what follows how Evelin Lindner transformed a difficult past into an extraordinarily positive, productive, and generous life — and thereby models for our entire world the journey we can be on together. We, too, are coming from a very difficult past as a world. We, too, are capable of transforming what we've lived through into a life, a future, a world that is positive, productive, generous — and much happier.

This is a story of how, out of the experience of a home that was not a home, Evelin's life project and the insights she now brings to the world took root and grew:

My early years were deeply affected by the atmosphere in my family marked by this post-war trauma. During my studies of psychology and medicine, I spent several months abroad each year. I worked in hospitals and related institutions in Israel, Norway, Thailand, the U.S., China, and New Zealand. I was continuously in search for an answer to the following question: Is there a basic structure in human thinking, common to all cultures, which could lead to better global understanding?

On my path...I have learned that human beings all over the globe share deep commonalities and that we are thus perhaps much less divided than is often assumed. Over the years my intuition grew that, basically, all human beings yearn for connection, recognition, and respect, and that its withdrawal or denial, experienced as humiliation, may be the strongest force that creates rifts between people and breaks down relationships.

I believe that the desire for connection, recognition, and respect...unites us human beings, that it is universal and can serve as a platform for contact and cooperation. I suggest that many of the rifts that we can observe around the world stem from the humiliation that is felt when recognition and respect are lacking.

I do not believe that ethnic, religious, or cultural differences create rifts by themselves; on the contrary, diversity can be a source of mutual enrichment. However, diversity is enriching only as long as it is embedded within relationships that are characterized by mutual respect. It is when this respect and this recognition are failing, that those who feel humiliated are prone to highlight differences in order to "justify" rifts that were caused, not by these differences, but by humiliation.

[It was this] specific biography [that] made me acquire a profoundly global perspective and identity. The lack of a clear sense of belonging during childhood (being born into

a family of displaced people) made me particularly sensitive
to identity quests that urged me to learn about and become
part of the rich and diverse *world culture* that belongs to *all
of us*, as opposed to being part of any particular national
sub-culture.

School Years

After completing elementary and secondary school, Evelin graduated with distinction at the Mathematical and Natural Science Department of the Viktoria-Luise Schule. She writes of that time:

> Already as a schoolgirl, I was interested in the world's
> cultures and languages, and I eventually learned to famil-
> iarize myself (to various degrees) with many languages,
> among them the key languages of the world. My aim was
> to become part of many cultures, not only "visit" or "study"
> "them." I wanted to develop a gut feeling for how people in
> different cultures define life and death, conflict and peace,
> love and hate, and how all look at "others.

She then studied at the University of Frankfurt (in law, psychology
and Chinese) for a year and went on to study social and clinical
psychology, graduating from the University of Hamburg with the
equivalent of a Masters Degree in 1978. From then to 1984 she
engaged in medical studies in Heidelberg and Hamburg in Germany,
and in Dunedin, New Zealand.

During this time, her passion to explore other cultures and to live
more globally emerged in strength. She completed a two-month
course in practical nursing in Oslo, Norway; a two-month internship at the Department of Surgery at the Paolo Memorial Hospital
in Bangkok, Thailand (with a study of Thai culture and society);
conducted an information-collecting journey through Malaysia and
Indonesia with a brief internship at the University of Kuala Lumpur,
Malaysia; a one month course at the Environmental Health Center in
Dallas, Texas, with a one-month information-collecting visit to the

Navaho, Pueblo, and Havaupai Indians becoming acquainted with different Indian medical and psychological philosophies; a two-month information-gathering journey through China, visiting medical institutions in different parts of the country and becoming familiar with Chinese language, culture, and history; a three-month internship in Internal Medicine and in Psychiatry at Dunedin University Hospital in Dunedin, New Zealand, with a study of the culture and history of the Maoris; and conducted research on the role and rank of the medical profession, the concept of disease, and medical care as seen by different cultures with approximately 100 physicians from Thailand, the U.S., New Zealand, Australia, Singapore, Norway, and Germany.

She graduated as a physician at the masters level in 1984 and completed a medical doctorate in the field of cross-cultural quality of life research at the Department of Medical Psychology at the University Hospital of Hamburg. She then became a Doctor of Medicine in 1994 with a thesis on *The Definition of Quality of Life in Egypt and Germany*. Susequently, she was licensed as a psychologist in Norway in 1995 and as a physician in 1997.

The world of cultures had become her passion. To the degree that we all look toward one another with wonder, with interest, this alone would change our experience of who we are to each other and what our shared life on the planet can be like. But it takes something more as well. For Evelin this journey of cultural exploration was not only a matter of curiosity but a reflection of her desire to answer the questions her background had made so urgent: How is it we, who are so different, can become at home with each other?

How indeed, and why has it proven so difficult? The key obstacle began coming into focus in the years that followed.

Cairo Years

After graduating as a physician in 1984, she worked as a counselor at the American University of Cairo in Egypt and developed a private practice in Cairo for all strata in society: from wealthy to poor; Egyptians and non-Egyptians of many nations, members of

Western embassies, institutes and schools; managers of Western companies; partners in mixed marriages and their children, offering both psychotherapy and trans-cultural counseling, from 1984 to 1991. She writes of this time:

> I offered clinical psychology and counseling in English, French, German, Norwegian, and, after some years, also in Egyptian-Arabic. My clients came from diverse cultural backgrounds, many from the expatriate community in Cairo, such as Americans, Europeans, Scandinavians, Palestinians, and citizens of other African countries, as well as from the local community, both Western-oriented, and traditionally-oriented Egyptians. Part of my work was "culture-counseling," meaning that foreigners working in Egypt asked me for my support in understanding Egyptian culture, Arab culture, and Islam.

During this time, she began to understand more deeply what it means to be in an honor culture. "I was particularly impressed by the skills of the people in the Nile Delta in handling aggression; people typically behaved with a certain degree of tolerance and flexibility towards aggression, however, at the same time were able to confine its excesses." It was also during this time that humiliation as the obstacle to relationships came to be central to her thinking.

> I increasingly felt that the severity of rifts caused by humiliation called for research. I started designing a research project on humiliation in 1995/6, and conducted it at the University of Oslo, beginning in 1997, and concluding in 2001 with a doctoral dissertation in social psychology...The research project was titled "The Feeling of Being Humiliated: A Central Theme in Armed Conflicts. A Study of the Role of Humiliation in Somalia, and Rwanda/ Burundi, Between the Warring Parties, and in Relation to Third Intervening Parties." Throughout the main phase of the four years of research, I carried out 216 qualitative

interviews addressing Somalia, Rwanda, and Burundi and their history of genocidal killings. From 1998 to 1999, the interviews were conducted in Africa (in Hargeisa, capital of Somaliland, in Kigali and other places in Rwanda, in Bujumbura, capital of Burundi, in Nairobi in Kenya, and in Cairo in Egypt), and from 1997 to 2001 also in Europe (in Norway, Germany, Switzerland, France, and in Belgium).

The initial research questions were: What is experienced as humiliation? What happens when people feel humiliated? When is humiliation established as a feeling? What does humiliation lead to? Which experiences of justice, honor, dignity, respect, and self-respect are connected with the feeling of being humiliated? How is humiliation perceived and responded to in different cultures? What role does humiliation play in aggression? What can be done to overcome the violent effects of humiliation? Where can I observe cases of humiliation? If humiliation played a role after World War I for Germany, is humiliation just as relevant in more recent cases of war and genocide, such as Rwanda, Somalia, Cambodia, and so on? Is humiliation also relevant for relationships at even higher macro-levels, for example between "civilizations" or cultural regions such as was described by Samuel P. Huntington (1996)?

Since 2001, I have concentrated on building a *theory of humiliation*...I have in many ways contributed to creating a new multidisciplinary field in the academic landscape, namely *humiliation studies*...as entry point into broader transdisciplinary analysis. Humiliation...permeates everything, from micro to macro level, from the global and local political realms, to the inner workings of organizations and corporations, to our private lives, and reaches even into every person's inner dialogue and how we frame ourselves.

She had focused on issues of humiliation in her earlier counseling work in Germany, and was now seeing the toxic role humiliation plays in relationships between family members and between people from different cultures. She began to consider the possibility that it is humiliation that lies at the heart of violence, at all levels of life from the intimate and domestic to genocide to world warring — and that the only real path to a better future for the world lies in a collective journey out of the habits of humiliation into sustaining one another's dignity.

Something was changing in Evelin as she continued her counseling. The problem was that people from different cultures were coming to her, deeply upset with one another, because they were unable to find in their differences a bond of common humanity. She set out to help them discover that common bond. And in doing so she was learning the art and skills of translating cultures to one another — not with the intent of maximizing someone's profits or power, but in the spirit of psychotherapy. She was driven by a desire to help people who had been divided by not knowing each others' culture to discovering they really could understand one another, have a positive feel for each others' life experience, and do better together.

And so the groundwork for the next step in her life journey was laid. Her future work would center on translating cultures to one another and to themselves, giving dignity and context to experiences, hopes, sufferings, and conflicts, so this world of different cultures could find a common humanity together.

We need people who will get to know us and our cultures well enough to introduce us to each other so we find that bond of common humanity, as well as our capacity for making a better life together. We need people like Evelin who have learned how to translate us to each other in just such ways — and want to. During her Cairo years Evelin was honing the skills to take up just that task. Ever since she has been blazing the trail for a different kind of leadership for our world, the only kind of "global leadership" that can actually help us to become safe in each others' presence and happier thanks to all of us being here on this planet.

Global Activist

She was awarded the doctoral degree in 2001 and was teaching at the Universities of Oslo and Trondheim, as well as making presentations to the corporate sector on globalization and culture difference. She was leaving behind the life of individual and family counseling to become something of a therapist to the world's cultures in their need to discover each others' humanity. The first step took place in Germany.

> In 1991, I found myself again in Europe. Perplexed by the lack of a sense of global responsibility in Germany, I founded the NGO *Better Global Understanding* in 1993 in Hamburg...

Events had been unfolding in Germany that led to her creating an event in 1993 "to convert the idea of a *Global Village* or *World House* into an event or happening that would illustrate...our inescapable responsibility to care for [our world] together."

> In 1986, conditions in asylum-seekers' "homes" in Germany had become increasingly inhumane. The outburst of hostilities against foreigners in Germany eventually led to counter-reactions, for instance, the organization of *Lichterketten* (*Chains of Lights*), which became a familiar image to all citizens, when thousands of people demonstrated with candles against the discrimination [against] foreigners. Inspired by this image, and after many rounds of reflections, we developed our concept of a *Vision of a World House* on the big lake in the middle of the city of Hamburg, called *Alster*, and the *Thread of Human Solidarity* stretched around the *Outer Alster*, which, together were named *Hamburger Ideenkette* (*Chain of Ideas*). The *Vision of a World House* was created to remind all living in a globally interlinked world of the fact that we cannot dissociate ourselves from this interdependence.

The aim of the *Thread of Human Solidarity* (a 7 kilometers long red rope fixed on the trees of the park around the lake) was to invite the citizens of Hamburg to attach, like laundry, their ideas, opinions, thoughts, suggestions, letters to politicians, or anything else they wished to express in writing or painting to this thread. Moreover, the site around the *Outer Alster* was opened up to become the setting for whatever means of expression people would wish to develop, such as dance, song, performance, or theatre… [Evelin] invited the citizens of Hamburg to participate in the IDEENKETTE on many radio and TV channels that served the area of Hamburg. Articles in the printed media explained how school children [could prepare] for the IDEENKETTE, or [whatever] ideas people planned to present…The local radio was to contribute live music and comments so that the audience watching from the shores of the lake could enjoy this both as a visual and acoustic event.

About twenty-thousand people came. It was a Saturday afternoon. People came to the park around the *Alster* with two-thousand "ideas" that they had prepared in advance, "ideas" in prose, drawings, or paintings. These objects were attached to a red rope, the *Red Thread of Human Solidarity*, that the helpers of the association BETTER GLOBAL UNDERSTANDING had fixed on trees around the lake. The participants of this unique festival walked around the lake for many hours, both as actors and audience, reading and viewing the objects. Furthermore, many came who had conceptualized other happenings, such as meditation groups, drawing groups, or mobile musicians bands. People with cultural backgrounds from outside of Germany came with their indigenous clothes and music, and a groups of photographers asked foreigners and German citizens to walk ten steps together and agree to have their pictures exhibited in a subsequent exhibition. Yet another group, which stayed anonymous, had placed crosses with the names of those who had been killed in right-wing violence in Germany after 1945.

In June 1993, a selection of the objects that had been attached to the *Red Thread of Human Solidarity* were displayed in a first exhibition in Hamburg. In July 1994, these objects were shown to the public in an exhibition in Bonn that was organized by the Ministry of Foreign Affairs. Ultimately, the Museum für Hamburgische Geschichte accepted to store the objects in their premise

The project was a great success, with Evelin hoping that it would "serve as a blueprint for further comparable initiatives and not remain a one time event." Aspiring to play a larger role in furthering global understanding, in 1994 she also stood as a candidate for the European Parliament. But this would not be her path.

Life as a Global Citizen: Building the Ship While at Sea

In 2001 Evelin was teaching Conflict Resolution and the Psychology of Humiliation at the International Center for Cooperation and Conflict Resolution at Teachers College, Columbia University in New York, while being a guest lecturer at the Maison des Sciences de l'Homme and the Laboratoire europeen de psychologie sociale-LEPS.

> [While at Columbia] I met Morton Deutsch, whose work I had admired for years, and was deeply touched by the encouragement that he, together with Andrea Bartoli, Peter Coleman, and Betty Reardon, extended to me. They encouraged me to found an institute or center or global network for humiliation studies and affiliate it, among others, with the Columbia University Conflict Resolution Network, which...has been superseded, in 2009, by the Advanced Consortium on Cooperation, Conflict, and Complexity (AC4).

Since Evelin began to build the HumanDHS network in 2001, her original approach to all facets of this work has embodied her radical commitment to respecting everyone's dignity and to finding people around the world who share those commitments, encouraging them and linking them together.

This meant Evelin took a radically different approach to creating and being a network. Donald Klein was especially helpful in this regard, encouraging Evelin in the first tentative steps toward holding meetings as a network. Linda Hartling, now the director of the HumanDHS (Evelin continues as its Founder and its Ambassador to the World) soon joined Evelin, and together they became co-nurturers of a new way of being a network that is non-hierarchical, not money-driven, a humiliation-free zone as much as possible; a network where everyone is treated with respect and appreciation, disagreements are handled with appreciative inquiry, apology, and forgiveness are considered foundational skills in building relationships of enduring trust; and everyone is considered to be in need of everyone else's "listening [them] into voice." Together they have given birth to a different kind of network — and a different sense of how to build a future together.

A Global Network

What is a truly global network? You will notice that usually global networks comprise many members from the so-called "West," and fewer from the "rest." In other words, in a global network your first task would be to design your global life in ways that bring you to the "rest."

> When I began creating our HumanDHS network...I started out with inviting those people I already knew through my doctoral dissertation on humiliation. Since my dissertation was located in Europe, with strong links to North America, and my field work had brought me to Africa, we soon had members from Europe, North America, and Africa. However, Asia, and South America, to name just two regions, were not well represented. As a consequence, I accepted an invitation of friends of our network to use their

apartment in Japan as a platform to include more members from Asia into our network. In this way, I spent altogether three years in Japan, China, and Australia (2004-2007).

Conferences: Her intention to bring people from all over the globe into a shared network has been pursued on a number of fronts. Every December a conference is held at Teachers College in New York. But the vast majority around the planet cannot afford to come to New York even though their voices are essential to charting the future, and their energy and contributions would give that better future a chance to emerge. Evelin therefore decided that if the world cannot get to the conferences, the conferences could come to the world. Every summer, a second conference is held in some other part of the planet, organized with and by people from that area who want to create their own exploration of the themes of dignity, humiliation, and healing across cultures.

After the first conference held at Columbia in New York in 2003, subsequent conferences were held in Paris, France (2003, 2004); Berlin, Germany (2005); San Jose, Costa Rica (2006); Hangzhou, China (2007); Oslo, Norway (2008, 2012, 2014); Honolulu, Hawaii (2009); Istanbul, Turkey (2010); Dunedin, New Zealand (2011); Portland, Oregon (2012); Stellenbosch, South Africa (2013); Chiang Mai, Thailand (2014); Kigali, Ruwanda (2015); Dubrovnik, Croatia (2016); Indore, India (2017); Cairo, Egypt (2018); and Marabá, the Amazonian State of Pará, Brazil (2019), with future conferences planned, including Madrid, Spain (2020).

And, whenever a conference takes place in close proximity to indigenous peoples, Evelin has made it a practice to go to those peoples, meet them and their elders, and to bring their wisdom into the worldwide community that she has been nurturing into existence.

A Global Team Effort. From the first, Evelin very actively reached out to people from all corners of the planet and all disciplines who shed light through their own work, in their own way, on dignity and humiliation and creating a better quality of global life by transforming our world of cultures into a genuinely functional, cooperative global village. Early on, she believed that insights into what makes home a reality and what makes life good were to be found everywhere, among all cultures, and that our search for being better together depended on learning from all of us. She likes to say she, and we, are on the hunt for more Nelson Mandela's around the world.

Discovering people around the planet, she has invited them to become members of the HumanDHS's Global Advisory Board, its Research Team, its Global Coordinating Team, and/or to become Global Partners, and has prominently featured them on the network's website, with statements about themselves and their work. Every person there is cited in a spirit of appreciation for their spirit and their work. *It's all about making these facilitators of the future known around the planet.*

Spirit. While many members of HumanDHS are successful and recognized in their own fields, this is a network that recognizes the painful reality that many people worldwide who share our values (regarding dignity and humility rather than humiliation, and pulling together in the spirit of being a global village) are in fact not valued where they are, are not noticed, or are in danger. Many (by no means all) who are devoted to everyone's dignity are themselves impacted by difficulty or humiliation.

Our world so often honors other values while so frequently denigrating or threatening those who espouse these values that all of us can be vulnerable one way or another. As a network, HumanDHS is committed to recognizing the value and the courage each brings to this work, the gift each is bringing or trying to bring. Together we support each other in encouraging our world of cultures to dare to be better together. We are wiser, stronger and able to contribute more because we support each other. This is the spirit Evelin and Linda have encouraged throughout the network.

Nurturing a Network, Creating a Community. That spirit is an embodiment of Evelin's sense of her role in the network. Both she and Linda see their role as nurturing the rich, diverse range of contributors to the future who are not only providing good ideas but also are living those ideas, "walking the walk, not only talking the talk."

> In the early twenty-first century the world finds itself in transition from a traditional culture of coercion to a culture of creativity (though still in its infancy). Creativity will be central to building a sustainable future for the bio- and sociosphere of our human family.
>
> I do not wish our members to "subscribe" to my personal research approach, because this would diminish the full range of diversity. As a researcher, I am merely one among many, hoping that my approach is useful, and wishing to encourage others, through my work, to develop their own perspectives. As an enabling nurturer of our overall fellowship, I wish to bring to the fore the flourishing of a rich diversity of approaches to our topics of dignity and humiliation.
>
> In other words, I wish to sow as many global seeds as possible, and multiply our message locally and globally, at all levels, and in all segments of society, and this in a long-term fashion, not just as a short-term business, or project, or enterprise, or campaign.

She and Linda focus on sustaining among the membership a common spirit of mutual respect, appreciation for contributions whoever they come from, avoidance of humiliating others, taking care with each other even while inquiring into disagreements. Those who venture to view the world so differently from what it is today, and to try and make it so, need to be valued, encouraged and given a platform for their voice. This is what the network Evelin created strives to do.

But is "network" the right word for what Evelin and Linda have been nurturing into existence? The culture of "networking" so prevalent today communicates that your value lies in connecting with others who can empower your next steps, provide information or ideas that enable you to take a next step, or increase your status in the world of those who are listened to. While all this is of value, and can be found in this network, there is something very different that is at the heart of what we are developing together. And yet it's hard to say just what that is. Maybe it has something to do with not having to impress each other, with being valued for the depth of your presence rather than your position in the larger world. Maybe it has something to do with being welcomed into each others' hearts, if I can use that phrase. Whatever it is, everyone at these conferences remarks on how different this feels from what they're used to. Whatever it is, maybe it's captured in a question Evelin and Linda have been asking themselves lately. Maybe they should stop calling this a "network." Maybe they should call it a community.

And maybe that says something about how we can go from being the kind of world we are to the kind of world we would prefer to be living in.

The Web. Human Dignity and Humiliation Studies, www.humiliationstudies.org, is our presence on the web. This is our electronic platform for connecting with many others who are striving to sustain and support the transition of our world from a humiliation-centric way of being to a mutually-supporting, mutually-dignifying way of being a world is reflected in this website, of which Evelin is the webmaster. This is no small task, as she receives about a thousand emails a day from around the planet, in addition to keeping the site current and creating a web-presence for new members. To put it in context, Evelin wrote: "I regard our HumanDHS network as a seed for an alternative global community," and for the this community, that's what being on the web is all about.

Money is considered a key to survival in most organizations, not so here. From the first Evelin has believed that focusing on money sooner or later humiliates someone. Consequently there are no membership fees in this network, and no fees for participating in Conferences lest some who would want to be involved but could not afford the fee would thereby be humiliated.

People who do the work of the network are all volunteers, while

"Director of Dignifunding" Rick Slaven, maintains the books on donations, expenses, etc. At the New York conferences, the minimal expense required to hold the event is divided by the number of people there, and Rick presents the figures and makes it clear that while everyone can help defray that expense to the degree they can and wish to, no one should feel they need to do what they can't do. The biggest donation they make, he points out, is their presence. This is the kind of community Evelin wanted to bring into existence and, together with Linda, has achieved. While many an organization feels forced to be money-centric, this community is appreciation-centric.

World Dignity Press, World Dignity University

To further support members and others in putting their thoughts and work out into the world, Evelin conceived the idea of a publication branch of HumanDHS: Dignity Press and World Dignity Press (www.dignitypress.org). Ulrich Spalthoff took up the challenge and has become a key publisher of books for the HumanDHS community. In three short years, he has published books from more than twenty-six authors. The press is faithful to the values driving the network in that contracts are issued that first and foremost protect and reward authors as much as possible. We believe that those who create and contribute need to do so in dignity. Dignity Press aims to bring authors' contributions to the wider world in a way that respects them for the important work they do.

By way of making this kind of thinking more available to more people around the globe, Evelin conceived the idea of a web-based World Dignity University initiative (WDUi; www.worlddignityuniversity.org) that would partner with specific universities and professors wherever they may be, while making content available not only to institutions but to anyone anywhere. This is a work in progress, another vehicle for nurturing the seeds of the future across our world today.

A World of Diverse Cultures,
But One World All Together

Evelin...

> I believe that both my personal [maturing and thinking have been] nurtured by a growing awareness that humankind is *one single family*. As long as people lived rather apart, it was not seen as possible, for example, that people from different cultures could indeed *understand* each other. Cultures were regarded as a priori separate, and not as part of one single culture of homo sapiens, where people react to each other in relational ways, and altogether are perhaps more similar than different.
>
> My conclusion after three decades of global experience is that we, the human inhabitants of Earth, are more similar than different and that there is ample common ground on which we can build. I suggest that this common ground connects people and draws them into relationships, and, if this trend is cherished, respected, and nurtured, and if people are attributed equal dignity, it can help turn differences that separate into valuable.. sources of enrichment as opposed to sources of disruption.

Evelin, as one person who grew up in a home whose members felt homeless, grew to create this vision of what we all can be together, of how it is we all can be at home with one another and at home on this planet. The pain of the past need not define who we are or what we can be together. If this one person could make such a life journey, we can all, as a world, embark on that same kind of journey out of the painfulness and suffering of our historical past and present, and journeyed into establishing ourselves as a home for all of us. Evelin does not want so much a belief in her as she wants us to have a belief in ourselves — all of ourselves. She did it, we can do it too. Together.

On Being Helped

As Evelin herself says, over and over, she has become able to do all she does because all of us are involved with her. There are so many people who have helped and continue to help in so many ways that I dare not single any of them out in particular. From making computers work to arranging for invitations to hold conferences to mentoring her soul as she has gone forward, her gratitude is immense to one and all — and to an immense number of writers and practitioners worldwide. I will only mention a few mentors who stand out: Morton Deutsch, Donald Klein, Arne Naess, and Kjell Skyllstad. Beyond that, those of us who walk together with her on this path, inspired by her and inspiring her, are too many to name. Please consider that she is grateful to one and all. In her case, this is not simply words but rather a deeply felt reality. And in this too she models a key to transforming our world from its global fractures into global community. Gratitude to one another, appreciation for the gifts we bring to each other: With these attitudes we become the different, better world we long to be living in.

A Global Citizen

Evelin calls no one place her home. She has no "home base," but considers the whole world her home. She refers to herself as a global citizen, a citizen of planet earth:

> I am often asked: "Where are you from?"...I explain that the usually expected answer, in my view, is prone to undermining world peace and that I therefore have developed an alternative answer.
>
> I avoid saying sentences such as "I am..." and then complete this sentence with the name of a nation, or the name of a profession, or a gender label. Why? Because my essence is not to belong to a nation or a profession or a gender category. My essence is to be a living creature and human being. This is my primary identity. This does not

mean that I am not in love with or attached to certain places or people more than to others. But all these attachments are secondary. The core essence is to be a fellow human being of all other human beings on our planet, ready to shoulder our joint responsibility for our tiny home planet.

In my view, my intuition that humiliation, a deeply relational concept, plays a core role in a globalizing world is deeply anchored in my global life..

Few people from the rich West try to enter into deep relationships with the rest of the world. Even when they travel, they pay *visits*, from *my* country to *your* country, and maintain the illusion that the West is somewhat independent from the rest and that discord can be attributed to cultural differences, to *them* and *their* (backward) culture, or *their* unfathomable evil motives. Many travelers overlook that the rest of the world is deeply connected with its rich parts and that this relationship is probably more relevant than cultural differences. And, this relationship may be characterized by feelings, such as admiration, or envy, or, when we talk about serious disruptions such as terrorism, by feelings of humiliation.

Even though having a "global horizon" is on the increase, still most people respond to the question "where are you from?" with the name of a country. This outlook entails a framing of the world in terms of *my* people, *my* history, in relation to *your* history and *your* people. In my case, I have developed an identity of being a citizen of the global village, and thus *all* people's history is *my* history and *all* people are *my* people.

Developing a global identity does not mean erasing local identities. On the contrary, it means adding a global layer on top of local layers of identity, and at the same time strengthening those local layers. It means "harvesting" from all cultural spheres their wisdom in support of Unity in Diversity.

I wish to strengthen both global and local identities. However, this can only have benign effects, in my view, when it is clear that our shared humanity, our common mindset of humility, and our mutual respect for equal dignity for all, trumps the seed of division that can lurk in diversity.

I feel responsible for not repeating atrocities perpetrated by Stalin, or Hitler, or any other dictator...My history is all humankind's history, and I wish to carry the shame and disgust for the destruction that all humankind ever perpetrated, and shoulder the responsibility to build a better world for all of humankind.

I cherish the beauty of humankind's cultural achievements, in all cultures. They are my aesthetic homes. What hurts me deeply is the fact that these achievements are not necessarily valued and visible locally. Currently, the desire for higher status, often translated into an urge to imitate the wealthy West, leads to a degree of global ugliness and dysfunctionality that often crowds out local beauty and functionality. This state-of-affairs pains me deeply..

By searching for the often unfulfilled potential for beauty and functionality, I try to enjoy and nurture this potential for more diversity.

There are still few people around with such broad backgrounds and global anchorings, yet their number is increasing and more and more people are drawn into this trend at least to some extent. Thus, my perspective and standpoint is not only particularly "global" but also future-oriented. My experiences and analyses will probably become more common in the future.

How can anyone tell the world stories of what is happening, on the ground, in everyday life as well as "at high levels," in cultures elsewhere, everywhere? Without such stories, we are only abstractions to each other. I think only those who move around inside the global village, spending time living with people in one neighborhood and then another, can really do this.

I think people like Evelin, who are rare, hold the world in their hearts. Because of this they can hold us and our possible better future in their hearts in a real way, not an idealized or rhetorically-correct way. This is what Evelin does thanks to her sharing lodging with people in such different places, moving around the world. I think people who do this can bring us to each other via the stories they can tell, so we can learn to trust and appreciate one another, along with the possibilities of organizing our shared existence on this planet to work better for all of us — because we now hold each other in our hearts.

All of this is possible only because, as she moves around, she is taking people, with their lives and historical and cultural situations, into a heart that wants everyone to do well together. Hers is a heart bent on making life together rather than on dividing some against others. This is the attitude of heart she searches out everywhere and tries to evoke in all of us. Because it is in this attitude of our hearts, worldwide, we can make a future, a tomorrow morning, we all want to be living in.

On Being Home

Evelin…

Today, I design my life as a global citizen without a house of my own, living in the "global village," being housed by our HumanDHS network and supporters of our work, living digitally (not using paper), and with a minimum of possessions. Wherever I go, I search for three gifts: 1) a loving context in a family home, I avoid hotels, 2) a mattress, since I work with my laptop on my knees, 3) if possible, a reliable online access, since I am the webmaster of this website and the nurturing of our work is done via email. I decline being full-time part of any local institution. I wish to stay globally flexible.

I cherish being part of many families around the world

and living many parallel lives. I never look for "a place to stay," but always for "a way to be part." Having an extended global family, with members from many cultural backgrounds, all with diverse sets of perspectives on the world, teaches me firsthand understanding and respect for the diversity in our world. This is what helps me to bring my life to scale with the global challenges that we, as humanity, face.

It is important for me to make clear that my global life is not a homeless or restless life. I do not even use the term "travel," since I live in the global village and in a village one does not travel, one lives there, even if one moves around in it...I am at home wherever I am, and this is not an idea, it is not a hope, it is my personal and deeply lived experience.

The result is a profound anchoring that I feel in the world. And it is not just my imagination that gives me this feeling. My way of presenting myself as a fellow human being, indeed opens hearts and minds of many people I meet around the world to our human commonalities. Their warm-hearted love that they then extend to me is what anchors me in this world and gives me a deep sense of belonging and roots.

I refrain from defining a small geographical locality as "my home" and the rest as "not my home." My home is the entire global village, all of humanity, all the people living in that village. I do not see my life as nomadic, and, as mentioned above, I do not resonate with the notion of travel...I prefer to "stay still" in the realm of love...I move between different relational contexts of love and "a place to stay" is secondary to being embedded into relationships of mutual care. In other words, I see myself being much more "still" and true to "my place," namely love...

My new-won global identity has healed my trauma of displacement and painful search for "who am I?" and "where do I belong?" The trauma of displacement that my family suffers (together with millions around the globe who ask "where do I belong?") can, to my view, best be healed by inviting all attachments and losses that are locally defined into the global care for a sustainable bio- and sociosphere for the entirety of our human family.

In the end, this seems to be the most important thing about Evelin, her spirit of love, the depth of her heart, her responsiveness to love and to the pains of the world that cry out for love and for tapping the ability to respond to each other with love.

On the Nature of Research

Evelin:

In order to understand a globalizing world, we need "global" research, as well as the participation of researchers who have a global outlook and global experience. In my case, a specific biography of displacement made me acquire a profoundly global perspective and identity. As a result, in my conceptualization, psychology is embedded within broader historic and philosophical contexts and is profoundly intertwined with global changes. The aim is to avoid single interest scholarship, work transdisciplinarily, and probe how even local micro-changes may be embedded within larger global transitions.

Historical trauma can be the springboard to historically transformative creativity. The past is a curse only if we let it be. We are a species meant to morph trauma into the world we need to be living in. And we need the researchers among us to help us do just that by studying closely what it is we need and how we can get from where we've been to the home we've needed all along.

Earth

Many indigenous peoples have developed cultural

knowledge of how to utilize a wide variety of resources of their land, knowledge that may become as important for humankind as biodiversity, which in turn often depends on cultural diversity.

As to planet Earth's resources and the fear that there may not be sufficient resources to support billions of global citizens, to my view, again, humankind has to sit together, gauge the "carrying capacity" of "spaceship" Earth, and design public policies, together, to reach a balance. There are many strategies available, from educating women (among other reasons to alleviate them from having to produce too many children as a form of old-age security) to more creativity with regard to technological solutions for producing energy and food, and so forth. Basically, the solutions are on the table already. What is lacking, at the current point in history, is the "political will," around the world, to implement solutions. In other words, we observe a lack of informed citizens, citizens who push politicians to take care of the common good of all humankind instead of losing this focus in struggles at local levels.

The ecological footprint of a global life does not have to be large. I have moved about not just by plane, but by foot, bus, ship, and train; I know the desert on horse, donkey, and camel; I also have trained to build and fly simple gliders. And there is no need to become a hyperglot like me either; I have successfully communicated by simply being human. Global citizenship is also no intrinsic part of casino consumerism. On the contrary. It can be used as a path to avoiding unnecessary consumerism and bringing indigenous gift economy to the entire human family.

On Danger and Hope

The most significant danger at the current point in

human history stems from the risk that the path toward a culture of dignity may be hampered by ubiquitous feelings of humiliation, which, when translated into retaliatory acts of humiliation, might send humankind back into the past of a divided world. I call this risk the danger emanating from "clashes of humiliation" (rather than Huntington's "clashes of civilization"). Clashes of humiliation need to be healed and prevented, not taken as pretext to turn back into the past.

[Building blocks] for hope are, among others:

1. Knowledge as the resource for livelihood. This offers a win-win frame that is more benign than the win-lose lose frame that is forced into the foreground when limited resources such as land are the main resource.

2. All humankind defining itself as one single in-group is more benign than many out-groups confronting each other.

3. The ideal of equal dignity for all invites everybody into developing their full personal potential; no longer need there be underlings serving as tools in the hands of their masters.

4. Cooperation with everybody is more constructive and benign than cooperating only within one's in-group to keep out-group enemies at bay.

5. Avoiding, preventing, and healing humiliation has a higher probability of succeeding than [focusing on security issues as we normally think of them].

Enlarging the Vision

It is not possible in this short piece to list all of Evelin's publications, all the presesentations, the committees she sits on, or the awards received. All of this is on the HumanDHS website. She has now five published books exploring the realities of humiliation and the possibilities of dignity: *Making Enemies: Humiliation and International Conflict*; *Emotion and Conflict*; *A Dignity Economy*; *Gender, Humiliation and Global Security: Dignifying Relationships from Love, Sex, and Parenthood to World Affairs*; *Honor, Humiliation, and Terror: An Explosive Mix and How We Can Defuse It With Dignity*. Even as this chapter is being written, she is writing a new book, *From Humiliation to Dignity: For a Future of Global Solidarity*.

Evelin's writings are original in vision, marked by clarity of moral perception seamlessly interwoven with deep compassion for all parties, careful to humiliate no one while summoning all of us to make a better world together, to be responsible for our shared future. She places the issues that divide us along fissures of humiliation, hate, and mistrust into much larger contexts we have forgotten or not recognized, historical contexts that extend backward for tens of millennia which set us up for mistakes and suffering we no longer wish to endure. She poses a future we long for but frequently don't dare to embrace. It is cultural systems and mistaken ideas, and the unhelpful habits of the heart they foster, that are the obstacle.

She wrote that "Bertha von Suttner (1843–1914), a pacifist, and the first woman to be a Nobel Peace Prize laureate...showed the way to creating future-oriented organizations by placing them in the future as much as possible and as close to the present as little as necessary."

This is what Evelin Lindner does, over and over again: creating a vision of the future that is as little moored to the mistakes of the present and is as much located in the future. This is the world that we would all prefer to be living in but could not have imagined until she spelled it out.

What comes through in her work is the goodness of her spirit. She would respond to that comment by immediately pointing out that she is better because of the goodness in the rest of us. The goodness we see in her is the goodness that resides within all of us, and that that goodness has the power to make our lives together so much better if we but trust this place within ourselves.

In the end, this daughter of displacement speaks to us of love of home, where everywhere is home to all of us. She speaks to us of taking care with real life and our real future, as these are our home. She writes and speaks of compassion and the realities of suffering, of hope, of generosity and mistakes, of the dangers of violence and of the consumer/wealth way of being a world. She mourns the losses of traditional ways of life worth keeping — from foods to clothing, languages and relationships — and talks with us about the ultimate importance of nature, of this planet, to all our lives. Embrace vulnerability, she might say, embrace compassion, and let go of humiliating and feeling humiliated. As one of her treasured mentors, Donald Klein, would say: "See through all of 'what is' to the deep gift of being here in this miracle that is life."

Final Words

I would like to leave you with a few closing thoughts from Evelin..

Today, social and ecological resources are being hollowed out all around the world. I do not want to stand *by*, I want to stand *up*. To do so, I have to identify with *all* of humankind, I have to make *all* of humankind my primary identification, and relegate local identities to an important, but secondary place.

Elements that violate equal dignity and/or are divisive can no longer have a place. Cultural diversity needs to be boosted in today's world — it is as crucial to protect and nurture cultural diversity as biodiversity.

We, as humankind, need to sit together and think through how we can protect not only biodiversity, but also cultural diversity.

I wander in the global village because I wish to do more than decry the world's ineptitude in addressing its global challenges. I wish to adapt my personal life to the world's global challenges, bringing my life "to scale" so-to-speak.

My personal desire is to nurture as much as possible

our shared vision of building a world which transcends humiliation, a world in which we hold hands in mutual respect for equal dignity. I wish to contribute by building relationships of shared leadership. With the HumanDHS network and fellowship, and the humiliationstudies.org website, *we wish to invite everybody to contribute as equals, as equals in dignity.*

[Citing Joseph Campebell] If you follow your bliss, you put yourself on a kind of track that has been there all the while, waiting for you, and the life that you ought to be living is the one you are living. Wherever you are — if you are following your bliss, you are enjoying that refreshment, that life within you, all the time.

I see myself as a paradigm shifter toward love, on the background of the humility of awe.*

---

* The words of Evelin Lindner have been culled from the HumanDHS website: www.humiliationstudies.org. For their fuller context, see her writings there.

Chapter Two

Growing Human Dignity and Humiliation Studies: Without Falling Prey to Neoliberal Norms

David C. Yamada

Introduction

Since its inception in 2001, the Human Dignity and Humiliation Studies network (HumanDHS) has been forging a global learning community of scholars, activists, practitioners, artists, writers, and students devoted to the advancement of human dignity. This unique assemblage brings together individuals from around the world, physically and virtually, through conferences, workshops, publications, courses, webpages, and online communications. Blessed with neither monetary wealth nor its own brick and mortar building, HumanDHS nevertheless enjoys a welcomed place in the lives of its community members.

For many associated with it, HumanDHS provides a source of genuine fellowship and support for our work. This quality is especially welcomed in an era when exercises of raw abuse and greed are so prevalent, traditional institutions can be so alienating, and the dominant social, economic, and political climate often feels ominous and threatening. It follows that our connections with this community invite us to consider how we might grow it so that human dignity serves as a stronger foundation for our world society.

This essay explores some of the opportunities and challenges that may arise as part of a concerted effort to expand HumanDHS as an influential voice for positive change. It will first assess the current state of HumanDHS and its core community. Next it will examine the neoliberal norms that confront any nontraditional learning community dedicated to advancing human dignity. It will then contemplate the potential growth of HumanDHS and the challenges we face in expanding the network's reach and influence. Ultimately, I hope this will serve as a supportive and constructive invitation to consider the future of HumanDHS and the human dignity movement in general.

Human Dignity and Humiliation Studies: Mission, Philosophy, and Structure

Founded by Dr. Evelin Lindner in 2001, the HumanDHS network is a global, "mutually supportive learning community designed to foster the growth and development of all involved" (Hartling, Lindner, Britton & Spalthoff, 2013, p. 138). From the outset, HumanDHS has embraced the cultivation of "mutually dignifying relationships" as "its highest learning priority." Accordingly, equal dignity has been "wired into the infrastructure of learning and practice," with the network "organized to be dignifying by design." Evelin has likened this process to "building a ship while it is at sea."

In terms of leadership, Evelin (Founding President) and Linda Hartling (Director) serve as primary officers and guiding spirits. They are assisted by fellow members of a small board of directors comprised of individuals who have been associated with the network for many years. With no paid staff, board members and core members of HumanDHS perform the essential work tasks of the organization on a pro bono basis. Decision-making tends to be rather informal; the board normally meets only once a year, in conjunction with the HumanDHS December workshop described below.

In addition to officers and board members, HumanDHS has

assembled a Global Advisory Board of over 300 individuals and many smaller working groups that contribute to the heart of this community. In total, more than 7,000 individuals have been invited to become part of the HumanDHS circle, which includes approximately 1,000 active members. HumanDHS is a tax-exempt, non-profit entity, but it undertakes very little formal fund-raising activity beyond figuratively passing the hat at its events. Even its website does a good job of concealing the link to its Paypal-hosted donations page (Hint: Look for the "DigniFunding" link at the bottom of the home page.). Although budget and fund-raising figures are not publicly circulated, I can verify as a member of the Board of Directors that the organization's annual revenue qualifies for the "extreme grass roots" category. The de-emphasis on raising money is intentional. The leaders of HumanDHS do not wish to burden themselves with the demands of fund-raising chores, choosing instead to concentrate on more substantive work, even if it means operating on a shoestring.

Indeed, HumanDHS's many activities seem improbable given its modest funding base. They include two larger events, a non-profit publishing house, and a unique university learning initiative, as well as a steady stream of books, articles, papers, and studies. Two major gatherings each year, a December workshop at Columbia University in New York City and a conference held in different locations around the globe, serve as primary catalysts for bringing together members of the community. A defining characteristic of these events is a series of interactive "dignilogues" using these two formats: (1) panel-like groupings of short presentations by individuals invited to discuss their work, followed by questions and discussion; and, (2) breakout sessions on topics chosen by participants, followed by short presentations to the full conference from each breakout group. Addresses, talks, music, artistic work, awards, and an open public event are also mixed into these programs.

The two-day New York City workshop is built around the theme "Transforming Humiliation and Violent Conflict," joined by a major sub-theme, recent examples being "The Globalization of Dignity" (2016), "Honoring Alfred Nobel's Message" (2015), and "Work that

Dignifies the Lives of All People" (2014). Upwards of sixty to seventy-five people participate in this workshop, including a fair number who travel from outside the U.S.

The annual conference features a variety of themes and formats, with a heavier programmatic emphasis placed on the specific location. Recent conferences have been held in Indore, Central India, 2017 (theme of "Dignity in Times of Globalisation"); Dubrovnik, Croatia, 2016 ("Cities at Risk — From Humiliation to Dignity"); and Kigali, Rwanda, 2015 ("A Life of Dignity for All"). Typically the annual conference draws several dozen participants.

Especially for the most active members of the HumanDHS community, the two annual gatherings help to foster lasting connections and friendships. Many regard them as welcomed sources of fellowship and mutual support. The framing values and practices of respectful dialogue and appreciative enquiry help to create a norm of thoughtful exchange, even when inevitably hard differences of opinion arise amid discussions of difficult topics.

Another major HumanDHS undertaking is its dual-division publishing house, Dignity Press and World Dignity University Press, launched in 2012 to offer publishing options for members and friends of this community. As of summer 2019, it has published twenty-two books under the Dignity Press label and eight books under the World Dignity University Press label, mostly on topics related to human rights and human dignity, often in a global context.

A third major endeavor is the World Dignity University initiative (WDU), started in 2011. WDU is an evolving collection of educational offerings developed and offered in partnership with other individuals and institutions, all under the broad rubric of human dignity studies. WDU embraces the dignifying of both the processes and content of education, thereby recognizing that positive learning experiences relate directly to the sharing of insight, understanding, and knowledge.

Many members of the HumanDHS community are active writers, researchers, and scholars on topics related to human dignity, producing a wealth of books, articles, papers, studies, and social media entries. This body of work is difficult to measure quantitatively. Among core members of the community, Evelin Lindner is a prolific writer and scholar. Linda Hartling publishes frequently as well. Michael Britton and Ulrich Spalthoff often join them in coauthoring articles and book chapters.

Dozens of other members of the community produce scholarship and creative work related to human dignity. However, not every publication or project inspired or guided by HumanDHS lists or includes this affiliation, and the leadership of HumanDHS makes no attempt to covetously "own" or claim such work on the group's behalf. Accordingly, it is fair to assume that HumanDHS's intellectual and creative influence stretches far beyond those works that expressly mention it.

In terms of network communications, HumanDHS sends out a periodic e-newsletter containing news items and event announcements. Its filled-to-the-brim website is heavy on substance and serves as an online organizational archive of sorts. However, the website does not have any interactive forum components, and existing blogs and social media pages are only intermittently active.

In sum, Human Dignity and Humiliation Studies has grown into an authentic, deeply humane, and morally grounded community of individuals who are committed to creating a better society. Operating efficiently on a modest scale, as a collective network it embraces the challenge of walking its talk. It is that rare institutional entity that helps us to become better people as we try to make a difference in our respective spheres of activity and influence.

Thus, at first blush, it may seem obvious that HumanDHS should expand its reach by bringing its words and deeds to bigger and broader constituencies. Could it be as easy as growing this model of dignity and caring until it takes over the world? Before we ponder this possibility, it may be useful, though sobering, to look at the prevailing status quo in the world of learning and ideas.

The Neoliberal University and Ideas Industry

HumanDHS exists against the backdrop of a higher learning paradigm that has become increasingly immersed in a neoliberal value system. Market competition, commoditization, prestige obsessions, and accompanying assessment and outcome measurements are its dominant features. Thus, amid the conventional realms of academic discourse, scholarly research, and adult education, HumanDHS's self-styled learning community stands as something of an outlier.

The very neoliberal economic values that have profoundly shaped global society during the past half-century have now gained a foothold in the world of ideas and higher learning. Leaders of higher education institutions talk of running their schools in a more business-like fashion, emphasizing returns on investment as reflected in post-graduate salary reports. Vocational disciplines are on the rise, while the liberal arts are in decline. Colleges and universities are increasingly evaluated and compared by so-called objective measures, such as rankings regularly sponsored and published by *U.S. News & World Report* and *Times Higher Education.*

Scholarly work has become commoditized, especially publication in academic journals. Within many scholarly circles, the worthiness of an article is measured in impact factors, citation counts, and prestigious journal placements. Hiring decisions for full-time academic appointments are grounded heavily in scholarly records and reputations built on these metrics. In many disciplines, access to scholarly research is limited by expensive subscriptions and online paywalls.

In addition, academic conferences, workshops, and symposia often buttress this value system. Donald Nicolson concludes his assessment of this realm with "the argument that academic conferences are a (neoliberal) commodity; that is, they are something of use/value, being bought and sold" (2017, p. 66). Building on this point, he asserts that conferences serve as marketplaces for knowledge, compete with other conferences for attention and participation, and reinforce the core notions of the neoliberal academy.

I find these tendencies especially in play at the flagship conferences of academic and professional disciplines, replete with individual and collective status obsessions and insecurities and varying airs of superiority, ambition, striving, and desperation. The unhealthy cultures of these events can be exhausting to witness, engage, and navigate.

Academic dysfunction aside, the commoditization of knowledge may be bypassing even the conventional university setting. For example, Daniel Drezner (2017) invokes the term "ideas industry" to posit that "thought leaders" are supplanting traditional public intellectuals in shaping public discourse. He further argues that these thought leaders are contributing to waning public trust, increased societal polarization, and the growth of plutocracy.

Drezner's thesis helps us to understand that we are bearing witness to the frequent mal-framing of the human condition in ways that are influencing millions. If we have any doubts, we can simply tune in to the latest servings of cable television news coverage and commentary and talk radio shows. This may, in turn, help us to grasp the sources of our anger, despair, or disappointment when we watch and listen to the programming served up by these media outlets.

Growing HumanDHS on a Human Scale

Faced with this dominant framework, the task of expanding the influence of HumanDHS appears to be quite formidable. Here are three questions for our consideration:

- How can HumanDHS grow in numbers and influence without succumbing to the neoliberal values and practices of conventional learning institutions and networks?

- How can HumanDHS expand in size while maintaining its smaller, very human scale?

- How can each of us play a meaningful, constructive role in helping HumanDHS to make an even greater difference in the world?

I offer several responses as food for thought:

Maintain Core Values

First and foremost, any efforts to expand the HumanDHS community must be undertaken with a deep commitment to retaining the qualities of respectful dialogue and appreciative enquiry that have guided it from the beginning. This is much easier said than done. It means growing with careful intention, while keeping interactions on a human scale. It means remembering that small is still beautiful. It means not compromising these core values even when opportunities to "go big" might seemingly justify certain trade-offs.

The question of how to grow the broader human dignity movement is even more challenging. Consider, for example, what might happen if a nascent academic field of "human dignity studies" suddenly goes mainstream. (This seems unlikely given current circumstances, but it helps to be imaginative!) Does this mean that a terribly ironic calculus of journal impact factors, program returns on investment, etc., will be used to measure the success of this new field? Given this real risk, how can we prevent it from occurring without marginalizing ourselves?

Claim Our Power

Many within the HumanDHS community have seen so many abuses of power that we are somewhat reluctant to claim our own. But a responsible exercise of that power may help us to expand our community and its influence. In a reflection on the 2013 annual workshop in New York City, I posted a blog entry on this subject. Here is a snippet:

> I submit that those of us who have witnessed excesses of power may be wary or downright fearful of it, and with good reason. All too often, power is exercised by those who use it to hurt others. Consequently, many of us have come to associate power with abuse.
>
> …My larger point is that such ambivalence can cause us to cede our own power to make positive change. Perhaps some feel comfortable with the term "empowered," which is more likely to be invoked at gatherings of social activists. But I think we need to face down the beast. We need to build our individual and collective power, exercise it effectively and judiciously, and keep it in check when we are tempted to use it excessively.
>
> …Power can be heady stuff, like holding a live wire.

Those committed to advancing human dignity should carefully but decisively embrace it and use it. (Yamada, 2013)

Claiming our power also includes taking personal risks. Especially
for those assuming an "edgewalker" role described below, it likely
requires stepping out of our respective comfort zones and potentially
facing rejection or even ridicule in trying to bring unconventional
ideas about human dignity to the fore. Our supportive connection
with HumanDHS helps to provide the fortitude and resilience we
need to remain steadfast in these efforts.

Nurture Cross-Generational Involvement

HumanDHS should devote significant attention to expanding its
cross-generational outreach. This is, to put it gently, a very mature
community. It needs to diversify in terms of age in order to sustain
itself over time. We should be constantly asking ourselves, who will
nurture this community in the decades to come?

That said, we should also acknowledge that HumanDHS is more
likely to appeal to those who are committed to a search for meaning
rather than personal advancement in a more traditional, careerist
sense. For some, the HumanDHS community is a special place
precisely because we have played, tried to play, or been pressured
to play, certain games of ambition and climbing up the greasy pole,
only to find them to be soul-depleting exercises. It can take years to
get to this place of understanding.

Lifespan and career development issues notwithstanding, we can
do things to expand our generational diversity. We have to keep
our eyes open to younger individuals who might be a good fit for
HumanDHS and cultivate their interests in becoming a part of the
community. This may not always come naturally for those focused
on the substance of their endeavors and perhaps used to working
within their age cohort, but it is vitally important.

In terms of communications, building and refining HumanDHS's
digital presence may help to soften our generational imbalance.
Social media activities are currently one of the less advanced aspects
of HumanDHS's work. Among other things, there is no truly active

online forum for the sharing and exchange of ideas and information and for organizing projects and events. The HumanDHS main website is rich and deep in content, but it may lack the visual appeal and ease of use that members of younger generations are used to encountering.

Play an "Edgewalker" Role

Author and personal coach Judi Neal writes that an "Edgewalker is someone who walks between the worlds," by building bridges, working at the boundaries and soft edges, and operating in a visionary way (Neal, 2006, p. 14). Neal draws heavily from diverse cultural and spiritual traditions in defining this role.

Many members of the HumanDHS community are actual or potential edgewalkers. Associated with standard-brand universities and institutions, they may often find themselves navigating these environments in ways that are personally and professionally challenging. Despite these negotiations, they can serve in this bridge-building capacity. They can bring the values and practices of HumanDHS into their more conventional realms. They can also inform HumanDHS of the realities that confront change agents.

This can be slow, halting, and frustrating work. However, by assuming this role, we can help to infuse our disciplines and vocations with the values and practices of the human dignity movement and work toward the day when the better alternatives become the norm.

Organize Local Events

Community members can organize and host local events, guided by inclusive practices modeled at the annual workshop and conference. This can also serve as a way to connect HumanDHS with others who are unable to attend our major events.

To illustrate, in the aftermath of the 2016 annual workshop, a group of HumanDHS community members began organizing periodic get-togethers in the New York City area. Sitting side-by-side in cozy Manhattan apartments, participants have shared stories, project updates, and personal news in an informal setting. This book project emerged from one of those gatherings.

The New York metropolitan region happens to be home to a strong concentration of HumanDHS community members, making this a natural location for hosting meet-ups. Perhaps those in other localities will be inspired to host similar events as well.

Build Partnerships

HumanDHS should also strive to build partnerships with like-minded institutions and networks. While making such connections may seem easy on the surface, in reality they are a blend of careful matchmaking and negotiation. They require not only shared values, but also similar sensibilities and often some degree of patience.

Let me offer an illustration. In 2015 I helped to forge a partnership between HumanDHS and the Western Institute for Social Research (WISR), a tiny, independent, non-traditional university dedicated to social change and community activism, located in Berkeley, California. WISR has long offered, among other things, flexible, learner-centered graduate degrees in higher education and social change. As a board member of both organizations, I brought together Evelin Lindner and Linda Hartling with John Bilorusky, WISR's president and co-founder. We designed a partnership between the World Dignity University initiative and WISR that would enable students to pursue a WISR degree with a Dignity Studies specialization.

The creation of this program was a perfect match of educational content, values, and sensibilities. To date, the partnership has not yielded the hoped-for flow of students, but we are hoping that more individuals will become interested in pursuing this unique learning opportunity.

Serve as a Model for Other Organizations

Finally, HumanDHS can serve as a model of healthy institution building for other organizations, especially in the nonprofit sector. Unfortunately, nonprofit entities can be as dysfunctional, hierarchical, and toxic as some of their for-profit counterparts. HumanDHS, by contrast, strives to put its values into practice. It stands for the proposition that nonprofit and community groups can operate in a healthy, engaging, and humane manner.

I can attest to the value of HumanDHS's example. I am currently serving as the founding board chairperson of the International Society for Therapeutic Jurisprudence (ISTJ), a new, global, nonprofit learned organization dedicated to advancing therapeutic jurisprudence, an interdisciplinary field of philosophy and practice that embraces psychologically healthy outcomes in legal disputes and transactions. Law professor Michael Perlin, another long-time member of the HumanDHS community, serves as an honorary president and board member of the ISTJ.

Although the ISTJ is structured a bit more formally than HumanDHS in several key aspects, I am consciously attempting to infuse into it with values and practices that affirm human dignity. The selfless servant leadership practiced by the creators of HumanDHS has given me plenty of ideas and inspiration toward doing so.

Building HumanDHS and the human dignity movement requires hard, concrete thinking and contemplation to complement our vision, commitment, and heart quality. I hope that these observations and insights will contribute to that conversation. It is worth the effort. At stake is nothing less than creating opportunities to positively change the world around us.

Sources

Much of the unquoted information about Human Dignity and Humiliation Studies has been drawn from its main webpage (http://www.humiliationstudies.org/), the Dignity Press webpage (http://www.dignitypress.org/index.php), and the World Dignity University webpage (http://www.worlddignityuniversity.org/), as well as the author's general knowledge of HumanDHS in connection with his role as a board member and long-time participant.

References

Drezner, D. W. *The Ideas Industry*. (New York, NY: Oxford University Press, 2017).

Hartling, L. M., Lindner, E. G., Britton, M. & Spalthoff, U., "Beyond Humiliation: Toward Learning that Dignifies the Lives of All People," in Hampson, G. P. & Rich-Tolsma, M., (Eds.), *Leading Transformative Higher Education Volume Two: Studies, Reflections, Questions*, pp. 134-146, (Olomouc, Czech Republic: Palacký University Olomouc Press, 2013), retrieved from: http://www.humiliationstudies.org/documents/evelin/BeyondHumiliationMatthewRich.pdf.

Neal, J. *Edgewalkers: People and Organizations That Take Risks, Build Bridges, and Break New Ground.* (Westport, CT: Praeger, 2006).

Nicolson, D.J. *Academic Conferences as Neoliberal Commodities.* (Cham, Switzerland: Palgrave MacMillan, 2017).

Yamada, D. "Dialogues About Human Dignity, Part III: Claiming and Using Power to Do Good." *Minding the Workplace* (Dec. 13, 2013), retrieved from: https://newworkplace.wordpress.com/2013/12/12/dialogues-about-dignity-part-iii-claiming-and-using-power-to-do-good/.

Yamada, D. "Infusing Good Core Values Into a New Organization." *Minding the Workplace* (July 24, 2017), retrieved from: https://newworkplace.wordpress.com/2017/07/24/infusing-good-core-values-into-a-new-organization/.

Chapter Three

Everyday Dignity:
The Surprising Power of "Small" Acts

Claudia E. Cohen

Introduction

The role of "dignity" and "humiliation" in conflict resolution has received well-deserved attention over the last fifteen or so years [1][2][3] Evelin Lindner, a pioneer in promoting the importance of "dignity" in human rights work, has extensively studied violent intercultural and identity-based conflicts. She cites the role of "humiliation" as a root cause of intractable conflict, defining it as a "profound and enduring relational violation [of dignity]" and "demeaning treatment that transgresses established expectations."[4] Lindner cites as examples of humiliation-based conflict the tragic cases of genocide in Cambodia, Somalia, and Rwanda. The preservation of dignity in human interactions is posited to be incompatible with humiliation. "Humiliation is prevented and counteracted when the human rights concept of equal dignity for all is heeded and respected."[5] When an individual or group is humiliated as part of a conflict dynamic, Lindner's framework suggests that dignity may be restored through the behavior of other actors at the interpersonal, intergroup, or international level.[i]

---

i. See the Human Dignity and Humiliation Studies website for a description of the breadth of their work (www.humiliationstudies.org.)

Donna Hicks reports discovering the importance of "dignity" in her work as an international mediator in conflict zones, including Cambodia and Northern Ireland.[6] Citing Lindner and Hartling's work, Hicks suggests that all conflicts involve "underlying, unaddressed" violations of an individual's dignity and links dignity violations to the experience of shame. She also equates dignity with "the recognition of our inherent value and worth."[7] Hicks confirms that dignity has not been operationalized sufficiently to describe the behaviors that constitute treating others with dignity, nor their mirror, behaviors that comprise dignity violations. She proposes a "language" of dignity, based in John Burton's human-needs theory of conflict[8] plus other elements she observed in facilitated discussions between "warring parties."[9] The ten elements she proposes (e.g., acceptance of identity, safety) are defined in broad, conceptual terms. In order to use this needs-based language to promote a shared understanding of dignity-enhancing behavior, more scenarios describing acts of dignity enhancement…and dignity violations are needed.

What do I mean by "Everyday Dignity"?

I have participated in the Human Dignity and Humiliation Studies (HumanDHS) Annual Meetings at Teachers College in New York since 2009. Previously, I had considered "dignity" to be a word too grand for common speech, a lofty concept as in the U.N. Declaration of Human Rights.[10] "Dignity," as in affirming the inherent dignity and worth of each individual, had seemed to be the purview of governments and nations, not ordinary citizens. Becoming familiar with the work of the HumanDHS community, over time I developed an hypothesis that "dignity" affirmations and violations might be more pervasive and yet more mundane than I had previously believed. As a cognitive social psychologist, I became curious about whether I could readily identify commonplace human interactions in which dignity affirmations (or violations) were playing a role and if so, what would be the impact? Can dignity affirmations (or violations) occur even in brief, micro-level interactions? How powerful are the impacts of these small actions? Will participants and observers recognize them as triggering dignity-based responses?

Over time, I have begun to "collect" acts of dignity affirmation in small daily interactions, or what I now call instances of "Everyday Dignity." Rather than waiting to develop a comprehensive definition of dignity-affirming acts, I have chosen an inductive, "bottom-up" approach. In this chapter, I present several examples of Everyday Dignity and analyze how these acts and their impacts constitute dignity affirmations.

This approach has two potential benefits: 1) documenting instances of Everyday Dignity may encourage others to observe and document other examples and scenarios, and 2) these examples provide a basis for discussing, in this chapter, how and in what ways Everyday Dignity may be a useful construct for understanding interpersonal interaction, conflict, and potentially, healing.

Everyday Dignity: Underground

Here's the first Everyday Dignity example. I have commuted into New York City via train almost daily for many years.[11] The train terminates in Pennsylvania Station. In the past I dreaded disembarking from the train and merging with a seemingly endless throng of other passengers pushing toward an "up" escalator. Our shared but unstated goal: to get as close as possible to the front of the crowd. Meanwhile, I perceive that the crowd has transformed from individual, almost amiable, commuters into a competitive mob. It appears that we are no longer viewing one another as fellow human beings, equally worthy of the most efficient commute possible. Rather, as others push past, I begin to feel less than human, an obstacle to someone else's goal.

So, one day, I tried this experiment. Instead of pushing through the throng, single-mindedly, I made contact with a commuter on my right. I made the universal "you first" sign with my right hand and murmured "after you." He startled and stopped. Then, he looked me in the eye, smiled, and waved me ahead, mumbling "after you!"

Enjoying this outcome, I did this experiment over and over again.

The responses varied. But, the vast majority of the time, the "subject" appeared to be both surprised...and appreciative. Once in a while, a commuter appeared not to have heard my offer and went ahead, heads down, often reading a text. More often, they accepted my offer, smiled and/or nodded, and preceded me...or waved me ahead. In all cases, I felt empowered...as if I retained my sense of agency. I have come to understand that as I honored the dignity of a fellow traveler my "Everyday Dignity" was affirmed.

Understanding Everyday Dignity: Some Useful Psychological Constructs

How shall we understand the abrupt transition from the "me first" to the appreciative and/or "after you" mindset of my fellow commuters? One psychological lens through which we can view this mini-experiment comes from the work of Morton Deutsch. Morton Deutsch, the eminent psychologist who spent most of his career at Teachers College, Columbia University, posited what he called (with self-mocking immodesty) "Deutsch's Crude Law." He defines it as "the characteristic processes and effects elicited by a given type of social relationship also tend to elicit that type of social relationship, and a typical effect tends to induce the other typical effects in the relationship (p. 12.)"[12] He goes on to specify that an act of coop-eration induces and is induced by "perceived similarity in beliefs and attitudes, readiness to be helpful, openness in communication, trusting and friendly attitudes, sensitivity to common interests and deemphasis of opposed interests, orientation toward enhancing mutual power rather than power differences (p. 12)," and so on. And, competitive actions induce and are induced through the use of coercion or threats and attempts to emphasize one's relative power advantage over another, as well as other behaviors associated with competition. For our purposes, the takeaway is that *an individual has the power to influence and change another's behavior by leading with either a cooperative or a competitive "move."* So, by leading with cooperation, e.g., inviting another commuter to precede me, I elicit (or in Deutsch's terms "induce") cooperative affect and behavior on the part of my fellow travelers.

Everyday Dignity: The Notebook Incident

Here is another subway example.[13] It also demonstrates the reciprocity of behavior (as per Deutsch's Crude Law) and the power of one individual's action to change the dynamics of an interaction. I was seated, riding the New York City subway Number 2 train uptown to my office at Teachers College. Two things about the trip are worth noting. First, I was admiring my beautiful new, lined, black Moleskine notebook and jotting down some thoughts, as best I could on a bumpy subway ride. Second, I was wearing brown slacks.

A man boarded the subway car, looking quite disheveled. He was wearing a jacket and tie, but his tie was loosened and his blue Oxford shirt partially untucked. His battered leather attaché case was unzipped and papers and folders were spilling out. His hair was mussed and held in one hand, rather precariously, a takeout coffee cup with the familiar "Greek diner" logo. As the train lurched, the man stumbled and — you guessed it — a stream of coffee headed right for me and my brand new notebook.

As the recognition of what was happening slowly penetrated my consciousness, it occurred to me that many of the students in the conflict resolution courses I teach (at Teachers College) also ride the Number 2 train and so my behavior might be observed. Since I teach about the benefits of cooperative behavior (and Deutsch's Crude Law) I decided to intentionally model "cooperation." The disheveled man looked horrified by the coffee spill and began to apologize. I smiled and told him not to worry. He seemed surprised by my calm response, and stammered further apologies, offering me a handful of napkins (undoubtedly from the deli where the coffee had originated.) As I calmly dabbed at my coffee stained notebook and my (brown) slacks, he ratcheted up his apologies, offering to pay my cleaning bill! I declined, responding that my pants were washable and anyway, they were brown. Apparently unable to think of anything else to offer, he held out a peanut butter and jelly sandwich, imploring me to take it. Once more I told him not to worry...and declined the sandwich!

I interpret this scenario as an example of Deutsch's Crude Law at work. In all honesty, I was upset and maybe even outraged by the permanent coffee stain on my brand new notebook. Had I responded with more visible anger (rather than embodying cooperation for an unseen student audience), my co-commuter might have felt humiliated ... and responded with defensiveness or even hostility. With a few words (and consistent nonverbal behavior), my reaction seems to have influenced the behavior of an embarrassed stranger and transformed the trajectory of our interaction. Perhaps it helped to preserve his dignity.

Microinvalidations and Their Counterpart

A second psychological frame useful for understanding Everyday Dignity is that of "microaggressions," popularized by Prof. Derald Wing Sue, also at Teachers College, Columbia University. *Microaggressions* are defined as "brief everyday exchanges that send denigrating messages to certain individuals because of their group membership (people of color, women, LGBTs). [14] [ii] Wing Sue frames these exchanges exclusively in terms of race, ethnicity, gender, and sexual orientation in order to raise our awareness of the subtle ways in which such "isms" (e.g., "racism") may be expressed, as well as of the impact of such microaggressions on the target or recipient of these exchanges.

Wing Sue identifies three forms of microaggressions: *micro-assaults, micro-insults and microinvalidations. Micro-assaults* are "conscious, deliberate...racial, gender or sexual-orientation biased attitudes, beliefs or behaviors that are communicated to marginalized groups"[15] through words, behaviors, or environmental cues. *Micro-insults* are similar, however they are usually occur *outside the awareness* of the perpetrator and may convey stereotypes or insensitivity about the

---

ii. The term was first coined by Pierce in 1970 in his work with Black Americans where he defined it as "subtle, stunning, often automatic, and nonverbal exchanges which are "put-downs." (Wing Sue, 2015; p. 24)

groups in question. Finally, *microinvalidations* are "communications or environmental cues that exclude or nullify the thoughts, feelings or experiential reality of certain groups (e.g., people of color, women, LGBTs)."[16]

While each form of microaggression is powerful, I think that the construct of *microinvalidation* is most useful here to apply to the practice of Everyday Dignity. If microaggressions promote humiliation in those who are on the receiving end,[17] then exchanges between individuals that affirm their humanity and/or counter messages of "denigration" should promote the enhancement of dignity. I propose that one way we affirm the Everyday Dignity of another individual is through what I am calling *microvalidations*.

Note that I am using the construct of "microaggressions" to apply to the actions and words directed toward an individual separate from, or not motivated *solely* by their membership in an oppressed or marginalized group. I do not intend to dilute the meaning of Wing Sue and colleagues' powerful research and insights. Rather, my purpose is to build on the utility of the construct and explore the "inverse" of microinvalidations, i.e., "microvalidations"…communications or environmental cues that acknowledge an individual's thoughts, feelings or experiential reality.

The framing of "*micro*aggressions" calls to attention the brief, mundane and often below the level of awareness acts that occur in everyday exchanges between people, and the power that these actions can have upon the recipient. We may believe that we reveal — or conceal — our attitudes and biases through purposeful action and well-considered comments or stated opinions. In fact, the study of human communication teaches that the "messages" that are encoded, sent, received, and decoded may be minute and fleeting ones, such as facial expressions and tone of voice.[18] [19] We are almost always communicating — emotions, attitudes, reactions, and values — both when we intend to and when we do not.

I suggest that act of acknowledging the dignity of another individual can be conveyed in a very limited interaction, with a few words or indeed a gesture. By the same token, one can violate or diminish the dignity of another in an equally brief exchange.

Dignity is a "Noun": Is there a Verb? How to Talk About the Act of Honoring Another's Dignity

As noted above, Lindner, Hartling, and Spalthoff [20] and Hicks[21] each equate "dignity" with "recognition of our inherent value and worth." A glance at a standard dictionary offers the following definition of dignity (noun): The state or quality of being worthy of honor or respect, e.g., "the dignity of labor."[22] There are also two secondary definitions, also nouns: "a high rank or position" and "a composed or serious manner or style." The first definition is silent on the Universal Declaration of Human Rights' assertion that dignity is inherent in all people. Note, however, that the two other definitions imply that "dignity" applies to some people, but not to all. The implication is that those without rank and/or those who do not behave in a "composed or serious manner" have less dignity than those that do.

There is another element about "dignity" to be called out that is not a part of the English Oxford definition but is both implicit and explicit in the work of Lindner and Hicks. It may seem almost contradictory that "dignity" is held to be both: a) inherent in all human beings, and b) highly susceptible to the actions of others. Donna Hicks states in a recent blog post, "The other truth about dignity is that it is as vulnerable to injury as the physical aspects of our humanity. Violations to our dignity need attention, just like a physical wound."[23]

So, if dignity is a noun, what term should we use for actions and behaviors that affirm another's dignity (and perhaps help to heal the injury that Hicks describes)? I suggested previously that the term "micro-validations" could refer to communications or environmental cues that demonstrates an individual acknowledges the thoughts, feelings, or experiential reality of another. While this is useful for describing specific acts, it would be helpful to identify a more general term to describe interpersonal actions that acknowledge and strengthen the "dignity" of another. I propose as a candidate term: *dignify* (verb, with object): *make* (something) seem worthy and impressive, e.g., the Americans had dignified their departure with a ceremony.[24] While the dictionary definition may seem to imply that "to dignify" can be used in an inauthentic manner (i.e., make [something] seem worthy and impressive even if you don't believe that it is), I intend to use the term to mean *"sincere communications and actions that acknowledge the worth of another."*[iii] For example, I might say when speaking about a friend who sent me a kind note when I required surgery, "I want to dignify her thoughtfulness with a phone call."

Everyday Dignity: A Criminal Justice Example

The third Everyday Dignity example was not drawn from my lived experiences. On a recent Friday morning, while half-listening to National Public Radio,[25] I found myself riveted by a story. It was a conversation between a District Court judge and an Afghan war veteran who had appeared in his court. The story was moving, with a surprising twist. But what kept me transfixed for those few moments was a jolt of recognition, i.e., here is a powerful example of Everyday Dignity.

In 2013, Green Beret Sgt. Joe Serna retired from the Army after 18 years of service and several tours of duty. Several years earlier, in Afghanistan, Joe and three buddies were trapped in their truck after it landed upside down in a river. The water rose and Joe was unable to save his comrades. Difficulties adjusting to civilian life led to struggles with drugs and alcohol; ultimately he received a DWI and a parole violation. He appeared before District Court Judge Lou Olivera, who sentenced him to spend a night in jail. Sgt. Serna remembered being alone for a little while in the small windowless cell, shaking and sweating, remembering being trapped in that truck. Hearing some keys jingle, he looked up to see Judge Olivera. Knowing Serna's wartime history, the judge had decided to spend the night in the cell,

---

iii. It is beyond the scope of this chapter to discuss how "dignify" could be modified (e.g., "fail to dignify"; "un-dignify") to describe injuries done to another's "dignity."

with him. After the judge entered and the door was locked behind him, Sgt. Serna reported that the terror left, being replaced by a deep calm. The two spoke all night, about themselves and their families; also about war. "I've never seen this kind of act from anyone," Sgt. Serna reported, with awe in his voice.

How do Judge Olivera's actions illustrate the phenomenon of Everyday Dignity? First, Sgt. Serna's words suggest that Judge Olivera's presence in the cell interrupted the psychological damage that he would have experienced if he had spent the night alone in the dark, windowless space. Also, Sgt. Serna also expressed that Judge Olivera's actions made him feel valuable and worthwhile, i.e., restored some of his damaged dignity.

Let's contrast that with an alternative path Judge Olivera could have taken. He could have shown "leniency" and not sentenced Sgt. Serna to the night in jail knowing how traumatic it would likely be for him. I suggest that would have been an act of mercy perhaps, but not one that would have nurtured Sgt. Serna's dignity. Bending the sentencing rules for this defendant might have left the judge feeling out of integrity. Instead, he threaded with precision a very narrow needle; he held Sgt. Serna accountable for his current mistake while mitigating with his presence the disproportionate potential damage of the jail sentence to Sgt. Serna's well-being.

There is one other piece of information useful in understanding this particular instance of Everyday Dignity: Judge Olivera is himself a veteran (of Desert Storm) and has served in the Cumberland County, North Carolina, Veteran's Treatment Court. So perhaps his access to deep empathy is less surprising; he experienced war and has had ongoing contact with veterans. And yet…this makes his actions no less remarkable and illuminating.

Concluding Thoughts and Appreciation

Some readers of this volume will be advanced students and scholars of the topics of dignity and humiliation. For others, this framing may be new. I want to leave all readers with two messages. First, I want to appreciate, affirm, and celebrate the life and life's work of Evelin Lindner. She has devoted most of her adult life to raising up the power and importance of humiliation and dignity in countless aspects of our social, cultural, political, and environmental lives. (You will have read more about the remarkable breadth of her work elsewhere in this volume). She has created, in partnership with Linda Hartling and many, many dedicated others, the Human Dignity and Humiliation Studies Network (HumanDHS) and continued to draw the circle of inclusion in this work wider. Through Evelin's speaking and writings — and via my exposure to other thought leaders in the HumanDHS Network community — I came to see something that was always before my eyes — the power of Dignity — and to recognize its value and its centrality to my understanding of human behavior.

Second, in honor of Evelin's work, I ask the reader to consider doing the following. First, notice when, in your daily life, an interaction leaves you feeling affronted or humiliated. The action or words that triggered your reaction (the "microinvalidation") may be very small and seemingly inconsequential. You may not at first recognize just what the stimulus was. But allow yourself to examine the interaction and mentally "file it" for future reference. Also notice brief exchanges that have the opposite impact, i.e., you feel recognized, honored, or affirmed. What was the stimulus that led to your reaction? Does the term "microvalidation" seem to fit. Keep track of these examples and see whether you find them illuminating.

Similarly, pay attention to the impact that *your* words and actions seem to have in even the briefest interactions. Are you setting a tone of shared dignity or are you promoting your own worth and welfare without considering the dignity of others? Through self-reflection and through the sharing of examples and instances, we will continue to discover the power of Everyday Dignity and our role in it.

Notice also those extraordinary acts of Everyday Dignity, such as that performed by Judge Olivera. Not only did he "thread the dignity needle" (or "dignify") with extraordinary skill — both maintaining his own dignity and affirming Sgt. Serna's — but he acted from a position of great power, amplifying the impact of his actions.

As more of us recognize these small but powerful Everyday Dignity interactions, and document them, the greater will be our shared understanding. I believe that acts of Everyday Dignity — both in "dignifying" and in receiving microvalidations — have the power to enhance psychological well-being and even to help heal previous "wounds."[26] I encourage you to conduct your own micro-experiments. I will be most interested to hear from you about what you discover.

Notes

1. Evelin G. Lindner, *Making enemies: humiliation and international conflict.* (Westport, CT: Praeger, 2006)
2. Linda M. Hartling, *"An appreciative frame: beginning a dialogue on human dignity and humiliation."* Paper presented, April, 2010. *15ᵗʰ Annual Conference of Human Dignity and Humiliation Studies,* Istanbul.
3. Donna Hicks, *Dignity: The essential role it plays in resolving conflict.* (New Haven: Yale University Press, 2011)
4. Evelin G. Lindner, Linda M. Hartling & Ulrich Spalthoff, "Human Dignity and Humiliation Studies: a global network advancing dignity through dialogue." *Policy Futures in Education* 9, no. 1 (2011: 67.)
5. Evelin G. Lindner, Neil R. Walsh & Judy Kuriansky, "Humiliation or dignity in the Israeli-Palestinian Conflict." In *Terror in the Holy Land: Inside the anguish of the Israeli-Palestinian conflict.* Edited by Judy Kuriansky (Westport, Praeger, 2006: 96.)
6. Hicks, *Dignity.*
7. Donna Hicks, "What is the real meaning of dignity?" Blog post, April, 2013. http://drdonnahicks.com/2013/04/what-is-the-real-meaning-of-dignity/
8. John Burton, *Conflict: Human needs theory.* (London: Macmillan, 1990.)
9. Hicks, *Dignity.*
10. United Nations. Declaration of Human Rights.
11. Claudia E. Cohen, *"Everyday Dignity"* Keynote paper presented, December 2015. Annual Conference of Human Dignity and Humiliation Studies, New York.
12. Morton Deutsch, "Cooperation, Competition and Conflict" in *The Handbook of Conflict Resolution.* 3ʳᵈ edited by Peter Coleman, Morton Deutsch & Eric Marcus (San Francisco, Jossey-Bass, 2014, 12.)
13. Cohen, "Everyday Dignity"
14. Derald Wing Sue, *Microaggresssions in Everyday Life: Race, Gender, and Sexual Orientation.* (Hoboken, NJ: Wiley and Sons, 2010)
15. Ibid, 28.
16. Ibid, 37.
17. Lindner, Hartling & Spalthoff, Human Dignity and Humiliation Studies.
18. Robert M. Krauss & Ezequiel Morsella, "Communication and conflict" in

The Handbook of Conflict Resolution. 3rd ed., edited by Peter Coleman, Morton Deutsch & Eric Marcus (San Francisco, Jossey-Bass, 2014.)

19. Paul Ekman, *Emotions Revealed: Recognizing Faces and Feelings to Improve Communication and Emotional Life*, 2nd ed. (New York: Holt, 2007.)

20. Lindner, Hartling & Spalthoff, Human Dignity and Humiliation Studies.

21. Hicks, Dignity.

22. Dignity. In Oxford English Living Dictionaries. n.d. Accessed July 28, 2017. https://en.oxforddictionaries.com/definition/dignity

23. Donna Hicks, "If indignity has torn us apart, then dignity can put us back together again." November 16, 2016. Posted http://Drdonnahicks.com

24. Dignify. In Oxford English Living Dictionaries. n.d. Accessed July 28, 2017. https://en.oxforddictionaries.com/definition/dignify

25. WNYC StoryCorps

26. Donna Hicks, "If indignity…"

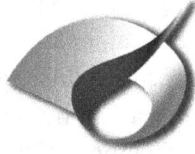

Chapter Four

Reclaiming Common Bases of Human Dignity

Janet Gerson

> We want to live our values...create an innovative global network...emphasize respect for equal dignity...refrain from old style autocratic communication modes...and create a humiliation free, collaborative learning environment.
>
> — HumanDHS

Introduction

Evelin Lindner's model of human dignity and humiliation studies brings in core interpersonal values. She exemplifies the agency of a global citizen and coordinates global networks of thinking, feeling, inquiring, and connecting others into the dignity-based Human Dignity and Humiliation Studies (HumanDHS) network which coordinates conferences, the World Dignity University, and Dignity Press as alternative counter-institutional models that invite rather than divide. Twice annually, the HumanDHS coordinates conferences and workshops. HumanDHS is a network of scholars, researchers, and practitioners that is independent of any ideological, religious, political, or material agenda. At the core of our work is the use of transdisciplinary approaches for generating and disseminating knowledge about human dignity and humiliation. We are committed to a wide range of knowledge creation and dissemination, from shifts in awareness and practice at the local micro-level to larger changes at the level of the global community.

These conferences are organized using the practice of dignilogues, a practice of dialogue with an emphasis on dignity and reciprocal respect, as well as appreciative inquiry and open-space practices. These practices are designed to widen space for collaboration, conversation, and mutually energizing connections. We strive to move beyond the conventional lecture/presentation format to meet in a spirit of shared humility and equal dignity. In what follows, I briefly review Evelin's conceptualizing of dignity. Next, I connect it to my emerging thinking on a neo-Kantian understanding of democracy, justice and peace. The intersubjective democratic paradigm of justice and peace engages a relation theory of justice building on the work of John Rawls (2001a, 2001b, 2005 2011), Jürgen Habermas (1984, 1998, 2011a, 2011b), Rainier Forst (2011, 2014a, 2014b, 2014c), and others being co-developed with Dale Snauwaert and Jeffrey Warnke. The intersubjective paradigm is based on dignity, human-to-human connections, and communicative action as practices that all people can engage in and as capacities for which we can educate.

Finally, I offer an excerpt from my work "Public Deliberation on Justice: The World Tribunal on Iraq" (Gerson, 2014). The excerpt "Reflective Inquiry as a Pedagogy for Reclaiming and Democratizing Justice" summarizes a descriptive analysis of the World Tribunal on Iraq, an alternative global civil society initiative to stop the 2003 War in Iraq and hold those accountable for what was deemed an illegal, illegitimate, and immoral war. The quasi-legal tribunal project was organized with the understanding that human dignity was at stake. People from all over the world coordinated twenty hearings, associated events, and a "Culminating Session," and then compiled the findings into a book, *The World Tribunal on Iraq: Making a Case Against War*

(Sökmen, 2008), and a film, *For the Record: The World Tribunal on Iraq* (Dadak, Z., Ertür, B., Köstepen, E., and Lebow, A., 2007) and archival and documentary films (Deep Dish TV, 2005).

This chapter about the World Tribunal on Iraq describes my analysis and then, based on communicative action used by the WTI, elaborates on how coordinating social action for justice might reclaim people's voices, human dignity, and a moral basis for deliberating on global justice. Lastly, the section addresses the problem of teaching public deliberation given the limits of classroom settings. Reflective inquiry is a more detailed and elaborate cousin of the "appreciative inquiry" brought into the HumanDHS conferences originally by Don Klein and continuously through the fine planning and facilitation of Linda Hartling with support from Michael Britton and Philip Brown.

Background

Dr. Evelin Lindner is the daughter of German parents who were displaced, repatriated, and traumatized in the systemically organized dehumanizing actions of World War II. With deep reflection and accomplished scholarship, Evelin came to understand humiliation as the result of violations of dignity and integrity of people and societies. As a psychologist and medical doctor, Evelin delved first into the implications of humiliation imposed on Germany by the victor nations at the end of WWI, then expanding her research to study of the Rwandan and Somalian genocides, and, beyond that, to the impact of humiliation on individuals and societies in Egypt, Indonesia, Japan, and Brazil, among others. Her work consistently integrates investigations of scholarship in relation to on-the-ground experiences with people and places.

Dignity, as I have learned in my work as a feminist activist working in/on global civil society, is the fundamental principle underlying human rights. Since 1945, the end of the global destruction enacted by humans in World War II, dignity and the inherent worth of each human being have been inscribed in the Universal Declaration of Human Rights and formally institutionalized in the United Nations

(UN Charter). The struggle for valuing each human person and human society has a long history. The devastation of WWII can be viewed as the apocalyptic culmination of human societies excluding and abusing, enslaving, torturing, maiming, raping, plundering, and dominating others, animals, and nature. Dignity serves as a core moral value and guiding ethical principle in peace education movement to further global civil society relationships toward what Lindner identifies as powerful contemporary forces — egalization and globalization.

In "The Concept of Human Dignity" (2007) Evelin reviews this history. Her radical work pushes the concept of dignity beyond deeply embedded historical versions:

> Medieval Christianity stressed the misery and worthlessness of homo viator, earthly man. Life on earth meant suffering and this had to be accepted with dutiful and obedient humility and meekness — this was a worldview not only in Christianity. Perhaps, ruling elites found it convenient to have their underlings believe in such a world order so as to make it palatable to them to be bonded into ranked collectives. At best, rewards could be expected in an afterlife. (p. 8)

Moral teachings embedded in religious worldviews have promoted human life and suffering as the norm against which humans must struggle for individual salvation and for social order. Order was dependent on hierarchical social-political arrangements. These "arrangements" in the predominately Christian societies of Europe were dominated by the local to transnational institutions of the church in conjunction with the state. Yet, Lindner's understanding of dignity transcends both of these interlocking hierarchies:

> The concept of dignity, as it emerged in European history, opposes precisely those two discourses of collectivism and this-worldly suffering. The concept of dignity embraces life on earth as something positive and rejects collectivist hierarchy, instead emphasizing individual rights. In a way,

dignity links up to former more benign hunting-gathering times of human history. (p. 8)

As Lindner explains, in hunter-gatherer societies, people had overlapping relationships and face-to-face encounters. However, in our current world, it is clear that peace and the well-being of people anywhere are affected by others' actions. Human actions generate global forces as in WWII. Yet, many of these forces are invisible:

> Globalization represents a push toward egalization, albeit with a hurtful time-lag. Globalization, among others, raises our awareness that there is but one humankind inhabiting a tiny interdependent planet that can only survive if all cooperate (and cooperation is difficult to achieve with force), and that furthermore, in an upcoming global knowledge society, creativity is needed (and creativity cannot be ordered either but thrives when conditions are enabling). (p. 16–17)

Evelin Lindner's fine work on humiliation and dignity as articulated in "The Concept of Human Dignity" (2007) leaves us where we actually are, living inside the conundrums of transition. While the form and practice of conferences and dignilogues offer experiences on a kind, warm and intelligent path forward, as of this writing in Fall 2017, the rise of the neoconservative right and populist fundamentalism in severe tension with the welfare state stands in marked contrast. In the U.S., the Trump Administration erupts daily with provocative, destabilizing verbal assertions while simultaneously gutting protective regulatory measures, dismissing international diplomacy, and threatening military escalations. In this publicly divisive context, where are the hopes for dignity, civility, social coherence, healing, and constructive collaboration?

As a peace educator and political theorist, I share with Evelin Lindner the urgent questions: what can ordinary human beings do? Where lies our power and agency? This chapter addresses our common aspirations for our global future and our shared sense of the importance of dignity in achieving a promising future. This chapter explores the processes within which dignity develops, which in turn relies on dignity to bear fruit. As a peace educator and an educator of peace educators, I have found these processes to be essential in the quest for both dignity and an emergent better life together. This first section considers dialogue as containing the kernels of dignity, recognition, and acknowledgment that constitute culture through civility and mutual understanding, which holds the promise of a path forward.

Creative Construction: Co-Creating Dignilogues and Discussions

The basic unit of dialogue has important features constitutive of the concept and practice of justice. By talking to another who listens with mutual engagement, the two people co-create an interaction that has the potential to reach a shared understanding. This is constituted through demonstrating mutual respect and mutual acknowledgement that constitute civility. This type of dialogic interaction, expressed as an ideal and simplified in order to lay out this line of reasoning, this dialogic unit constitutes an element of dignity. The dialogic unit is a container for the qualities of respect, acknowledgement, and dignity. These qualities are described to express the positive constructive potential of dialogue that engages in reciprocity, civility, and justification. The kernel of understanding contained in the dialogic unit of dignity has generative potential.

This elemental kernel of understanding combines with other similar kernels which are shared and subsequently often repeated, thereby combining to constitute socially shared understandings. These socially shared, mutually constructed, and reiterated understandings form a web of connectedness. This web binds people together with social understandings and bonds the individuals to the subsequent social formation. Habermas called this a binding/bonding effect and considered it a fundamental capacity in the use of communication through language (1994, 1998, 2011a, 2011b). This is a rudimentary description of social group formation. In Open Space technology this is referred to as the innate human capacity for self-organizing (Owen, 2008).

We can think of situations where this self-organizing becomes the more prominent and emergent dynamic, for example in the much-isolated, post-hurricane catastrophe in Puerto Rico (Dickerson, October 16, 2017). So many supports for communication, interaction, and sustenance have been disrupted — electricity, phone service, television, and internet, as well as road transportation and shipping deliveries of food, medicines, and supplies of all sorts. In this context, people have had to rely on their pre-technological, pre-globalized, innate abilities to help themselves and their neighbors.

Presumably self-organizing is always ongoing. But perhaps we are more conscious that humans are generally born into already formed societies laden with assumptions, beliefs, and values about what is important, how to behave, and what to strive for, as well as ideals about how living together should unfold for communities, individuals, and structures of governance. We are socialized into the social imaginary through our parents, teachers, neighbors, peers and the media (Taylor, 2004; Kumar, 2005).

To illustrate how I see human dignity and human-to-human connections as the fundamental connection for global society organizing (for a more just, peaceful and dignified global human community), I would like to excerpt text from my dissertation "Public Deliberation on Global Justice: The World Tribunal on Iraq," which I wrote in 2014. It summarizes a descriptive analysis of the World Tribunal on Iraq, an alternative global civil society initiative to stop the 2003 War in Iraq and hold those accountable for what was deemed an illegal, illegitimate, and immoral war. The descriptive summary is followed by a comparison of the processes of dialogue and deliberation. It describes the tribunal as a form for challenging injustice and a form for simultaneously practicing the creative construction of justice by people who see themselves as interconnected global citizens. It exemplifies human dignity and human-to-human connections that are central to the work of Evelin Lindner and fundamental to global society organizing for a more just, peaceful, and dignified global human community.

The World Tribunal on Iraq as New Form: Reclaimative Post-Conflict Justice

> Global citizenry is a human-to-human experiment in dignity and reciprocity, and of mutual reflection toward co-creating coordinated action. (HumanDHS, 2019)

The 2003 war and occupation of Iraq provoked worldwide antiwar protests and continued activism against domination of Iraq. At the same time, political theorists, peace scholars and educators, philosophers and legal theorists called for further conceptualization of post-conflict justice. Post-conflict justice has been conceptualized along two lines, retributive or restorative post-conflict justice. The World Tribunal on Iraq, I argue, enacted a third form, reclaimative post-conflict justice.

Reclaimative justice, as exemplified by the WTI, calls for transforming global reaction to injustice into coordinated global deliberation in order to demand more justice and accountability from those responsible for the war and deadly conflict. The WTI coordinated a flexible, polycentric group of variegated hearings in twenty cities that subsequently converged into an intensive Culminating Session in Istanbul in 2005. The WTI challenged two principles of post-conflict justice, the temporal principle that the deadly conflict must be over and the social-political principle that all parties to the conflict must participate. In fact, the WTI offered a radically distinct geopolitical difference to previous post-conflict justice conceptions in that the WTI was coordinated and populated with people from most continents of the world; however, Iraqis, although represented, met with great difficulties in regard to participating despite determined efforts of all concerned. Furthermore, the leaders of the war and occupation did not participate either.

The WTI based their validity and legitimacy instead on universal moral and human rights principles as the bases of global justice. The coordinators did not claim to be what they were not — official or legal authorities. Instead, they aimed to reclaim the common bases of human dignity and human-to-human connection of all global society. The violations against the Iraqis were a threat to all of us, and the dismissal of the concerns of the global antiwar movement and the global citizens who said "no" to the war were in themselves acts of violation and injustice.

The most radical claim of the WTI was to reclaim the voice of authority of people of the world and to reclaim the promises for justice in the UN Charter, the Universal Declaration of Human Rights, and the International Court of Justice. The WTI called itself an "experimental assertion" (Sökmen, 2008, p. x) and a "creative act of resistance" (p. x) intended to reclaim the future of humanity by finding alternative bases for justice, judgment, and the institutions that failed to prevent the destruction of Iraq.

The WTI operationalized deliberations using principles of a democratic ethic of participation in which consensus could be reached without anyone dominating others. The principles included non-hierarchical organizing, volunteer participation, and inclusion of diverse and pluralistic participation to bring in divergent debates and views. They achieved some of their aims by leaving an alternative record of the war and occupation of Iraq, by working together for more justice, and by asserting a form that could be used as a future model for global citizen participation in bringing about more justice.

The WTI's Democratizing Global Justice

The WTI's central experimental assertion was that people can mobilize their sense of injustice into a collective project to advance social justice on a global scale. The tribunal form provided the cohesion and integrity to coordinate diverse and divergent deliberations. This illustrates a significant role for civil society tribunals — to experiment in ways that official institutions and procedures are too restricted to attempt. The WTI's documentary account of the war and occupation of Iraq from 2003 to 2005 is immensely informative, diversely argued, an astounding account.

The WTI advanced the processes of democratizing justice by practicing nonhierarchical, horizontal social relations of shared authority. The inclusion of diverse conflictual positions is an important example for conflict-resolution processes and peace education as well as real world political conflicts. Models for deliberation can reasonably be expanded to include diagnoses of injustice as well as solution-finding. Reclaiming ethical-moral promises within the already existing mandates of international and national institutions can ground people's collective claims to advance justice. This includes the effects of war on people who are directly victimized and people all over the world who are also affected, albeit indirectly. Thus, post-conflict justice as a sub-theory of justice and just war theory should ground itself in claims of those both directly and indirectly affected. Dialogical practices must also include skills in defining the group and organizing the group's aims through deliberative processes. Global citizenry is a human-to-human experiment that we political theorists and peace educators can help to advance by considering the WTI's collective resistance and their coordinated tribunal accomplishment.

Reflective Inquiry as a Pedagogy for Reclaiming and Democratizing Justice

> Peace education is education for responsible global citizenship.
>
> — Betty Reardon (2013b)

> For those of us who believe in the right of artists, intellectuals and ordinary, affronted citizens to push boundaries and take risks and so, at times, to change the way we see the world.
>
> — Salman Rushdie (2013)

> We believed in ourselves … as active subjects, capable of
> making evaluations and reaching a judgment to reclaim
> justice, as well as taking action to have these decisions
> implemented.
>
> — Ayşe Berktay, World Tribunal on Iraq (2008)

The World Tribunal on Iraq (WTI) accomplished noteworthy political actions with implications for peace education. To distill and apply learning from the WTI case, what follows addresses a key question using the WTI: How can we prepare the next generation of citizens to be capable of participation in processes of reclaiming and democratizing justice? I think this is a central and timely question for peace educators, especially in light of the work of peace educator, scholar, and activist Betty Reardon. As Reardon (2011) describes it, the work of peace educators is "educating toward political efficacy in the formation and pursuit of citizen action and public policy intended to move the world toward the achievement of a more just and less violent global order" (p. 2).

In what follows, I explore this central task by using Reardon's pedagogy of reflective inquiry in relation to content from WTI documentary text and film. The WTI will be explored as an example of global citizens working in concerted effort for political accomplishments. Through a learning unit and simulation activity, I hope to demonstrate how reflective inquiry can be used as a method for transformative peace education so that "ordinary, affronted citizens" can cultivate the capacities needed to contribute to "chang[ing] the way we see the world" (Rushdie, 2013).

Reardon states that reflective inquiry is a method for political efficacy. But what does that mean? How can classroom work be connected to political efficacy? This captures the seemingly problematic relationship of political theory, peace politics, and peace education. I hope to shed light on their relatedness through conceptual explanations and a discussion for a course that uses the transformative pedagogy of reflective inquiry.

Reflective inquiry is a pedagogy that combines question formation with empirical and textual investigations followed by dialogue. Facilitated dialogue, focused by a guiding question and supported by valid information, are the materials for the transformative pedagogy of reflective inquiry. Being informed is complemented by each participant's experiences, perspectives, and reactions to the valid information. Through sharing responses, participants are challenged by others' views. In listening to others, we may hear unfamiliar views, and we can learn much more about our own assumptions, expectations, and deeply held beliefs. In peace politics, all of this is significant and valid and, therefore, constitutes relevant information.

Focused dialogue is a key process in reflective inquiry. Focused dialogue opens up individual and collective positions through responses of others. The subsequent challenges to an individual's opinions, beliefs, and worldviews can then be examined.

Opening and re-examining worldviews in light of others' views opens the potential for new thinking. Under the conditions of dialogic exposure, the whole group can engage together in reasoning, explaining, justifying, and rethinking even deeply held positions and beliefs. Under the conditions of cooperative dialogue, new thinking for individuals furthers new shared understandings. The aspiration here is not for one way of thinking to emerge that wins out over others. Instead, the goal is that various views can co-exist. In addition, what the group as a whole can agree upon can also emerge.

Thus, reflective inquiry is a method for learning how to think in relation to a focused inquiry. It is also a means to examine one's own and others' views. Furthermore, reflective inquiry is a method for collective rethinking on how these can be shaped for the group to respond in action to the political peace problems at issue. According to Reardon (2013):

> …inquiry into obstacles and possibilities for transformation should form the core of peace pedagogy, so as to provide learning in how to think and to act for political efficacy in peace politics, complex learning that requires

pedagogies of multiple forms of reflective inquiry. (p. 4)

Reardon refocuses the understanding of political efficacy on thinking for transformation, rather than on more common explanations. These are typically solutions such as concrete outcomes and measurable "results," for example, winning elections or bringing about a socialist, Islamist, or democratic state. In other words, she emphasizes the processes and capacities that precede coordinated actions. These processes and capacities are what can be cultivated in peace education classes and courses.

But peace education should not be limited to dialogic interactions. There are other dimensions to contentious politics (challenging injustice) and coordinated action (practicing justice) (Forst, 2014b), that leads to understanding that deliberation is an additional vital process that must be considered. While dialogue is an interactive exchange among people, deliberation is a dialogic process used to make decisions and solve problems. Deliberation is more intensive than dialogue, as used here. In deliberation, contention and creative construction are combined.

To enlarge on this understanding, it is useful to consider that political efficacy, according to Betty Reardon (2001), depends on learning *how to think*; not, as is frequently supposed, *what to think*. In peace politics, transformation of understanding reached through creative constructive contention can lead to new ways of transforming current obstacles and power relations toward ethical political and social complementary outcomes, wherein justice aligns with peace. Peace, Reardon explains, consists of not only achieved conditions, but also in processes that are based on universal moral and ethical principles, most fundamentally, respect for human dignity and moral inclusion of all human beings.

Reardon identifies reflective inquiry with the ethical perspective of political cosmopolitanism. Political efficacy, grounded in the ethical considerations of political cosmopolitanism, would include having all those impacted voice their ideas in a place for public reason. Dale Snauwaert elaborates Reardon's theory of reflective inquiry by explaining how it is a method for including diverse perspectives in open and public deliberation. The following quote is useful in seeing the connections between reclaiming the ethical bases of inclusion and democratizing justice through public deliberation.

> If we take into consideration the almost incomprehensible scope of human diversity, the ideals of universal human dignity and moral inclusion, including the principles of recognition, inclusion, and fairness as well as equal political consideration and participation, require open impartial public deliberation.
>
> It requires that everyone submit their values and ideas to open impartial scrutiny as a test of their objectivity, value, and validity. Given that our perspectives tend to be confined, exposing our positions to open impartial scrutiny is a means of transcending our positional confinement. This call for impartial scrutiny is central to Reardon's advocacy of reflective inquiry and her critique of the narrowness and partiality of the positioning of critical, reflective pedagogies as ideologies rather than as methods of inquiry and educational liberation. (Snauwaert on Reardon, 2011, p. 5)

The processes of impartial scrutiny and public reason are not easy to bring about in a classroom. Students are rarely pressed by necessity to make decisions and solve problems together. And they do not necessarily have a cosmopolitan sense of interconnectedness and interdependence. But in the global community, this paradigm is gaining recognition. Global ecological, economic, and war crises are among the shared problems that challenge the survival of human society today.

But public deliberation needs mediating forms. Public opinions stated in newspapers, on the internet, or in politicians' speech do not constitute public deliberation. A tribunal form offers a communication structure for public challenges to injustice, for the presentation of relevant research, and for diverse perspectives and experiences to be presented. A tribunal form offers a public space for the presentation of public argumentation to be submitted to public reason. Proposals from various sectors are presented with justifications that are open to scrutiny from a variety of perspectives of the participants and those concerned. In a tribunal form, conclusions must be drawn that reflect the deliberations. Knowledge of these steps is an important learning for global community and global citizens.

Three related forms of communication have been discussed in relation to the World Tribunal on Iraq: *dialogue, deliberation*, and *tribunal* project. The differences are summarized in the following:

Dialogue. On the classroom level, dialogue means open and respectful communication as an interchange of opinions and experiences. Dialogue, in the sense used here, constitutes a way of thinking together toward new understandings. New knowledge and understandings are necessary, since political peace remains an aspiration. Dialogue enables people to delve into their sense of injustices brought out by historic issue events for the political purpose of arriving at arrangements for more justice, as Amartya Sen described in *The Idea of Justice* (2009).

Deliberation. In political actions such as the World Tribunal on Iraq, dialogue is incorporated into deliberation. Deliberation is a dialogic interchange of proposals, reasoned justifications/explanations, and scrutiny of proposals in order to make shared decisions toward solving problems and taking action. Thus, deliberation is a more intensive process than dialogue, as the terms are used here. Decisions, strategies, and planned actions must be reached as conclusions of successful deliberations.

Tribunal project. The phrase "tribunal project" is used to distinguish formal, official, and/or institutional tribunals that are based on violations of criminal and procedural law. The WTI is one example of civil society or people's tribunals that fill in gaps in law or representation or jurisdiction to address what a multitude of people consider as violations of justice. Tribunals are public spaces for presentation of political concerns of injustice.

From a perspective of peace politics, both dialogue and deliberation are transformative in that the action of engagement with others is intended to reach understanding and a "congruence of opinion" (Snauwaert, 2009). Reaching congruence of understanding is the objective of coordinated action, which does not necessitate one proposal or position to dominate over others. In peace politics, diversity, pluralities, and differences are viewed as the reality of global relations. Therefore, the principles and processes of peace politics must respect the range of perspectives and at the same time engage communicative, respectful means for people to work together toward a common purpose. In peace politics, ethical and inclusive means are as important as political aims. This was the case in the WTI processes from inception in 2003 through the two-year engagement to the "Final Statement of the Jury of Conscience" in July 2005.

As we have seen, the WTI also claimed an ethical basis to their political process. The WTI project used an innovative tribunal form for reclaiming and also for democratizing justice. This was done in part by invoking a cosmopolitan ethic of global humanity as a common base for investigating the global injustices related to the 2003 war and occupation of Iraq. The political cosmopolitanism of the WTI was enacted through ethical principles of, and through democratic principles for, participation (Gerson, 2014). Political cosmopolitanism entails the cosmopolitan ethic for equality, dignity, and inclusion of all human beings. As enacted by the WTI, political cosmopolitan philosophy was guided by democratic principles for participation — inclusions, diversity, plurality, and contradictory perspectives; non-violence and non-coercion; horizontal and equal value of all voices; and consensus decision-making.

Reardon's pedagogy of reflective inquiry offers a method for political cosmopolitanism as a basis for peace politics. In other words, the ethical dimensions of political cosmopolitanism provide a basis for critical analysis of unjust power relations, on the one hand, and, on the other hand, provide some guidance in how political practices can be ethically constructed to model — to exemplify and prefigure — the arrangements for justice that might constitute peaceful relations. This is experimental rather than empirical, because sustained peaceful relations for a global humanity have not yet become a reality.

Reardon and Snauwaert offer a typology of reflective inquiry to which I have added two more types. Using these five types together offers a method for mapping the complementary dimensions of issues of war, peace, and justice (See Reardon, 1988, 1999). Together this mapping provides one focused example of what comprehensive peace education can look like (Reardon, 1988). The WTI documentary text did this kind of mapping and provides a comprehensive understanding of the violence, injustices, and illegalities of war from the human-to-human perspective, using the specific evidence of what happened in the 2003 war and occupation of Iraq.

In peace education classrooms, a cosmopolitan ethic of equality, respect, dignity, and inclusion can be upheld. This is also true for democratic principles for participation. In fact, these are easier to enact in a classroom than to enact and sustain in public settings. Consensus decision-making can be practiced, but the weight of classroom decision is minimal in comparison to the life and death decision-making of peace politics. Horizontal coordination of dialogue and deliberation within political bodies is obviously much more demanding and rare in political decision-making. Nevertheless, the classroom provides a space for experimentation with these democratizing alternatives.

Given these differences, the balance of this chapter will first review Reardon's pedagogy of reflective inquiry as a method for exploring the question: How can we educate peace education students to develop the skills and capacities for participation and contributing in learning dialogue and deliberation? I will then outline how the WTI experience could be used as a case study in a course that might be called "Global Citizens/Global Community" using Reardon's pedagogy of reflective inquiry. Finally, I will end with a reflection on a dilemma that arose when a peace education intensive program conflicted with the February 15, 2003, worldwide protests against the U.S./U.K. proposed invasion of Iraq.

Building on Reardon's Typology for Reflective Inquiry

> ...the action of reflecting together leads to a sense of inter-
> connectedness as well as moving toward bases for norma-
> tive consensus. In other words, a kind of community of
> understanding ideally arises. (Gerson, 2014, p. 290)

Reardon's pedagogy of reflective inquiry offers a philosophy and
method for transformative learning for political efficacy in peace
politics. Reardon contrasts this pedagogical strategy to that of those
whose aims are already formulated, for example, formulated to achieve
a particular kind of state or economic or political solution. Instead,
the starting point for Reardon in peace education is not the outcome
per se — the means are as important as the outcome. This is because
the processes of moving toward the peace politics we envision are a
part of that vision. In other words, how we think and how we work
together form the basis of a kind of practice for peace politics. Practices are not only prefigurative; they are also the means to "being the
peace we want to see," as Gandhi and others have said.

At the same time, the practices are informed by thinking, conceptualizing, and theorizing. In a sense, the practices are a way to zoom
in to the hands-on action. The theorizing is a way to zoom out, to
take perspective, to get an overview, and to focus that overview. Both
the form of a tribunal and the form of an educational course provide
a structure to move back and forth between theory and practice. The
moving between theory and practice engages participants in a learning
process. A tribunal as a form for political participatory action can be
characterized as engagement as learning. A formal education course
in peace education can be characterized as learning for engagement.

The global citizens who participated in the WTI were learning
on their feet, so to speak. Students in a peace education course,
also global citizens, have come together with the intention to learn,
presumably to go back out into a public world being wiser about how
they will participate. Moreover, having learned more about how to
engage others would include learning more about themselves (e.g.,

building values, skills, and capacities to engage) and learning more about the obstacles and possibilities for engaging with global problems of injustice.

The inquiry in reflective inquiry is organized by forming guiding questions. Inquiry questions are not ones that have answers. Instead, inquiry questions are epistemological—their purpose is to guide the formation of new knowledge. As Reardon (2013) explains, they are queries intended to guide the "quest in question and the search in research" (p. 12). Inquiry questions drive the quest for learning more, a process for developing knowledge. At the same time, inquiry questions shape these processes. An inquiry needs focus and direction toward an aim, but also needs to be narrowed. The inquiry question sets the scope of the inquiry process — not all dimensions will be addressed. The typology of reflective inquiry, which will be explained soon, offers five dimensions from which to shape the learning inquiry based on the example of the WTI coordinators. A good inquiry question is one that will focus, guide, and direct an inquiry. In doing so, the inquiry question generates movement toward the intended aims.

But what kind of movement? In the pedagogy of reflective inquiry, the reflective interaction of the participants is emphasized in addition to the usual sources of information and already-developed knowledge that constitute the field of study. In the classroom, additional material is drawn from experiences, views, and perspectives of the people who have come together into the temporary learning community. Reflective dialogue among the students and facilitated by the teacher generates another type of movement. In relation to each other and in response to the question directing the inquiry, the dialogic interactions move the participants' thinking into new areas. In addition, the action of reflecting together leads to a sense of interconnectedness as well as moving toward bases for normative consensus. In other words, a kind of community of understanding ideally arises. This community of understanding is, as Habermas (1998) claimed, the result of coming together because of the shared interactions. These shared understandings constitute a transformed normative understanding, at least among the participants who shared the dialogic experience of the reflective inquiry process, including drawing conclusions. In using reflective inquiry as a pedagogy for peace education, the conclusions drawn are then reflected upon for relevance to each student's work and toward formulating applications of peace politics.

One of the goals of peace politics is the transformed understanding on a public level. In the background is the ethical query, "What are our assumptions and expectations of what is good and right?" and the political query, "What are our assumptions and expectations with regard to minimizing violence and enlarging justice?" These are not questions for reflective inquiry, as they are too broad. However, reflective inquiries on peace politics would hold these queries in the background, as the core ethical-political concerns. The transformation of these assumptions and expectations — the political imaginary of the global public — is what is possible through classroom dialogue and through public deliberation.

In a pedagogy for peace politics, what is possible is the quest to uncover public norms and assumptions that allow them to be scrutinized and submitted to public reason and argumentation so that they can be reconsidered from multiple views in order to find ways to address the political problem at hand. When this transformed understanding results from open and democratic public dialogue, and when this results in a congruence of opinion and shared understanding, then political efficacy can be understood as at least setting the platform for transformative political action (Reardon & Snauwaert, 2011, p. 3). This platform for action is political will, which can be generated from shared understanding. This was the case in the transformation of participation in coordinated global protests in which participants again came together for the sustained WTI tribunal project.

Reardon divides the pedagogy of reflective inquiry methodology into (at least) three types. The types that she has identified are the relevant dimensions of comprehensive peace education (Reardon, 1988, 1995, 1997, 2001). These are: critical/analytic, moral/ethical, and contemplative/ruminative. Reardon describes these interrelated areas as complementary and necessary for addressing obstacles to and possibilities for peace (Reardon, 1988, 1993, 1996, 2013a, 2013b).

In reflecting on the WTI and peace education pedagogy, I believe that the WTI experience suggests two types of reflective-inquiry methodology in addition to those of critical/analytical, moral/ethical, and contemplative/ruminative. I call these types constructive/collective and future/projective. By "constructive/collective," I wish to highlight the success of the WTI, especially during the final session in Istanbul, which created and maintained what might be called a coalitional consciousness (Sandoval, 2000). This allowed a highly diverse assembly to find common purpose and sustain unity. While a good teacher will inspire a "constructive/collective" atmosphere in a classroom, the differences between a classroom and a non-classroom setting are substantial. Yet in both the WTI and the classroom, teachers, facilitators, or leaders are tasked with facilitating dialogue. As Dale Snauwaert (2011a) notes:

> ...reflective inquiry...must not only engage and develop the inward reflection of the student; it must constitute a social and political dialogue. The pedagogy of reflective inquiry that leads to political and social transformation mirrors the nature of public reason and democratic deliberation. (p. 14)

Public reason and democratic processes for public deliberation are common practices that can translate from classroom discussion to public-sphere deliberations. In suggesting that "future/projective" is yet another type of reflective inquiry, I am calling attention to the task or opportunity afforded the WTI in deciding what should be the product or outcome of the Tribunal and whether it should continue beyond the Final Session. While it is possible that a classroom of students might organize a project together, their relationship is not a given beyond the end of the semester or the school year.

Moral/Ethics Reflective Inquiry

Guiding questions that direct moral/ethical reflective inquiry lead the participants to delve into questions of *what is good* and *what is right*. For Reardon, this is the place to start a comprehensive peace education inquiry. Moral/ethical dimensions guide all thinking about peace. For example, the Universal Declaration of Human Rights (UDHR) is the result of deliberations among people from around the world following the devastation of World War II (Adami, 2012). The result of these deliberations was the Declaration, which proclaimed a vision for peace and the normative expectations for the United Nations. The UDHR is not law itself, but rather a statement of principles and aspirations. Many treaties for international law elaborate these principles for human rights. Through due process, the treaties become instituted as official international laws.

In a classroom, ethical principles can be laid out first. They provide the foundation for questions of (in)justice. However, in the applied politics of the WTI, the issues of injustice raised by the war in Iraq were put forth first. The ethical considerations were raised to help clarify the questions of injustices. Importantly, the ethical principles that the WTI agreed upon provided the framework of commonality for the diverse participation. Betty Reardon (in Reardon & Snauwaert, 2011) describes the moral/ethical dimension of reflective inquiry like this:

> Moral/ethical reflection addresses questions of fairness and moral inclusion with queries focused on issues of the goodness, distribution of advantage and harm, the justice and potential detriments and benefits of relationships, effects upon quality of life and the biosphere. Transformative moral/ethical reflection is guided by normative principles consistent with the values designated as the indicators of what is considered to be socially good and humanly enhancing. (Ibid., p. 3)

Norms are the expectations that people generally can agree upon about what is right and good. Inquiries in the WTI focused on ethical questions, in other words, questions of right and wrong. Snauwaert adds that ethical inquiry involves "principled practical reason … [which] is most fundamental to political efficacy and the education of cosmopolitan citizens" (Ibid, p. 3). Furthermore, moral/ethical dimension of reflective inquiry follows "the ethical imperative of cosmopolitanism, which mandates that we see the other as a person, transcending the objectification of persons in favor of the recognition of their humanity and their rightful standing in the moral community" (Ibid., p. 4).

In moral/ethical reflective inquiry, both questions and the dialogical processes that follow imply democratic principles of participation. Each and every person is viewed with respect and dignity, their views are valued and included, and their concerns are relevant to critical analyses and proposed strategies for action. In this sense, peace politics differs from other political theories in which moral/ethical dimensions are not taken to be core.

Critical/Analytic Reflective Inquiry

Critical/analytic reflective inquiry questions delve into power relations and their impact on issues of war, peace, and justice. The WTI was instigated by what was perceived as the illegitimate attack on Iraq and subsequent occupation. The antiwar movement from which the WTI arose critiqued the failure of the United Nations to stop the war, the "pre-emptive strike" justification used by the invading powers, and the lack of decision-making power of the Iraqi people on how the international community might help them to deal with their own dictator. These "outrageously unjust arrangements" (Sen, 2009, p. 26) were protested worldwide. However, to make a tribunal project, those individuals and groups who wanted to follow through had to further develop their sense of injustice into an elaborated critique and analysis of the unjust power relations. Many different types of researchers contributed critical analysis from their various areas of expertise — anthropology, law, philosophy, medicine, diplomacy, international relations, economics, history, journalism, etc. Together their critical analyses comprised a comprehensive mapping of the war and violations that took place in and related to Iraq.

Reardon explains the type of critical/analytic reflection as delving into the issues of power relations, institutional relations, and other kinds of structural relations and their effects on human life and society. Critical/analytic reflection

> ...is more directly political than the other two [types of reflective inquiry], as its primary inquiry is into the nature, functions and distribution of power, the political institutions and social structures through which it is mediated and the consequences of these circumstances to human lives and relationships. (Reardon & Snauwaert, 2011, p. 11)

Critical/analytic inquiry is the most used type of political inquiry. Many political analysts and activists focus almost entirely on critique and analysis without engaging the moral/ethical dimensions (p. 11). As was the case with moral/ethical reflective inquiry, critical/ analytical inquiry leads directly to political implications. However, from a peace-politics and education perspective, critical/analytic reflective inquiry always takes place in relation to the moral/ethical considerations. As Snauwaert (Reardon & Snauwaert, 2011) notes:

> Critical/analytic reflection is a constitutive imperative of political equality and thus of cosmopolitanism, for the sustainable institutionalization of individual political empowerment is based upon individual awareness and knowledge of one's rights to consideration and participation and the internal capacities to effectively participate in the political process. (p. 4)

Snauwaert draws our attention to the aim of individual empowerment and the development of "internal capacities" for participation in peace politics. These are more directly focused on in contemplative/ ruminative reflective inquiry.

Contemplative/Ruminative Reflective Inquiry

Contemplative/ruminative reflective inquiry can be described as critical self-examinations of our internal motivations and moral capacities. In this case, "our" could be conceived as pertaining to either the individual or to the group of participants. The individual or the group reflects on what is meaningful and valuable. In explaining Reardon, Snauwaert states that the contemplative/ruminative reflective process "is essential for ethical commitment and for the empathic moral response to the dignity of other persons" (2011, p. 4). In addition, contemplative/ruminative reflective inquiry offers a space for students to integrate challenges, insights, and new possibilities into their worldviews.

As a pedagogy for classrooms, contemplative/ruminative questions generate space and focus for students to consider their own perspectives and experiences within the dialogue on the ethical and political dimensions. In complement, the self-reflection of each student in relation to the other students and to the issues raised helps to cultivate the capacities of students for political reasoning from an ethical foundation. Thus, "internal moral resources" become guides for political reasoning (Snauwaert, 2011b). In addition, students develop inner moral resources and capacities for critical analysis of global issues within an inclusive and democratic ethic of participation. In other words, the outcomes are relational.

Both Reardon and Snauwaert link the contemplative/ruminative dimension of reflective inquiry to the process of building global learning communities. They assert that this is what amounts to a dialectical relationship between building such communities, fostering an ethic of cosmopolitanism, and developing the capacities (individually and collectively) for ethical reflection. Thus, Snauwaert writes:

> The self-reflective, contemplative dimension of cosmopolitanism consists of the internal moral resources of the individual that provides the consciousness and capacity to be aware of and to ethically respond to the inherent dignity of every human being....Cosmopolitanism thus entails an internal disposition and capacity to respond to others empathetically with respect and care. It also entails a moral commitment to the ideals of human dignity and inclusion, which makes cosmopolitanism a deliberative choice. These

dispositions emerge out of critical self-examination and contemplative reflection wherein their meaning and value are contemplated and affirmed by each individual citizen. (Reardon & Snauwaert, 2011, pp. 3–4)

The question then becomes, how do individuals and groups develop these "internal moral resources" that are necessary to respond to others empathically, and how do they/we help ourselves and others to make "a moral commitment to the ideals of human dignity and inclusion"?

This is, in a sense, a lifelong project of the moral political person. But it is possible for classroom learning to encourage this process through posing questions and facilitating dialogue: toward building learning-community relationships that might endure beyond the classroom. Queries, questions that one holds onto throughout life, are shared in a learning community. One peace learning query is "How might war be de-legitimized?" In a sense, the WTI took on that question as evidenced by the subtitle of their documentary text *Making the Case Against War* (Sökmen 2008). Queries are larger, more far-reaching than inquiries. Yet, queries can be shared amongst the networks of people all over the world who are engaged in peace politics. The ability to formulate and hold queries to guide one's work is another type of inner resource that can result from peace education. As Reardon writes:

Reflective inquiry initiated by the posing of questions is deepened through the consideration of queries. In that it is in essence a process of thinking by interrogation, it is thus essentially dialogic, beginning with focusing on and encountering the subject of the inquiry as the entry point into the process of examination of what is to be further explored. In this respect, reflective inquiry begins with an inner process of confronting and questioning toward a basic understanding of the subject or issue. While it is possible for the process to remain inward and still be productive of learning, the practice of reflective inquiry as peace education — learning toward social and political change — must become outwardly dialogic in the form of a learning discourse through posing queries to elicit the individual reflections of all who comprise the learning community (or class). (Reardon & Snauwaert, 2011, p. 7)

What is of great importance here for my inquiry is the obvious bridge that the concept of "contemplative/ruminative reflection" provides between the peace-education pedagogy of Reardon and Snauwaert and the experience of the WTI. A fundamental part of the WTI project was to develop *outside* of a classroom or other institutional structure the "learning community" that Snauwaert sees as the foundation for peace education.

One must continually assess the relationships among inner development, ethical development, and political critique and actions. The classroom affords more examination of the individual and face-to-face dialogue. The political is more focused on external far-reaching concerns. But, in political projects there are two other dimensions of reflective inquiry that can be added to Reardon's three.

Collective/Constructive Reflective Inquiry

A classroom and a course are institutional arrangements that involve the teacher, department, academic institution or school, and governmental institutions — the school district, the Board of Education, the state and the federal government agencies. But a global citizens' project such as tribunal is not already formulated, nor is it bound by a rulebook of procedures. Thus, it is necessary to inquire into the nature of the project from the viewpoint of the citizens who are taking responsibility for it. This fourth type of reflective inquiry will be referred to as a collective/constructive reflective inquiry. The core general inquiry asks: Who are we and what kind of group/project are we constructing?

The WTI organizers began with these questions. One problem they faced was framed as a paradox in the WTI Mission Statement as follows:

> Being confronted with the paradox that we want to end
> impunity [for initiators of the war] but we do not have the
> enforcement legal power to do so, we have to steer a middle
> way between mere political protest and academic sympo-
> siums without any judicial ambition on the one hand,
> and impeccable procedural trials of which the outcome is
> known beforehand. This paradox that we are just citizens
> and therefore have no right to judge in a strict judicial
> way and have at the same time have the duty as citizens to
> oppose criminal and war policies should be our starting
> point and our strength. (WTI, Archived website)

To address this paradox, the WTI asked itself (in my paraphrasing),
"What can this global citizens' tribunal do?" and "What is the basis
of our legitimacy?" In addition to the questions of validity, there
were also practical questions to consider, such as "How can we set
the scope of this tribunal to be something we can actually accomplish?" In practical terms, "How can the form of the WTI enact our
principles to be inclusive, pluralistic, and nonhierarchical?" And at a
yet still-higher level, the WTI organizers asked: "How can we model
the world we want to see?" Because the WTI, in form and process,
was a rejection of US imperialism and the failure of the UN to stop
an aggressive war, the WTI organizers sought to establish a form and
processes for self-organization that reflected the peace-and-justice
values of their overall aims.

For example, the WTI decided to use consensus-based decision
making. Of course, consensus or achieving consensus are shorthand
ways of conveying a complexity of processes that, in the case of the
WTI or similar peace education activities, conducted in public spaces
with a "voluntary" constituency, are the building blocks of the activity
itself. In a classroom setting, the guidelines are often set by the teacher,
but nonhierarchical dialogical processes can be used to transcend a
teacher-dominated way of conducting the class. Every person can be
invited to hold the principles of interaction as their individual and
the group's collective responsibility.

In fact, the WTI core leadership experienced learning through their feminist, anarchist, or Quaker predecessors, drawing on decades and centuries of experiments with non-hierarchal self-government. Sökmen (2008), for example, states: "The process of preparing the tribunal was as important for us as its end result. We did our best to organize non-hierarchically in a horizontal network, and to include, rather than silence or exclude, debates and divergent views" (p. x).

In the end, of course, both the classroom and citizens' political projects such as the WTI are "temporary communities." One way in which they differ is that the participants have different expectations about the process or guidelines and differ in their commitment to participation. Yet, the problems of war, justice, and peace, as well as the challenges of cultivating global arrangements for moral/ethical relations, continue when a student leaves the classroom. How can peace educators encourage students to think of continuing relations and engagement as global citizens in the global community of peace learners?

Future Projective Reflective Inquiry

As Reardon has practiced peace education, there is always the question of how the individuals in the class will apply their learning to their lives and their work. This is also true for intensive collective projects such as the WTI. In their case, the WTI intentionally considered what follow-up actions would be recommended in the "Final Statement of the Jury of Conscience." This document had implications for future actions that could be taken up in other settings, for example, cases could be made in the International Criminal Court. The WTI concluded the Culminating Session at the end of June 2005. There was a commitment to publish the documentary text and to make a documentary film. However, there was no collective commitment to continuing the collective effort. Some people wanted to formalize the WTI beyond a coordinated network into a formal institution, perhaps most like an NGO. Others were completely opposed. This is frequently a question in social movement network-based projects.

Reflective inquiry on future/projecting delves into the question of continuing relationships, next campaigns and projects, and historic issue events that present obstacles and possibilities of enlarging justice and enhancing peace. In addition to the simple future-oriented questions of "should we keep going?" or "what should we do next?" the future/projecting dimension of reflective inquiry underscores the reality that the "temporary community" of peace educators is itself learning as it goes along. As Reardon and Snauwaert (2011) write:

> In all peace education, we need to make clear that all the knowledge necessary for the making and building of peace is not yet available to us; that our task as peace learners and peace makers is to contribute to the building of the fundamental peace knowledge base, involving all existing fields of human knowledge and perhaps inventing new ones. (p. 12)

Reflecting on the experience of the WTI, what is remarkable to me is how appropriately the dimensions of Betty Reardon's concepts of reflective inquiry can be used in practice to understand and illuminate what I take to be the strengths and contributions that the WTI has made to the world of peace education. And conversely, in developing a sustained practice of self-organization through consensus over a period of several years, the WTI has demonstrated that the best pedagogies of peace educators are not confined to the classroom, but can also guide peace activists wherever there are "temporary learning communities" in formation.

Conclusion

> What accounts for citizens being able to publicly respond to each other in ways that honor their dignity as free and equal citizens and human beings? (Snauwaert, 2011b).

Reflective inquiry is based on learning to form questions dialogically and then using the agreed-upon question to guide discussion on the problematic, the issue, and/or dilemma and/or challenge that the inquiry is meant to address. A guiding inquiry question, generally speaking, should have at least three characteristics: focus, scope, and a method for inquiring. With these perimeters articulated, each guiding inquiry question will yield a different account of the problematic.

Reflection on Peace Education and Political Efficacy

Political efficacy has different meanings for different groups, political communities, and institutions. The specific aims can vary according to the issues that are foremost at particular historic and geopolitical contexts. Often, individuals believe that it is only diplomats, people in powerful roles, or special people who can have influence to be politically effective. Another view is that political efficacy can only take place through concrete developments. For example, the WTI wanted to influence public opinion sufficiently so that the war-makers would end the war.

This analysis has found that the WTI constituted a post-conflict global citizen's tribunal based on reclaiming and democratizing justice. Although they were unable to end the war and occupation, or even to speak for citizens of Iraq, the WTI did…

> …organize non-hierarchically in a horizontal network …to include rather than silence or exclude, debates and divergent views … working together as a global subject, leaving a record for history, bringing together material that can be used in appeals to the ICC or the UN, or legitimate grounds for conscientious objection, and creating a spark of hope for future collective work. (Sökmen, 2008, p. x).

In classrooms, we know that we cannot end war. However, we can prepare students for political engagement as citizens and subjects. Reardon's pedagogy of reflective inquiry can prepare students for forming questions that will open dialogue along multiple dimensions of political issues, including ethical and relational dimensions. Deliberation requires more intensification of form than dialogue does. Deliberation requires more shared commitment in combination with problem-solving and decision-making necessities. These are aided by forms such as the WTI tribunal project and by discussions and agreement on the aims and concerns of the group. Furthermore, both dialogue and deliberation can result in shared understandings and a congruence of opinions. From these reached understandings, normative transformations can occur in the expectations, assumptions, and demands for justice. Through a pedagogy of reflective inquiry, students can engage in learning that prepares them for political participation. Through public reason and deliberation, global citizens can engage in political action for more justice while learning from their collective engagement. Finally, global communities of learners can engage and reengage in multiple forms of learning toward a more just and peaceful world.

Postscript

On February 15, 2003, I was teaching a peace education intensive course with Yohei Ichiguro at Teachers College, Columbia University, through the Peace Education Center. The students were all either graduate students or professionals enrolled in the weekend intensive. They wanted to attend the global antiwar protest in midtown New York City. But we only had that weekend to finish the course. Attendance for the two-and-a-half days was a requirement, as stated in the syllabus. One possible solution was for the for-credit students to accept incompletes for their grades and go to the protest. This was somewhat helpful in that the participants realized they had some choice. However, it did nothing to raise their spirits. In the end, people agreed that they wanted to complete and pass the course. We all felt glum, to say the least. We next asked ourselves: Was protest the only way on that weekend that we could work against the impending war? Was participating in this worldwide protest the only way we could work for peace?

These questions constituted a contemplative/ruminative type of reflective inquiry. As peace educators and the course facilitators, Yohei and I raised these questions. We offered the reasoned proposal that peace activism is a long-term commitment that takes many forms.

One student supported our reasoning. He stated that he had already attended eight protests and was sure there would be many more in the days to come. He proposed that we listen to the radio during our lunch break. Other students accepted this proposal. When the break came, some stayed to listen, while others went out to lunch.

The students did all stay for the weekend. They did engage in the course activities throughout. But they worked in a subdued way. Truly, there would have been a "high" from going together to the protest. However, being in the center of activity of the massive protest would have been very difficult. (For example, some activists I know from Westchester County got off the train at Grand Central Station, but never got more than a block or two from the station due to the massive crowds that packed into the streets, which were further congested by barricaded side streets and rows of police on horses backed up by police vehicles).

Only one student left for the protest. She was not taking the course for credit. She came back ebullient to tell us about her experience. Yohei and I, in our facilitator reflection, wondered if it would have been better for the other students' morale for her not to return to the class or share her happy account. Interestingly, she was not able to move close enough to hear the main speakers. But, she reported that she did hear some speeches on other protesters' portable radios!

In the final course reflection, there seemed to be a general agreement that the small group work was good. One person said she was unsure if we had made an impact on peace, but she herself felt better. The participants generally appreciated working together intensely on critical analyses of the issues and collectively focusing on how each person's work might move forward, given these analyses. This research is in part the result of my own personal reflection on the same inquiry.

Moving again to the focus of this chapter, it can be said that transformation of worldview is one aspect of transformative action. Enlarging the scope of justice in the minds of the participants is another. Reflective inquiry, as practiced in a peace education course, offers a means to see the world differently, to open spaces and dialogues. Transformative thinking, dialogues on shared issues, and introspection within a moral/ethical framework can contribute to citizens' capacities to work for more justice. Furthermore, this classroom practice builds experience for the more intensive experiences outside the classroom, in political deliberation.

Closing

The work of Betty Reardon and Dale Snauwaert in peace education is very closely connected to that of Evelin Lindner, Linda Hartling, and all those connected with Human Dignity and Humiliation Studies. Both start with dignity as the basic principle, the kernel from which human-to-human capacities and connections emerge. Equally important, both Lindner and Reardon emphasize global civil society as did the coordinators of the World Tribunal on Iraq.

This essay makes visible the span from individual and interpersonal dignity in dialogue through global citizens organizing communicatively, deliberating on justice as a practice of those citizens. The WTI coordinators engaged facts, norms, laws, and the violations of human well-being and justice as an intersubjective, collective aim for well-being. The WTI participants became authors of justice as a collective action of the global citizens' tribunal. This did not stop the war, nor did it have the authority to hold the criminals and violators accountable. Nevertheless, the model remains for us who participated and who can read about it to contemplate further communicatively-coordinated actions for dignity, justice, and peace.

References

Adami, R. (2012). "Reconciling universality and particularity through a cosmopolitan outlook on human rights." *Cosmopolitan Civil Societies Journal,* 4(2), pp. 22–37. Retrieved from http://utsescholarship.lib.uts.edu.au/epress/journals/index.php/mcs

Berktay, A. (2008). "The WTI as an alternative: An experimental assertion," pp. 468–470. In Sökmen, M. G. (Ed.), *World Tribunal on Iraq: Making the Case Against War.* Northampton, MA: Olive Branch Press.

Çubukçu, A. (2008a). "The WTI as an alternative: An experimental assertion," pp. 468483. In Sökmen, M. G. (Ed.), *World Tribunal on Iraq: Making the Case Against War.* Northampton, MA: Olive Branch Press.

Çubukçu, A. (2008b). *Humanity must be defended? Paradoxes of a democratic desire.* Unpublished doctoral dissertation. (UMI Number: 3317541)

Çubukçu, A. (2011). "On cosmopolitan occupations: The case of the World Tribunal on Iraq." *Interventions, 13*(3), 422–442.

Dadak, Z., Ertür, B., Köstepen, E., and Lebow, A. (2007). "For the record: The World Tribunal on Iraq" [video documentary]. Retrieved from http://www.youtube.com/ playlist?list=PL2D0 EE9948D8F5973

Deep Dish TV. (2005). "World Tribunal on Iraq" [documentary film]. Internet Archive, Iraq War. Retrieved February 10, 2011, from http://www.archive.org/details/worldtribunaloniraq

Dickerson, C. (October 16, 2017). "Stranded by Maria, Puerto Ricans get creative to survive." Retrieved October 19, 2017, from https://www.nytimes.com/2017/10/16/us/hurricane-maria-puerto-rico-stranded.html?_r=0

Finlayson, J. G. and Freyenhagen, F. (2011). *Habermas and Rawls: Disputing the political.* New York: Routledge.

Forst, R. (2014). *The right to justification: Elements of a constructivist theory of justice.* Translated by Jeffrey Flynn. New York: Columbia University Press. First published 2007, Suhrkamp Verlag, Frankfurt am Main.

Forst, R. (2014). *Rainer Forst in dialogue: Justice, democracy and the right to justification.* London: Bloomsbury Academic.

Forst: R. (2014). *Justification and critique.* Translated by Ciaran Cronin. Cambridge, UK: Polity Press. First Published (2011) in German, Suhrkamp Verlag, Frankfurt am Main.

Gerson, J. C. (2014). "Public deliberation on global justice: The World Tribunal on Iraq" [doctoral dissertation]. New York: Teachers College, Columbia University.

Habermas, J. (1998) *Between facts and norms: Contributions to a discourse theory of law and democracy.* Cambridge, MA: MIT Press.

HumanDHS (2019). Human Dignity and Humiliation Studies [website]: http://www.humiliationstudies.org

Küey, H. (2008). "The WTI as an alternative: An experimental assertion," pp. 475–476. In Sökmen, M. G. (Ed.), *World Tribunal on Iraq: Making the Case Against War*. Northampton, MA: Olive Branch Press.

Kumar, C. (2008). "Toward a new political imaginary." In Sökmen, M. G. (Ed.), *World Tribunal on Iraq: Making the Case Against War*. Northampton, MA: Olive Branch Press.

Lindner, E. (2007). "The concept of human dignity." Human Dignity and Humiliation Studies. Retrieved October 21, 2017, from: www.humiliationstudies.org/.../TheConceptofHuman-DignityforNoelleQuenivets.pdf

Rawls, J. (1971). *A theory of justice*. Cambridge, MA: Harvard University Press.

Rawls, J. (2001a). *Justice as fairness: A restatement*. Cambridge, MA: Belknap Press of Harvard University Press.

Rawls, J. (2001b). *The law of peoples*. Cambridge, MA: Harvard University Press.

Rawls, J. (2005) *Political liberalism: The John Dewey essays in philosophy* (Vol. 4, expanded ed.) (Originally published 1993). New York, NY: Columbia University Press.

Reardon, B. A. (1988). *Comprehensive peace education: Educating for global responsibility*. New York, NY: Teachers College Press. (ISBN 0-8077-2885-3)

Reardon, B. A. (1993). *Women and peace: Feminist visions of global security*. Albany: State University of New York Press.

Reardon, B. A. (1995). *Educating for human dignity: Learning about rights and responsibilities*. Philadelphia: University of Pennsylvania Press. (ISBN 978-08122-1524-3)

Reardon, B. A. (1996). *Sexism and the war system* (First published in 1985, Teachers College Press). Syracuse, NY: Syracuse University Press.

Reardon, B. A. (1997). "Human rights as peace education." In G. Andreopoulos and R. P. Claude (Eds.), *Human rights education for the twenty-first century* (pp. 21–34). Philadelphia: University of Pennsylvania Press.

Reardon, B. A. (2013a, June). "Criminalizing war and those who make it." *Global Campaign for Peace Education Newsletter,* Issue 105. Retrieved from http://.peace-ed-campaign.org/resources/CriminalizingWar.html

Reardon, B. A. (2013b). "Meditating on the barricades: Concerns, cautions and possibilities for peace education for political efficacy," pp. 1-29. In P. Trifonas and B. A. Wright (Eds.), *Critical peace education.* Dordrecht, The Netherlands: Springer.

Reardon, B. A., and Snauwaert, D. T. (2011). "Reflective pedagogy, cosmopolitanism, and critical peace education for political efficacy: A discussion of Betty A. Reardon's assessment of the field." *In Factis Pax, 5*(1), 1–14. Retrieved from http://www.infactispax.org/journal/

Sen, A. (2009). *The idea of justice.* Cambridge, MA: Belknap Press of Harvard University Press.

Sökmen, M. G. (Ed.) (2008). *World Tribunal on Iraq: Making the Case Against War.* Northampton, MA: Olive Branch Press.

Snauwaert, D. (2002). Cosmopolitan ethics and democracy. *Current Issues in Comparative Education, 4*(2), 5–16.

Snauwaert, D. (2004). "The Bush doctrine and just war theory." *OJPCR: The Online Journal of Peace and Conflict Resolution,* 6(1), 121–135. (ISSN: 1522-211X). Retrieved from www.trinstitute.org/ojpcr/6_1snau.pdf

Snauwaert, D. (2008). "The cosmopolitan ethics of the Earth Charter: A framework for a pedagogy of peace." *In Factis Pax* 2 (1) 88–130. Retrieved from http://www.infactispax.org/journal/

Snauwaert, D. (2010a, July). "Social justice, diversity and peace education." Plenary presentation at the International Institute on Peace Education, Cartagena, Colombia.

Snauwaert, D. (2010b, July). "Reflective practices of learning and change: Strengthening the inside for the outside work." Plenary presentation at Peacelearning Peacebuilding Institute, National Peace Academy.

Snauwaert, D. (2010c). "Democracy as public deliberation and the psychology of epistemological world views and moral reasoning: A philosophical reflection." *In Factis Pax,* 4(1), 120–126. Retrieved December 15, 2010, from http://www.infactispax.org/journal/

Snauwaert, D. T., (2011a, October 28). "The fundamentals of peace education in a democratic society." Paper presented at the First Annual Charles DeBenedetti Peace Conference, Toledo.

Snauwaert, D. T. (2011b, November). "Democracy, public reason, and peace education." *Global Campaign for Peace Education Newsletter* (Issue 88). Retrieved from http://www.peace-ed-campaign.org/newsletter/archives/88.html

Snauwaert, D. T. (2013, June). "Upholding the right to peace." *Global Campaign for Peace Education* (Issue 105). Retrieved from http://www.peace-ed-campaign.org/resources/Human-RighttoPeace.html

Sökmen, M. G. (Ed.). (2008). *World Tribunal on Iraq: Making the Case Against War.* Northampton, MA: Olive Branch Press.

Üçpinar, H. (2008). "The WTI as an alternative: An experimental assertion." In Sökmen, M. G. (Ed.), *World Tribunal on Iraq: Making the Case Against War* (pp. 468483). Northampton, MA: Olive Branch Press.

World Tribunal on Iraq (WTI). (n. d.). Archived website: http://www.worldtribunal.org/main/?b=1

WTI Istanbul Coordination (WTI-IC). (2008). The WTI as an alternative: An experimental assertion. In Sökmen, M. G. (Ed.), *World Tribunal on Iraq: Making the Case Against War* (pp. 468–483). Northampton, MA: Olive Branch Press.

WTI Platform for Action (2003, October 20). "Istanbul mission statement for the creation of an international tribunal of justice on the war and occupation on Iraq." Retrieved from http://www.wagingpeace.org/articles/2003/10/20_ istanbul_iraq-tribunal_print.htm

Chapter Five

The Language of Respect and Dignity for Intercultural Understanding and Conflict Resolution: Application to Diplomacy and Education

Noriko Ishihara

Introduction

In today's era of globalization, there is increasingly frequent travel and interaction across national, cultural, and linguistic borders. In such intercultural interactions, the language of respect and dignity is particularly important in establishing and maintaining rapport in all spheres of communication, including personal, social, educational, commercial, political, and diplomatic relations. However, research in linguistic politeness and intercultural communication shows that the notion and expression of *face* and *politeness* vary across cultures and can be a source of misunderstanding, embarrassment, humiliation, conflict, and essentialization of other cultures (e.g., Culpeper & Haugh, 2014; Holmes & Brown, 1987; Ishihara & Cohen, 2010; Spencer-Oatey, 2000; Piller, 2011). In fact, insights gained from work in Human Dignity and Humiliation Studies (HumanDHS) suggest that loss of face can further develop into intense emotions of aggression, anger, and humiliation. Humiliation has a cumulative impact, which, without connection and support elsewhere, may turn into isolation, depression, or sometimes violence (Hartling, 2007, personal communication cited in Lindner, 2009, p. 48). Lindner (2009, 2016) argues that experiences of humiliation can lead to depression or apathy when it is turned inward and to violence when turned outward. While the potential link between intercultural misunderstanding, humiliation, and violence needs to be further explored, I call in this chapter for enhanced awareness of the role of language and culture in globalized communication. I do so by providing two examples of how such (meta-)linguistic awareness can be stimulated and concrete linguistic strategies can be acquired in the contexts of diplomacy and education.

The Role of Language in Intercultural Communication

Let me begin by citing the wisdom of just a few among many scholars and writers who addressed the power of language in making positive social change and building peace. In their work on appreciative inquiry, Whitney and Trosten-Bloom (2010) argue that we create the world through language, meaning that the world becomes an embodied reality when it is described through language. Language therefore matters as it "bring[s] things to life, creating the world as we know it (p. 53). Along the same lines, in his inspirational poetic creation, peace linguist Gomes de Matos (2013) proposes ways to dignify our daily conversations. One is by speaking to others with "respectful language and optimistic vocabulary"; another is by "disagreeing through emphatic language," which he further explains as "placing oneself in other's shoes"; still another is by "using *positivisers*," or words that can enhance positive traits of others (p. 76).

Layers of complexity are compounded when it comes to intercultural communication. "Words create worlds" (Whitney & Trosten-Bloom, 2010, p. 51), yet different language speakers view the world they create in ways tinted by culture, thus at least partially differently. What is typically viewed as "respectful" behavior or "emphatic" language also varies across cultures. Our language use is so closely intertwined with our cultural orientations and subjectivities that without this activated awareness, we are inclined to evaluate others' behavior using our own yardstick, potentially leading to misunderstanding, conflict, negative cultural stereotypes, and possibly even humiliation. Let us explore a few examples from linguistic politeness research in the area of cross-cultural pragmatics.

Kirkpatrick (2015) cites a study in which the language of requests by Chinese and American speakers was compared (Kirkpatrick & Xu, 2002). While Chinese speakers of English tended to opt for prefacing a request by providing reasons for the request before making the actual request, American speakers of English preferred a reversed order, presenting the request at the outset. The researchers argue that Chinese speakers may perceive American English requests as "rude and abrupt," while Americans may interpret Chinese requesters as "unsure of their ground, tentative, if not inscrutable" (Kirkpatrick, 2015, p. 463). As stated earlier, these negative judgments can lead to an intercultural conflict. In this equation, English falls on the direct side and Chinese on the indirect side. Yet comparing English with some Slavic languages, formulaic English requests that take the rhetorical form of questions (e.g., *Could you close the door?*) fall at the indirect end as more direct imperative forms (e.g., *Close the door*) are normative in Slavic languages (Kirkpatrick, 2015). Given such variation in language use, awareness of various linguistic practices across cultures becomes crucial for respectful and dignified interactions in many social domains.

Another example is the language of refusal and relevant sociocultural values underlying such linguistic behavior. Relatively speaking, American English is found to prefer honesty in providing a reason for turning down an invitation, request, offer, or suggestion, whereas innocent social niceties, or *white lies*, are more socially acceptable in other languages, such as Japanese, as a face-saving strategy for both the speaker and addressee (Kubota, 1996; Moriyama, 1990). American learners of Japanese sometimes find this Japanese convention difficult to emulate at least initially, as they tend to interpret it as a sign of dishonesty (Kubota, 1996; Takamiya & Ishihara, 2013). After I made a presentation at an applied linguistics conference in Indiana in 2005 in which this intercultural challenge was mentioned, an American graduate student in the audience approached me to say how this information opened his eyes to a different interpretation of his Japanese wife's behavior, who would use innocently untruthful remarks in turning down invitations, a behavior he interpreted as deceitful, which led him to start doubting her morality. No thoughts occurred to him that this was an artifact of culture; he had attributed it to a personality issue on the part of his wife. This illustrates how we are prone to use our own cultural lens to evaluate others' behavior if awareness of intercultural differences is unavailable.

However, a cautionary note should be issued because with the rapid progression of migration and interaction across linguistic and cultural borders, identified cultural patterns may become increasingly blurred as multilingual individuals mesh languages and behavioral codes in a complex and unique manner (Canagarajah, 2013). It is important to bear in mind the contextual contingency and dynamic fluidity of these behavioral norms, especially for English used as an international language. The goal of a respectful communicator should be to not essentialize cultures or language users but to elevate a critical awareness of variations in behavioral norms in relation to face and linguistic politeness, as well as to cultivate interest in, respect for, and appreciation of such diversity. In the following sections, I discuss how this awareness can be capitalized on in two contrasting cases: the professional development of diplomats and a peace-oriented curriculum for elementary education.

Raising Awareness of Oppositional Talk in Diplomacy

In the context of diplomacy, much of the peace-keeping effort aiming at resolving or avoiding conflicts is made by way of language, typically English as an international language, which is used by at least 1.5 billion people in today's world (Selvi & Yazan, 2013; Statista, 2016; numbers vary depending on sources). While negotiating to advance national and international interests, diplomats can be mindful of dignifying language while maintaining attitudes of openness, empathy, and compassion (LeBlanc, 2016; Friedrich & Gomes de Matos, 2016). Their language should strike a fine balance between being direct and indirect (e.g., Bjørge, 2012), forceful and graceful (Scott, 2016), assertive and empathetic, and persuasive and compromising. Given this challenge, it is evident that verbal and nonverbal language assumes a crucial role if negotiators are to be contextually and interculturally tactful. Thus, awareness of the language of respect and dignity and concrete linguistic and meta-linguistic strategies of that language can be dealt with in professional development programs for diplomats in a manner informed by research in linguistic politeness. Below is an example of this type of linguistic awareness based on the notion of *face* and how it can apply to the expression of an oppositional stance such as disagreements, challenges, denials, or accusations.

As mentioned above, the expression of face and politeness varies across languages and cultures and can influence our perceptions of others as we are inclined to interpret others' manners according to the norms of behavior we are socialized into. The notion of *face* in linguistics (pragmatics) refers to the positive social value or public images of self we strive to uphold for ourselves and our partners in conversation (Goffman, 1967), a concept similar to respect or dignity. Face cannot be assumed to exist in all interactions but needs to be protected, saved, and maintained mutually. Loss of face can be equated with embarrassment and humiliation (Culpeper & Haugh, 2014; Lindner, 2009), and there always is a risk of threatening, losing, or aggravating face in communication (Bremner, 2013; Locher, 2012). That is, we must collaboratively engage in the *facework* of co-constructing mutual respect, dignity, and integrity in all human interactions.

The concept of *positive* and *negative politeness* (Brown & Levinson, 1987; Goffman, 1967) may also be useful in understanding different linguistic orientations in expressing politeness. In this case, the terms *positive* and *negative* refer to one's optimistic or pessimistic stance in expressing politeness rather than a value judgment of good or bad. Negative face wants consist of our desire for independence, freedom, and respect. To save or enhance our conversational partner's negative face, we typically express deference, stress our recognition of the importance of the other's time and freedom, apologize for imposition or interruption, or use self-deprecation. For example, when we say *Excuse me, I'm sorry to interrupt you, but if you have a moment…*we draw on negative politeness strategies through a formal attention-getter, an apology, a negative or pessimistic outlook that we may be infringing on our interlocutor's freedom or independence, and a cost-minimizer (i.e., *a moment*). Some cultures, such as British culture, generally rely more extensively upon negative politeness (Johnson, 2006).

In contrast, other cultures, such as Spanish and Greek, are generally oriented toward positive politeness (Johnson, 2006). To address positive face wants, we express solidarity with our interlocutors and stress our common goal or closeness in the relationship (Goffman, 1967). Positive politeness is often expressed through the optimistic standpoint that the addressee shares the same goal and thus must be helpful and cooperative. The language of positive politeness therefore draws on camaraderie and solidarity as in: *Hey guys, we've got some awesome news you wanna hear right now.* Instead of a formal address and an apology for interruption, the speaker uses an informal attention-getter, word choices, contractions (i.e., *hey guys, awesome, wanna*), the inclusive *we*, and a positive outlook on harmony, stressing the common interest.

As discussed earlier, the preference for and acceptability of the choice of positive or negative politeness strategies in a given context varies across cultures and communities. Misunderstandings may occur where there are differences in politeness orientations. For example, in speaking English with a friend from a culture where positive politeness is often emphasized, a request loaded with negative politeness strategies (e.g., *I realize your schedule is tight, but I was wondering if it might be possible to get some help with my relocation this weekend*) may be perceived as distancing and awkward. Conversely, emphasis on positive politeness (e.g., *Dude, you wanna help me move this weekend?*) may be interpreted as imposing or even self-centered by an addressee with a preference for negative politeness. Unfortunately, such negative perceptions and interpretations can readily be attributed to flaws in the speaker's personality rather than to different orientations in communication styles, possibly leading to negative judgments, animosity, or essentialization of cultures.

Likewise, in diplomatic negotiations involving interactants from a wide range of cultural backgrounds, positive politeness strategies that may be intended as amicable, friendly, or pleasant may be misinterpreted as intrusive, excessively informal, or simply rude. In turn, well-intended negative politeness strategies could create the misguided impression of being overly distant, alienating, or aloof. In diplomacy, being aware of various cultural orientations in the use of politeness may be conducive to remaining open and compassionate toward other cultures that may prefer different linguistic and social conventions. Furthermore, this awareness can assist in the strategic choice and use of linguistic politeness according to context and addressee. More specifically, in expressing oppositional views such as disagreements, negative politeness strategies function to minimize potential face threats, namely, discomfort, embarrassment, or humiliation caused by oppositional views. These strategies include the use of a variety of mitigating devices and pessimistic stance markers. A linguistically equipped diplomat may also strategically employ positive politeness, such as compliments, partial agreement, jokes, or inclusive pronouns (e.g., *we* and *us*) to stress commonality of opinion and collegiality (Holtgraves, 1997; Johnson, 2006; Malamed, 2010). For instance, an expression of disagreement such as *Great, that sounds like an excellent idea, but I think it might be a bit premature* includes a combination of positive and negative politeness strategies. (See Ishihara, 2016 in the edited book, *English for Diplomatic Purposes* for specific mitigating devices for expressing disagreement and meta-linguistic pointers for observing the negotiation of disagreements by expert diplomats.)

As noted in the last example, it should be stressed that various positive and negative politeness strategies are often employed jointly to express layers of nuances and that such language use is contextually dependent. That is, the interactants negotiate linguistic strategies based on factors including relative social status, age, level of acquaintance, gender, and the stakes involved in the situation in addition to their linguistic and cultural orientations. Therefore, the negotiation of linguistic politeness should be viewed as dynamic and subject to both diachronic and synchronic change (Culpeper & Haugh, 2014), interactively co-constructed, and contextually dependent.

Raising Awareness of the Language of Empathy in Education

In the educational context, the language of respect and dignity can be incorporated into language instruction. In fact, Gomes de Matos (2012, 2013) goes so far as to argue that children deserve a peace-oriented curriculum and encourages educators to always challenge students to elevate their sense of communicative dignity, justice, and peace. To illustrate this orientation, let me introduce a case study of elementary education in Japan (Ishihara, Orihashi, & Clark, under review) in which peace education content was integrated with instruction in the *Language of Empathy* from a *peace linguistics* perspective (Friedrich, 2012; Gomes de Matos, 2014) as well as theories of linguistic politeness (Brown & Levinson, 1987). (A short video featuring this instruction is accessible at: https://youtu. be/Kld11FuRZpU.) The instruction was designed collaboratively between elementary homeroom teachers, a district educational leader (Orihashi), an American assistant language teacher (Clark), and an applied linguist (Ishihara). The instructional objectives included (but not limited to): 1) learning about the history of the "friendship dolls" in the school community gifted by U.S. citizens as tokens of peace and friendship; and 2) developing compassion with the "friends" who experienced wartime atrocities via the *Language of Empathy.*

Back in 1927, over 12,700 dolls representing 48 U.S. States were gifted by American citizens to Japan as tokens of peace and friendship and distributed to kindergarten and elementary schools across Japan, attracting children's attention and admiration. During World War II, following a top-down military order, many of these dolls were destroyed, often cruelly, being burned or speared as they became identified as the symbol of the enemy. Only about 240 dolls survived thanks to brave protectors; one of them was found in one of the schools where this instruction took place. Since 2012, district educational leader Orihashi has been implementing instruction designed to address this local history as part of peace education on the one hand and to stimulate students' motivation to communicate in English on the other, as students were asked to interact with the surviving doll, whose voice was reenacted by Clark hiding behind a curtain (Orihashi, 2016). In 2016, Ishihara joined as a university researcher and suggested an additional instructional component on the *Language of Empathy* to incorporate the perspective of *peace linguistics* as well as research in *linguistic politeness*. The instruction was implemented in a small city in Central Japan with a total of 57 six-graders nearing graduation. The data for this ethnographic case study consisted of documents (e.g., lesson plans, worksheets), video recordings of the lessons, and reflective writings by the students and educators involved.

In the initial phase of instruction in social studies classes, students discussed the historical background and researched relevant facts according to their interests. Student reflections elicited at the end of this phase indicated that they gradually achieved a comprehensive understanding of the local history and a range of wartime mentalities and developed compassion with the "friend doll" who underwent hardships and survived to be 90 years old.

In the second phase, students prepared English questions for the doll and her new companion, gifted in 2007, and interacted with them in English, a most exciting activity for the majority of students, who had hardly ever used English for meaningful communication. While most were innocent questions, several were potentially offensive or hurtful to the dolls: *Why do you have blue eyes? Why does your skin break and fade?* Upon hearing these questions, Clark (in the dolls' voices) started to sob, asking a rhetorical question, *"Why are your eyes brown?"* back to the students, thus indirectly encouraging students to accept different appearances. Our intention was to have students directly experience the consequences of these questions.

With Orihashi supporting the interaction by meshing English and Japanese throughout, these teachers co-constructed with students a firsthand experience of how careless language use can seriously hurt the feelings of a conversational partner.

Subsequently in two moral education classes, students were afforded an opportunity to revisit their learning, drawing on the notion of the *Language of Empathy* at a meta-linguistic level. First, the instruction addressed possible strategies for phrasing potentially face-threatening questions. Informed by research on face and politeness, these meta-linguistic strategies included: (i) alerting the listener to an upcoming question (i.e., using *alerters*) (e.g., variations of *Can I ask you a personal question?*); (ii) asking indirectly through non-threatening language (e.g., *What happened to your friends?* rather than *Why did your friends die?*); and (iii) *opting out* of asking directly to ask someone else or explore another means or timing. The students' reflective writings showed that all of them understood the point and agreed on the potential impact of the Language of Empathy. They were also able to demonstrate their enhanced (meta-)linguistic awareness through a variety of language examples embodying empathy (e.g., Japanese equivalents of: *It may be a difficult question to answer, but may I ask...? You don't have to answer, but..., I'd be happy to hear if you could tell me...*; and retrospectively *I'm sorry for having asked*).

Second, the moral education class dealt with the application of the Language of Empathy in an activity in which students discussed specific language they could use in a similar but novel situation. The students demonstrated a sophisticated ability to use an array of expressions representing the Language of Empathy. In addition to alerters (see above) and apologies, they used a range of cost-minimizers (e.g., *if possible*), disclaimers (e.g., *you don't have to tell me if you don't want to*), and *keigo* honorifics to enhance the general levels of politeness (e.g., humble verb forms and polite particles). They even consciously focused on the positive and sometimes paid attention to the sequential organization of their messages to soften the blow of their questions. Their reflective writings showed that conducting this exploration as a group activity further provided a collaborative opportunity to notice and learn from each other's language strategies.

Moreover, Orihashi's informal observation of these students after graduation showed that at least some of them retained their awareness of the Language of Empathy and used it to cultivate friendships at a new junior high school. We hope to continue to observe the potential long-term impact of this instruction now that Orihashi and Clark teach them on a regular basis. The students' learning we have documented can be attributed to fruitful collaboration across various subject areas and academic fields. This allows recursive and iterative instruction to reinforce learning in several subjects from multiple perspectives. Our results indicate that respectful language use and awareness of it may be amenable to instruction at a young age. (See Ishihara, Orihashi, & Clark, under review and a video introduced above for details of this study.)

Conclusion

The preparation of this chapter provided me with an inspiring challenge as I attempted to discover how a common thread in linguistic politeness (pragmatics), peace linguistics, and HumanDHS mesh and can jointly reap the benefits of the shared insights, especially how peace linguistics and HumanDHS can contribute the broader perspective of peacebuilding and social justice to the type of research and second language education and teacher development I engage in on a daily basis. The two examples of diplomacy and education represent my emerging efforts as I strive to build this bridge. To go further, Lindner's (2009, 2016) notion of humiliation is broad enough to encompass aggression, conflict, rage, threats, and insults conveyed by way of language and clearly overlaps with the focus of investigation in pragmatics and peace linguistics. In fact, the field of pragmatics has recently started to direct greater attention to impoliteness and rudeness in addition to a conventional focus on politeness. An extension of this line of research can (and should) include a focus on humiliation, which in the field of pragmatics may develop into, for example, the structure of the language of humiliation and in-depth analysis of its co-constructed development in interaction. More importantly, holistic exploration of the emotions and impacts of experiencing humiliation on individuals and communities will shed a humanitarian light on issues of dignity, integrity, marginalization, bias, social justice, human rights, and peace and can perhaps be most effectively accomplished through cross-fertilization resulting from interdisciplinary research.

References

Bjørge, Anne Kari. 2012. "Expressing disagreement in ELF business negotiations: Theory and practice." *Applied Linguistics* 33 (4):406-427.

Bremner, Stephen. 2013. "Politeness and face research." In *The Encyclopedia of Applied Linguistics*, edited by Carol A. Chapelle, 1–6. Oxford: Blackwell Publishing.

Brown, Penelope, and Stephen C. Levinson. 1987. *Politeness: Some Universals in Language Use.* Cambridge: Cambridge University Press.

Canagarajah, Suresh. 2013. *Translingual Practice: Global Englishes and Cosmopolitan Relations.* London: Routledge.

Culpeper, Jonathan, and Michael Haugh. 2014. *Pragmatics and the English Language.* New York: Palgrave Macmillan.

Friedrich, Patricia, ed. 2012. *Nonkilling Linguistics: Practical Applications.* Honolulu, HI: Center for Global Nonkilling.

Friedrich, Patricia, and Francisco Gomes de Matos. 2016. "Toward a nonkilling linguistics." In *English for Diplomatic Purposes*, edited by Patricia Friedrich, 1-19. Bristol: Multilingual Matters.

Goffman, E. 1967. *Interaction Ritual: Essays on Face-to-Face Behavior.* New York: Pantheon.

Gomes de Matos, Francisco. 2012. *Innovation in Language Teaching: A Checklist.* ABA Poster Series. Recife: ABA Global Education.

Gomes de Matos, Francisco. 2013. *Dignity: A Multidimensional View.* Lake Oswego, OR: Dignity Press.

Gomes de Matos, Francisco. 2014. "Language, peace, and conflict resolution." In *The Handbook of Conflict Resolution: Theory and Practice*, edited by Peter T. Coleman, Morton Deutsch, and Eric C. Marcus, 182-202. San Francisco: Jossey-Bass.

Hartling, Linda M. 2007. Personal communication cited in Lindner, Evelin. 2009. *Emotion and conflict: How human rights can dignify emotion and help us wage good conflict*. Westport, CT: Praeger, p. 48, May 12, 2007.

Holmes, Janet, and Dorothy F. Brown. 1987. "Teachers and students learning about compliments." *TESOL Quarterly* 21 (3):523-546.

Holtgraves, Thomas. 1997. "Yes, but...: Positive politeness in conversation arguments." *Journal of Language and Social Psychology* 16 (2):222-239.

Ishihara, Noriko. 2016. "Softening or intensifying your language in oppositional talk: Disagreeing agreeably or defiantly." In *English for Diplomatic Purposes*, edited by Patricia Friedrich, 20-41. Bristol: Multilingual Matters.

Ishihara, Noriko, and Andrew D. Cohen. 2010. *Teaching and learning pragmatics: Where language and culture meet*. Harlow: Pearson Education (republished in 2014, Abingdon: Routledge).

Ishihara, N., and Terumi Orihashi. in preparation. "Innovations in elementary classrooms: Integrating the teaching of English, history, and peace linguistics." In *Innovations in Language Learning and Teaching: The Case of Japan*, edited by Hayo Reinders, Stephen Ryan, and Sachiko Nakao.

Johnson, Fiona. 2006. "Agreement and disagreement: A cross-cultural comparison." *BISAL* 1:41-67.

Kirkpatrick, Andy. 2015. "World Englishes and local cultures." In *The Routledge Handbook of Language and Culture*, edited by Farzad Sharifian, 460-470. Oxford: Routledge.

Kirkpatrick, Andy, and Xu Zhichang. 2002. "Chinese pragmatic norms and 'China English.'" *World Englishes* 21 (2):269-279.

Kubota, Mitsuo. 1996. "Acquaintance or fiancée: Pragmatic differences in requests." *Working Papers in Educational Linguistics* 12 (1):24-38.

LeBlanc, Josette. 2016. "Compassionate English communication for diplomatic purposes." In *English for Diplomatic Purposes*, edited by Patricia Friedrich, 42-74. Bristol: Multilingual Matters.

Lindner, Evelin. 2009. *Emotion and Conflict: How Human Rights Can Dignify Emotion and Help Us Wage Good Conflict*. Westport, CT: Praeger.

Lindner, Evelin. 2016. "The journey of humiliation and dignity and the significance of the year 1757." Retrieved May 10, 2017 from: http://www.humiliationstudies.org/documents/evelin/Significanceof1757.pdf

Locher, Miriam A. 2012. "Situated impoliteness: The interface between relational work and identity construction." In *Situated Politeness*, edited by Bethan L. Davies, Michael Haugh, and Andrew J. Merrison, 187-208. London: Bloomsbury.

Malamed, Lewis H. 2010. "Disagreement: How to disagree agreeably." In *Speech Act Performance: Theoretical, Empirical, and Methodological Issues*, edited by Alicia Martínez-Flor and Esther Usó-Juan, 199-215. Amsterdam: John Benjamins.

Moriyama, T. 1990. "'Kotowari' no houryaku: Taijin kankei chouseito komyunikeishon [Strategies of refusals: Interpersonal adjustments and communication]." *Gengo* 19 (8):59-66.

Orihashi, Terumi. 2016. "Kataraseru gengo katsudokara kataridasu gengo katsudoe: Aoi meno ningyowo daizaini shite [Improving English education: Change of focus from repetition and pattern practice to communication with motivation using the 'Japanese blue-eyed doll' story as a case study]." *JES Journal* 16:4-17.

Piller, Ingrid. 2011. *Intercultural Communication: A Critical Introduction*. Edinburgh: Edinburgh University Press.

Scott, Biljana. 2016. "Force and grace." In *English for Diplomatic Purposes*, edited by Patricia Friedrich, 149-172. Bristol: Multilingual Matters.

Selvi, Ali F., and Bedrettin Yazan. (2013). *Teaching English as an International Language*. Alexandria, VA: TESOL.

Spencer-Oatey, Helen. 2000. *Culturally Speaking: Managing Rapport through Talk Across Cultures*. London: Continuum.

Statista. 2016. The most spoken languages worldwide. Retrieved on May 14, 2017, from http://www.statista.com/statistics/266808/the-most-spoken-languages-worldwide/

Takamiya, Yumi, and Noriko Ishihara. 2013. "Blogging: Cross-cultural interaction for pragmatic development." In *Technology in Interlanguage Pragmatics Research and Teaching*, edited by Naoko Taguchi and Julie Sykes, 185-214. Philadelphia, PA: John Benjamins.

Whitney, Diana, and Amanda Trosten-Bloom. 2010. *The Power of Appreciative Inquiry: A Practical Guide to Positive Change* (2nd edition). Oakland, CA: Berrett-Koehler.

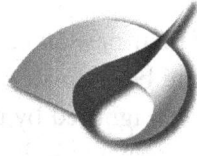

Chapter Six

Dignity and Therapeutic Jurisprudence: How We Can Best End Shame and Humiliation

Michael L. Perlin[*]

Introduction

I will begin with a few very short paragraphs about who I am, what I have done, and I what I continue to do. Before I became a law professor at New York Law School (a position which I held for over thirty years), I spent thirteen years as a lawyer representing persons with mental disabilities, including three years in which my focus was primarily on such individuals charged with a crime. In this role, during my time as a Deputy Public Defender in Mercer County (Trenton), New Jersey, I represented several hundred individuals at the "maximum security hospital for the criminally insane" in New Jersey habeas corpus hearings and in a class action.[1]

For eight years after that, I was the director of the New Jersey

---

*The author first came to an HumanDHS meeting in 2007, and has been a regular participant/presenter since. He is eternally thankful to Evelin, Linda and their colleagues for welcoming him with open arms, and for encouraging him to continue to write about the issues of shame, humiliation, and dignity. The first item filled in on his new calendar is always the December meeting.

Division of Mental Health Advocacy. This state division was part of a then-new office, the State Department of the Public Advocate, that had been created to provide legal representation to those who had been ignored by the justice system, a "voice for the voiceless."[2] We represented — literally — tens of thousands of persons in individual matters in civil commitment cases, post-insanity acquittal release hearings, refusal of treatment cases, and the full range of law reform and test case litigation that challenged the way patients were treated in state hospitals and in community settings.[3]

I then became a law professor, and continued to teach and write about these same topics. Mental disability law was the center of the Venn diagram of my scholarship, with concentric circles of criminal law and procedure, international human rights law, sexual autonomy and sexual offending, the quality of legal representation of the populations in question, and therapeutic jurisprudence. Although I retired from the full-time faculty in December 2014, and now have *emeritus* status, I continue writing about these topics to the present day.

Some twenty-one years ago, I wrote an article criticizing a then-current United States Supreme Court decision that allowed seriously mentally ill criminal defendants to represent themselves at trial. I titled it, *Dignity Was the First to Leave:** Godinez v. Moran, *Colin Ferguson, and the Trial of Mentally Disabled Criminal Defendants,*[4] because I thought that that line — of Bob Dylan's — was the perfect descriptor for what happened in trials when that set of circumstances occurred. As I have written elsewhere, something "clicked" with me when I did that, and I have continued to use Dylan titles and lyrics ever since (with no sign of let up).[5] But, for the purposes of this volume, *something else* "clicked," and that has significantly changed the focus of my scholarship in the subsequent years. When I was fortunate enough to meet Evelin Lindner and Linda Hartling, and become part of the Human Dignity and Humiliation Studies (HumanDHS) community over a decade later, my focus became even further sharpened. I believe that I first participated in an HumanDHS meeting in December 2007, when I presented a short talk on *Humiliation and the Criminal Justice System: How Our Desire to Humiliate Contributes to Recidivism and,*

Ultimately, Injures Victims.[6] Since that time, I have turned regularly to the issues of shame and humiliation — along with dignity — in my scholarship (and in my HumanDHS short talks), especially in the context of therapeutic jurisprudence,[7] and I owe Evelin and Linda a great debt of gratitude for their teachings, guidance, and inspirations.

In this short chapter, I will do the following. First, I will explain how, starting with the *Dignity Was the First to Leave…*article, I have come to focus on dignity in all the concentric circles of my scholarship. Then, I will do the same with my focus on shame and humiliation. Finally, I will explain the meaning of therapeutic jurisprudence (TJ), and how the HumanDHS's focus on "respect for equal dignity" is a perfect "fit" with the principles and precepts of TJ.

Dignity

Our legal system must be premised upon the dignity of the individual.[8] As Professor Tom Tyler has taught us in his groundbreaking work on procedural justice, perceptions of systemic fairness are driven, in large part, by "the degree to which people judge that they are treated with dignity and respect."[9] In a recent article about dignity and the civil commitment process, Professors Jonathan Simon and Stephen Rosenbaum embrace therapeutic jurisprudence as a modality of analysis, and focus specifically on this issue of "voice": "When procedures give people an opportunity to exercise voice, their words are given respect, decisions are explained to them, their views taken into account, and they substantively feel less coercion."[10]

Similarly, I believe that legal education must integrate dignity teachings into the curriculum. Learning to give clients dignity, voice, and validation will be critical skills to develop the empathy that can lead students to choose to pursue careers in public interest law.[11] Also, judges must incorporate dignity values into their day-to-day work in courtrooms; when "legal proceedings do not treat people with dignity, they feel devalued as members of society."[12]

Adherence to dignity values is one of the basic cores of the HumanDHS. In the second sentence of HumanDHS's website's homepage, it is made clear: "We wish to stimulate systemic change, globally and locally, to open space for dignity."[13] Core member Michael Britton described it in this manner: In HumanDHS, "the labors of inquiry, honesty, integrity, dignity, trust and trustworthiness, and humility are at the heart of who we are and what we do."[14]

Since I wrote about dignity in the 1996 article that I mentioned earlier, I have returned to it multiple times, both in articles and book chapters[15] and in a free-standing book, the latter entitled, *A Prescription for Dignity: Rethinking Criminal Justice and Mental Disability Law*.[16] There is no question in my mind that my yearly participation in the HumanDHS conferences — not just the fact that I have presented, but that I was fortunate enough to hear so many other gifted colleagues share *their* ideas about dignity — was the major inspiration for this collection of writings.

Shame and Humiliation

A goal of HumanDHS is also set out explicitly in its first web page: "Our goal is *ending humiliating practices*, preventing new ones from arising, and fostering healing from cycles of humiliation throughout the world."[17] In a recent article, Evelin Lindner and Linda Hartling explain how "some victims of humiliation may internalize their experience as shame, blaming themselves for their experience."[18] In another piece, co-authored with Britton and another, they argue — forcefully and compellingly — that "humiliation is the global-social nuclear bomb of emotions,"[19] noting that "crippling a target by triggering their self-protective sense of shame is precisely what perpetrators of humiliation attempt to utilize, often successfully, even though there is no reason for the target to feel ashamed."[20]

When I started to come to HumanDHS meetings, this resounded with me so forcefully. In the years that I had represented marginalized and indigent criminal defendants and persons in psychiatric hospitals (or subject to such hospitalization), I was always aware of the omnipresence of the feelings of shame and humiliation that befell my clients, but I had never been able to articulate the issues in the way

that Evelin and Linda did. As I indicated above, my initial presentation to an HumanDHS conference was on exactly this topic: *Humiliation and the Criminal Justice System: How Our Desire to Humiliate
Contributes to Recidivism and, Ultimately, Injures Victims.* In that talk,
I made these points: that (1) there is not a shred of empirical evidence
that [shaming and humiliating] sanctions have any utilitarian value,
(2) such tactics are more likely to be (a) counter-productive, leading
to further criminal activity, (b) utterly contradictory to the aims of
therapeutic jurisprudence and/or restorative justice, and (c) ultimately
demeaning to the victims of the initial criminal activity, and thus (3)
there should be ban on…such punishments.[21]

Again, when I did this short talk, something "clicked," and my
scholarly and advocacy foci immediately expanded to include these
issues. Some years later, with a colleague, I turned that short seven
minute presentation into a sixty-one-page law review article(!).[22]
I have since turned to shame and humiliation several times in my
subsequent writing,[23] and in my most recent presentation to an
HumanDHS conference.[24]

In these writings, I argue squarely that "humiliation and shaming
contravene basic fundamental human rights and raise important
constitutional questions implicating the due process and equal protection clauses,"[25] and that they "lead to recidivism, inhibit rehabilitation,
discourage treatment, and injure victims."[26] Laws that humiliate "can
provoke feelings of hopelessness, and unworthiness"[27] and can trigger
relapse in ex-offenders.[28] Importantly, this shaming is inevitably
public; thus, its dehumanization and social demotion occurs when
a shameful trait or act becomes "visible, and is exposed to others."[29]

Again, the environment that Evelin and Linda have created — not
just at the NYC conferences, but worldwide — has given us all a safe
space to assess the impacts of these pernicious influences on our lives

Therapeutic Jurisprudence

Finally, what is "therapeutic jurisprudence"?[30] One of the most
important legal theoretical developments of the past three decades has

been the creation and dynamic growth of therapeutic jurisprudence (TJ).[31] Therapeutic jurisprudence presents a new model for assessing the impact of case law and legislation, recognizing that, as a therapeutic agent, the law that can have therapeutic or anti-therapeutic consequences.[32]

Therapeutic jurisprudence asks whether legal rules, procedures, and lawyer roles can or should be reshaped to enhance their therapeutic potential while not subordinating due process principles.[33] David Wexler clearly identifies how the inherent tension inherent in this inquiry must be resolved: "the law's use of mental health information to improve therapeutic functioning [cannot] impinge upon justice concerns."[34] As I have written elsewhere, "An inquiry into therapeutic outcomes does not mean that therapeutic concerns 'trump' civil rights and civil liberties."[35]

Using TJ, we "look at law as it actually impacts people's lives"[36] and assess law's influence on emotional life and psychological well-being.[37] One governing TJ principle is that "law should value psychological health, should strive to avoid imposing anti-therapeutic consequences whenever possible, and when consistent with other values served by law should attempt to bring about healing and wellness."[38] TJ supports an ethic of care.[39]

How does this relate to the two themes I am writing about in this chapter: dignity and shame/humiliation? First, I believe that *dignity* is the core of the entire therapeutic jurisprudence enterprise, and do not think we can seriously write about or think about TJ without taking seriously the role of dignity in the legal process. One of the central principles of TJ is a commitment to dignity.[40] TJ may also lend dignity to the voice of those who are subordinated.[41] Boiled down to its most essential element, *therapeutic jurisprudence adds the dignity and value of the individual human being to legal analysis in a formal way."[42]

This is accentuated in the context of shame and humiliation. Keeping in mind that the law always has the power to shame and humiliate,[43] it is crystalline-clear that humiliation in the law utterly contradicts the aims of TJ and undermines the role of dignity.[44] These behaviors "directly contravene the guiding principles of therapeutic jurisprudence, especially in the context of its relationship to the importance of dignity in the law."[45]

Conclusion

As I indicated at the beginning of this chapter, I have spent most of my career representing, advocating for, and teaching about persons with mental disabilities. Disproportionately, this population is deprived of its freedom, dignity, and basic human rights,[46] and is subject to rampant shame and humiliation.[47] The work that Evelin Lindner, Linda Hartling, and their colleagues do represents a path out of this morass, and shines a light on approaches that can remediate some of what has gone on — and continues to go on — in matters involving these individuals. In a recent article, they issue this challenge: "we need an 'all hands on deck' approach to changing the global–social biosphere."[48] I concur.

Those of us in the therapeutic jurisprudence movement — lawyers, mental health professionals, criminologists, and sociologists — have been focusing on these issues for over twenty-five years. I believe that a coalition between those of us in that movement and those in the human dignity movement — my friend and colleague David Yamada, my friend and co-author Alison Lynch, and I are boundary spanners who are active in both — offers the best way to begin to solve the problems we face. I will eternally be grateful to Evelin, to Linda and to all the other HumanDHS stalwarts for creating a safe space in which these topics can be discussed, and for encouraging me to take this path in my own work.

Notes

1. Dixon v. Cahill, No. L30977/y-71 P.W. (N.J. Super. Ct. Law Div. 1973), reprinted in Michael L. Perlin & Heather Ellis Cucolo, MENTAL DISABILITY LAW: CIVIL AND CRIMINAL § 19-8 (3d ed. 2016).
2. Michael L. Perlin, *"John Brown Went Off to War": Considering Veterans' Courts as Problem-Solving Courts*, 37 NOVA L. REV. 445, 446 (2013).

3. *See* generally Michael L. Perlin, *Mental Patient Advocacy by a Patient Advocate,* 54 PSYCHIATRIC Q. 169 (1982) (advocating for legal advocacy at commitment hearings); Michael L. Perlin, *"Infinity Goes up on Trial": Sanism, Pretextuality, and the Representation of Defendants with Mental Disabilities,* 16 QUT L. REV. 106, 106-07 (2016); Michael L. Perlin, *"Justice's Beautiful Face": Bob Sadoff and the Redemptive Promise of Therapeutic Jurisprudence,* 40 J. PSYCHIATRY & L. 265, 265, 278 n.2 (2012).

4. 14 BEHAV. SCI. & L. 61 (1996).

5. See Michael L. Perlin, *Tangled Up In Law: The Jurisprudence of Bob Dylan,* 38 FORD. URB. L.J. 1395 (2011); see also, Michael L. Perlin, *Dignity and the Nobel Prize: Why Bob Dylan Was the Perfect Choice,* available at https://www.youtube. com/watch?v=HgRepQhW2xQ&feature=youtu.be.

6. http://www.humiliationstudies.org/whoweare/annualmeeting/10.php.

7. I believe I have missed one NYC-based meeting only in the past decade (if that), and, as I noted above, the dates for the 2018 conference are already on my calendar.

8. See generally infra text accompanying notes 31-40.

9. Michael L. Perlin, *'Everything's a Little Upside Down, As a Matter of Fact the Wheels Have Stopped: The Fraudulence of the Incompetency Evaluation Process,* 4 HOUSTON J. HEALTH L. & POL=Y 239, 251(2004).

10. Tom R. Tyler, *The Psychological Consequences of Judicial Procedures: Implications for Civil Commitment Hearings,* 46 SMU L. REV. 433, 442 (1992).

11. Jonathan Simon & Stephen A. Rosenbaum, *Dignifying Madness: Rethinking Commitment Law in an Age of Mass Incarceration,* 70 U. MIAMI L. REV. 1, 51 (2015).

12. Michael L. Perlin & Alison J. Lynch, *How Teaching about Therapeutic Jurisprudence Can Be a Tool of Social Justice, and Lead Law Students to Personally and Socially Rewarding Careers: Sexuality and Disability as a Case Example,* 16 NEVADA L.J. 209, 233 (2015).

13. Bruce Winick, *Therapeutic Jurisprudence and the Civil Commitment Hearing,* 10 J. CONTEMP. LEGAL ISSUES 37, 44-45 (1999).

14. http://www.humiliationstudies.org/ (emphasis added)

15. Id.

16. See e.g., Michael L. Perlin & Alison J. Lynch, *"She's Nobody's Child/The Law Can't Touch Her at All": Seeking to Bring Dignity to Legal Proceedings Involving Juveniles,* 56 FAM. CT. REV. – (2018) (forthcoming); Michael L. Perlin, *"Have You Seen Dignity?": The Story of the Development of Therapeutic Jurisprudence,* — N.Z. U. LAW REV. — (2017) (forthcoming); Heather Ellis Cucolo & Michael L. Perlin, *Promoting Dignity and Preventing Shame and Humiliation by Improving the Quality and Education of Attorneys in Sexually Violent Predator (SVP) Civil Commitment Cases,* 28 FLA. J. L. & PUB. POL'Y 100 (2017, forthcoming); Michael L. Perlin, *"The Judge, He Cast His Robe Aside": Mental Health Courts, Dignity and Due Process,* 3 MENT. HEALTH L. & POL'Y J. 1 (2013); Michael L. Perlin, *"There Are No Trials Inside the Gates of Eden": Mental Health Courts, the*

Convention on the Rights of Persons with Disabilities, Dignity, and the Promise of Therapeutic Jurisprudence, in COERCIVE CARE: RIGHTS, LAW AND POLICY 193 (Bernadette McSherry & Ian Freckelton, eds. 2013) (Routledge); Michael L. Perlin, *Understanding the Intersection between International Human Rights and Mental Disability Law: The Role of Dignity,* in The Routledge Handbook of International Crime and Justice Studies, 191 (Bruce Arrigo & Heather Bersot, eds.) (2013).

17. (Ashgate 2013).

18. http://www.humiliationstudies.org/ (emphasis added).

19. Linda M. Hartling & Evelin Lindner, *Healing Humiliation: From Reaction to Creative Action,* 94 J. COUNSELING & DEVELOPMENT 383, 385 (2016).

20. Linda M. Hartling et al., *Humiliation: A Nuclear Bomb of Emotions?* 46 PSICOLOGÍA POLÍTICA 55 (2013).

21. Id. at 62.

22. http://www.humiliationstudies.org/whoweare/annualmeeting/10.php

23. Michael L. Perlin & Naomi Weinstein, *"Friend to the Martyr, a Friend to the Woman of Shame": Thinking About The Law, Shame and Humiliation,* 24 SO. CAL. REV. L. & SOC'L JUST. 1 (2014).

24. E.g., Michael; L. Perlin & Alison J. Lynch, *"To Wander Off in Shame": Deconstructing the Shaming and Shameful Arrest Policies of Urban Police Departments in Their Treatment of Persons with Mental Disabilities,* in POWER, HUMILIATION AND VIOLENCE (Prof. Daniel Rothbart ed. 2017, forthcoming): Cucolo & Perlin, supra note 16; see also, Michael Perlin, MENTAL DISABILITY AND THE DEATH PENALTY: THE SHAME OF THE STATES (Rowman & Littlefield 2013).

25. Michael L. Perlin, Alison J. Lynch & Alexander J. Perlin, *"Them Who Are Slandered and Humiliated": How Marijuana Arrest Patterns Perpetuate a Racist Criminal Justice System and Shame and Humiliate Minority Youth* (to be presented Dec. 7, 2017).

26. Perlin & Weinstein, *supra* note 23, at 1.

27. Id. at 2.

28. Heather Ellis Cucolo & Michael L. Perlin, *Preventing Sex-Offender Recidivism through Therapeutic Jurisprudence Approaches and Specialized Community Integration,* 22 TEMPLE POLITICAL & CIVIL RTS. L. REV. 1, 30 (2012).

29. Jill S. Levenson & Leo P. Cotter, *The Impact of Sex Offender Residence Restrictions: 1,000 Feet From Danger or One Step From Absurd?,* 49 INT'L. J. OFFENDER THERAPY & COMP. CRIMINOLOGY 168, 169 (2005).

30. Perlin & Lynch, *supra* note 24, manuscript at 13, quoting, in part, Toni Massaro, *Shame, Culture and American Criminal Law,* 89 MICH. L. REV. 1880, 1902 (1991).

31. This section is largely adapted from Michael L. Perlin, *"I've Got My Mind Made Up": How Judicial Teleology in Cases Involving Biologically Based Evidence Violates Therapeutic Jurisprudence,* – CARDOZO JOURNAL OF EQUAL RIGHTS AND SOCIAL JUSTICE – (2018) (forthcoming). It also distills my work from nearly

the past quarter-century. See Michael L. Perlin, *What Is Therapeutic Jurisprudence?*, 10 N.Y.L. SCH. J. HUM. RTS. 623 (1993).

32. *See* e.g., DAVID B. WEXLER, THERAPEUTIC JURISPRUDENCE: THE LAW AS A THERAPEUTIC AGENT (1990); DAVID B. WEXLER & BRUCE J. WINICK, LAW IN A THERAPEUTIC KEY: RECENT DEVELOPMENTS IN THERAPEUTIC JURISPRUDENCE (1996); BRUCE J. WINICK, CIVIL COMMITMENT: A THERAPEUTIC JURISPRUDENCE MODEL (2005). Wexler first used the term in a paper he presented to the National Institute of Mental Health in 1987. *See* David B. Wexler, *Putting Mental Health into Mental Health Law: Therapeutic Jurisprudence,* 16 LAW & HUM. BEHAV. 27, 27, 32-33 (1992); David B. Wexler, *Therapeutic Jurisprudence Forum: The Development of Therapeutic Jurisprudence: From Theory to Practice,* 68 REV. JUR. U.P.R. 691, 693-94 (1999).

33. *See* Michael L. Perlin, *"His Brain Has Been Mismanaged with Great Skill": How Will Jurors Respond to Neuroimaging Testimony in Insanity Defense Cases?,* 42 AKRON L. REV. 885, 912 (2009); see also, Kate Diesfeld & Ian Freckelton, *Mental Health Law and Therapeutic Jurisprudence,* in DISPUTES AND DILEMMAS IN HEALTH LAW 91 (Ian Freckelton & Kate Peterson eds. 2006) (for a transnational perspective).

34. Michael L. Perlin, *"Everybody Is Making Love/Or Else Expecting Rain": Considering the Sexual Autonomy Rights of Persons Institutionalized Because of Mental Disability in Forensic Hospitals and in Asia,* 83 WASH. L. REV. 481 (2008); Michael L. Perlin, *"And My Best Friend, My Doctor, Won't Even Say What It Is I've Got": The Role and Significance of Counsel in Right to Refuse Treatment Cases,* 42 SAN DIEGO L. REV. 735, 751 (2005). *See also,* Ian Freckelton, *Therapeutic Jurisprudence Misunderstood and Misrepresented: The Price and Risks of Influence,* 30 T. JEFFERSON L. REV. 575, 585-86 (2008).

35. David B. Wexler, *Therapeutic Jurisprudence and Changing Concepts of Legal Scholarship,* 11 BEHAV. SCI. & L. 17, 21 (1993). *See* also, e.g., David Wexler, *Applying the Law Therapeutically,* 5 APPL. & PREVENT. PSYCHOL. 179 (1996).

36. Michael L. Perlin, A Law of Healing, 68 U. CIN. L. REV. 407, 412 (2000); Michael L. Perlin, *Where the Winds Hit Heavy on the Borderline: Mental Disability Law, Theory and Practice, Us and Them,* 31 LOYOLA L.A. L. REV. 775, 782 (1998).

37. Bruce J. Winick, *Foreword: Therapeutic Jurisprudence Perspectives on Dealing With Victims of Crime,* 33 NOVA L. REV. 535, 535 (2009).

38. David B. Wexler, *Practicing Therapeutic Jurisprudence: Psychological Soft Spots and Strategies,* in Daniel P. Stolle, David B. Wexler & Bruce J. Winick, PRACTICING THERAPEUTIC JURISPRUDENCE: LAW AS A HELPING PROFESSION 45 (2006).

39. Bruce Winick, *A Therapeutic Jurisprudence Model for Civil Commitment,* in INVOLUNTARY DETENTION AND THERAPEUTIC JURISPRUDENCE: INTERNATIONAL PERSPECTIVE ON CIVIL COMMITMENT 23, 26 (Kate Diesfeld & Ian Freckelton eds., 2003).

40. *See* e.g., Bruce J. Winick & David B. Wexler, *The Use of Therapeutic Jurisprudence in Law School Clinical Education: Transforming the Criminal Law Clinic,* 13 CLINICAL L. REV. 605, 605-07 (2006).

41. Perlin & Lynch, *supra* note 12, at 214

42. Keri K. Gould & Michael L. Perlin, *Johnny's in the Basement/Mixing Up His Medicine: Therapeutic Jurisprudence and Clinical Teaching,* 24 SEATTLE U. L. REV. 339, 354 n. 93 (2000).

43. Carol L. Zeiner, *A Therapeutic Jurisprudence Analysis of the Use of Eminent Domain to Create a Leasehold,* 2013 UTAH L. REV. 883, 890.

44. Perlin & Lynch, *supra* note 12, at 224 n 85

45. Perlin & Weinstein, *supra* note 23, at 9.

46. Id. at 2.

47. Id. at 30.

48. Michael L. Perlin, *"Merchants and Thieves, Hungry for Power": Prosecutorial Misconduct and Passive Judicial Complicity in Death Penalty Trials of Defendants with Mental Disabilities,* 73 WASH. & LEE L. REV. 1501, 1503 (2016) ("we should all be profoundly ashamed of a system that shames persons with disabilities").

49. Hartling et al, *supra* note 20, at 69.

50. *See* Michael L. Perlin & Alison J. Lynch, *"Had to be Held Down by Big Police": A Therapeutic Jurisprudence Perspective on Interactions between Police and Persons with Mental Disabilities,* 43 FORDHAM URBAN L.J. 685, 707-08 (2016), discussing the work of Henry Steadman, who defines "boundary spanners" as individuals whose positions "link two or more systems whose goals and expectations are likely to be at least partially conflicting," see Henry J. Steadman, *Boundary Spanners: A Key Component for the Effective Interactions of the Justice and Mental Health Systems,* 16 LAW & HUM. BEHAV. 75, 75-76 (1992); see also, Joel A. Dvoskin & Henry J. Steadman, *Using Intensive Case Management to Reduce Violence by Mentally Ill Persons in the Community,* 45 HOSP. & CMTY. PSYCHIATRY 679, 684 (1994).

Chapter Seven

Humiliation, Social Justice, and Ethno-Mimesis

Maggie O'Neill

Background and Conceptual Framework

In honour of the huge contribution Evelin Lindner has made to social justice by encouraging generations of students, researchers, practitioners and academics to think about humiliation and human dignity through the lens of appreciative enquiry, this paper, for Evelin, revisits my own contribution to my very first Human Dignity and Humiliations Studies workshop at Columbia University in 2005. The Workshop was on Humiliation and Violent Conflict and it was the 6th Annual Meeting of Human Dignity and Humiliation Studies in New York, December 15–16, 2005.

At this workshop and subsequent others, I met many incredible scholars, activists and people committed to the vision of a world free of humiliation and rooted in principles of human dignity. One person who stands out is Garry Davis, an international peace activist, former bomber pilot, who, renounced his U.S. national citizenship in 1948 and committed to world citizenship by creating a world passport. Garry told the workshop that he had travelled on the passport. I signed up for one, but have never travelled on it, and am certainly not as brave as Garry was. I think Garry was around 90 years old when we met at two of the annual workshops that Evelin Lindner, Linda Hartling and her husband Rick organise annually at Columbia University Teachers College. Garry invited me to be interviewed for his weekly radio show, World Citizen Radio. It was such an honour. Garry told us that the "Garry Davis Council of Solidarity" was co-founded by Albert Camus and he was mentioned by Eleanor Roosevelt for his commitment to world peace and world government. Garry died recently, but his spirit lives on in the tenacious commitment to a world without borders, without humiliation, embracing social justice as a principle embedded in the work of the global Humiliation and Human Dignity Studies movement.

Lazare (1987) suggests that the experience of humiliation among other things involves feeling stigmatized; feeling reduced in size, i.e., feeling belittled, put down, or humbled; being found deficient, i.e., feeling degraded, dishonoured, or devalued; being attacked, i.e., experiencing ridicule, scorn, or insult. The dynamics of humiliation are also embedded in the logic of the market and historically in the imperial impulse. The current importance of "humiliation" is due to the connection with human rights in an era of globalisation (Lindner 2006:173).

Lindner (2006) argues that globalisation brings with it the issue of resources and resource based conflicts; that there has been an increase in rights and a decrease in the political autonomy of nation states; and this growing cosmopolitan condition brings with it risks and uncertainties. Increased global dependency involves displacement and resentment. Humiliation can be described for Smith (2006) using the term "social displacement" in fact humiliation emerges by "outrageous displacement," and that displacement leads to conquest, relegation or exclusionary forms of humiliation.

In response to her understanding of these conditions, and based as well on her personal experience of social displacement, Evelin Lindner founded a global network (the Human Dignity and Humiliation Studies Network — HumanDHS) to address, understand, and move beyond the experiences of humiliation, non-recognition and lack of respect through transformative social action underpinned by the need for human dignity globally and locally.

For Lindner (2004) there has been a shift (*we could call it from modernity to late modernity or post modernity*) in global relations, "from a world steeped in Honor codes of unequal human worthiness to a world of Human Rights ideals of equal dignity." Influenced by anthropology Lindner (page 4) writes: in the new historical context (of equal dignity for all/Human Rights legislation), the phenomenon of humiliation[1] (expressed in acts, feelings and institutions), gains significance in two ways, a) because of the new and more relational reality of the world, and b) through the emergence of Human Rights ideals. Dynamics of humiliation profoundly change in their nature within the larger historical transition from a world steeped in honor codes of unequal human worthiness to a world of human rights ideals of equal dignity. Dynamics of humiliation move from honor-humiliation to dignity-humiliation, and, they gain more significance.

In developing this work Lindner (2006) conducted extensive empirical research that includes fieldwork in Somalia and in Rwanda and she states that the word "humiliation" points to an act, second at a feeling, and third at a process: I humiliate you, you feel humiliated, and the entire process is one of humiliation. Lindner suggests that "in a globalizing world in which people are increasingly exposed to human rights advocacy, that acts of humiliation and feelings of humiliation emerge as the most significant phenomena to resolve" (2001:1)

Moreover, Lindner asserts that "all humans share a common ground, namely a yearning for recognition and respect that connects them and draws them into relationships" and "many of the observable rifts among people may stem from the humiliation that is felt when

---

1 Lindner writes: "Humiliation means the enforced lowering of a person or group, a process of subjugation that damages or strips away their pride, honor or dignity. To be humiliated is to be placed, against your will and often in a deeply hurtful way, in a situation that is greatly inferior to what you feel you should expect. Humiliation entails demeaning treatment that transgresses established expectations. It may involve acts of force, including violent force.... Indeed, one of the defining characteristics of humiliation as a process is that the victim is forced into passivity, acted upon, made helpless" (2004:29).

recognition and respect are lacking" (ibid.). Hence, "only if the human desire for respect is cherished, respected, and nurtured, and if people are attributed equal dignity in this process, can differences turn into valuable diversities and sources of enrichment — both globally and locally — instead of sources of disruption" (ibid.).

For Lindner the human rights revolution "could be described as an attempt to collapse the master-slave gradient to a line of equal dignity and humility" that she defines as "egalization." Lindner writes that feelings of humiliation may lead to a) depression and apathy, b) the urge to retaliate with inflicting humiliation (she gives the example of Hitler, genocides, terrorism, or c) they may lead to constructive social change (she gives the example of Mandela). Lindner is committed to research and action that helps to foster new public policies for driving not only *globalization* but also *egalization* and helping to create a peaceful and just world, and she writes that three elements are necessary for progress to be made in developing institutions based on principles of dignification.

Firstly, new decent institutions should be built, both locally and globally, that heal and prevent dynamics of humiliation (see Margalit, 1996[2]). Secondly, new attention must be given to maintaining relationships of equal dignity. Thirdly, new social skills must be learned to maintaining relations of equal dignity. We need not least, a new type of leaders, who are no longer autocratic dominators and humiliation-entrepreneurs, but knowledgeable, wise facilitators and motivators, who lead toward respectful and dignified inclusion of all humankind as opposed to hateful polarization. Lindner calls for a *Moratorium on Humiliation* to be included into new public policy planning. The need for new decent institutions and leadership to heal and prevent the dynamics of humiliation, othering, de-humanization, and an examination of governance both nationally and globally.

Dennis Smith (2006) also focuses upon humiliation. He argues that unless globalisation changes direction "the cost in terms of

---

2 Margalit (1996) *The Decent Society* — draws our attention to the fact that we need to stand up not just against singular acts of humiliation. We have to build societies with institutions that do not humiliate their citizens.

freedom and human rights will be high" (2006:1). He also makes a distinction between what he calls globalisation's "public agenda" such as market opportunities, business interests, competition for energy resources such as oil and gas, the war on terror, and globalisation's "hidden agenda." This "hidden agenda" is shaped by three historical processes that he defines as a "triple helix": globalisation; the regulation of modernity; and the dynamics of humiliation. He suggests that these three socio-historical drivers (and their inter-relationships) are shaping the future of global society in the twenty-first century (2006:9).[3] "Globalisation causes people to be displaced or excluded in ways that make them feel outraged and resentful" (Smith 2006:9).

Globalisation is therefore a cause of humiliation. The two codes of modernity — the human rights code and the honor code, and usually a mixture of the two, influence the way humiliation is experienced. Historically the honor code is "particularistic" it "values strength: the capacity to maximise your stake in the world and to destroy your enemies" (p. 13). In contrast the human rights code is "universalistic", it respects and recognises "needs and makes demands that all human beings should be given access to the means of enjoying a decent life" (p13). There is, at one and the same time "the decreasing capacity of the nation-state to contain and structure our lives as influence shifts upwards to the global level" (p. 15). Being humiliated by the experience of forced displacement or exclusion, denied recognition, rights, security, and what you feel is rightfully yours can lead to three kinds

---

3 The dynamics of globalisation include the pursuit of power, prestige, and profit — and survival across three phases: European Imperialism (1600 – post WWII); Global Imperialism (end of Cold War/America/Europe);Global Multipolarity (21st century — uni-polarity coming to an end — European Union/ rise of China/revival of Japan/India, resurgence of Russia. The regulation of modernity involves social competition; provision of care and protection; control of access to socio-cultural benefits. Embedded in modernising processes is the tension between the honor code and the human rights code. The honor code that is very much alive in many part of the world involves a focus upon strength and the capacity to maximise your stake in the world and to destroy enemies. The human rights code focuses instead upon respect that all human beings should enjoy a decent life. Most societies operate a mix of the two codes.

of humiliation: conquest humiliation; relegation humiliation (being forced downwards in a hierarchy); and exclusion humiliation (being denied membership of a group you feel you belong to). Possible responses involve escape (fear cycles); acceptance (victimization cycles); rejection (revenge cycles).

Lindner (2006) and Smith (2006) both focus attention upon the role of "humiliation" in understanding the social processes that give rise to displacement and forced migration that includes analysis of increasing global interdependence. Lindner's (2006) work not only identifies the dynamics of Humiliation, but creates research, practice and productive collegial relationships globally through the interdisciplinary HumanDHS network she founded and leads. Her goal is no less than countering the destructive tendencies emanating from "the triple helix" of modernity, globalisation and humiliation (Smith 2006). Lindner's inter-disciplinary scholarship entails elements from anthropology, history, social philosophy, social psychology, sociology, and political science. She argues that in a globalizing world in which people are increasingly exposed to human rights advocacy, acts of humiliation and feelings of humiliation emerge as significant phenomena to resolve. Lindner's Ph.D. was carried out in Somalia, Rwanda, and Burundi addressing their history of genocidal killings. From 1998 to 1999 she conducted 216 qualitative interviews. On the basis of the empirical evidence she argued that:

> Feelings of humiliation may lead to violent acts of humiliation and spirals of retributive violence. Terrorists are hard to track and difficult to combat; they eclipse traditional warfare methods. Embracing new security strategies that include the mind-sets of people in violent conflicts appears one wise alternative. Humiliation-for-humiliation may represent the only real Weapons of Mass Destruction we face. High jacking planes (9-11) or hacking neighbours to death with machetes (genocide in Rwanda 1994) are all "cost-effective" methods of mayhem that work when leaders manipulate followers into becoming willing perpetrators.

Feelings of humiliation can represent the Nuclear Bombs
of the Emotions. (Lindner, 2002b, pp. 127-129)

She argues that given the shift from the honor code to the human
rights code, what was once accepted as normal could now be rejected
as humiliating (2006: xv). Using the Hutus as an example she states
that the Hutus lived under a hierarchical system ruled by Tutsi elites
for hundreds of years, that this was once regarded as "normal" and
with the shift in moral views and changing power of the Hutus,
"humiliation became a burning wound that led to a genocidal frenzy
against the Tutsi *inyenzi* ('cockroaches')." (Lindner 2006: xv). Lindner
also describes the ways in which tensions between the honor code
and human rights code can elicit feelings of humiliation such as in
the case of honor killings, "a family whose daughter is raped may
try to regain its honor by killing the girl; advocates of human rights
are appalled. While defenders of family honor are offended by what
they regard as...the humiliating devaluation of their culture" (p. xv).

Smith (2006) further argues that the lack of the following three
human needs is an indicator that you are in conditions of humiliation:
freedom (politics, economic, social, protective security — Sen 1999
and Nussbaum 2006 in Smith 2006); agency (Mary Kaldo/Arendt/
Bauman); security (Peter Singer and Barrington Moore); and recognition (Barrington Moore/Margalit). Global terrorism seems to follow
a similar logic, led by humiliation entrepreneurs who instrumentalize
feelings of humiliation among the broad masses using violence.

Lindner calls for a moratorium on humiliation and argues that
social change is a process and one must remain mindful of the goal.
She tells us that all humans share a common ground, namely a
yearning for recognition and respect that connects them and draws
them into relationships. Many of the observable rifts among people
may stem from the humiliation that is felt when recognition and
respect are lacking.

In the foreword to Lindner's (2006) pioneering text on understanding humiliation, Morton Deutsch states that her work enables
"understanding how attacks on one's dignity and the experience

of humiliation can foster destructive interactions at the interpersonal and international levels." Moreover, for Deutsch — we need to "enhance knowledge of the conditions which foster dignifying as well as humiliating relationships and, more importantly, which will enhance knowledge of how to transform humiliating relationships to dignifying ones." The need for dignifying relationships and awareness of the conditions that foster dignifying relationships demand engagement with constructions of social justice, "community" rights and recognition. For example, the conditions that fostered dignifying relationships for Garry Davis involved a profound and relational commitment to peace, world governance, and world citizenship.

Participatory Action Research as a Vehicle for Egalization

As an academic and researcher, my own action in relation to fostering dignifying relationships towards social justice involved conducting research with, not on or for, marginalised people and groups. I learned to value the expertise, knowledge and vision for social justice of the very people who are usually the subjects of research, and to support their ability to challenge and change social inequalities in their communities,

The role of participatory action and/or participatory arts research, through ethno-mimesis can lead to a radical democratisation of images and texts that can move us, pierce us, challenge identity thinking and bring us in touch with the micro relational worlds. This counter-hegemonic approach helps us to connect with our feeling worlds in a subjective reflexive relationship with the feeling worlds of the Other. It de-stabilizes the relation between us and them, self and Other into a subject-subject relationship. A politics of feeling that emerges through the potential space and the attunement that occurs in and through participatory research projects can counter identity thinking and mis-recognition, de-stabilise regressive discourses and help us move towards egalization (Lindner 2006, 2007), a recognitive theory of community and social justice. This kind of research runs counter to the kind of messages and images we find in the mainstream media and ultimately feeds into the public imagination.

In the context of Evelin Lindner and Linda Hartling's pioneering research and the HumanDHS this short paper contributes to the project by sharing some work I have undertaken with Bosnian and Afghan refugee communities in the UK and new arrivals (asylum seekers and economic migrants from various countries) to the East Midlands and the North East.

Drawing upon Evelin Lindner (2006), the concept of humiliation as an act, a process and an experience has a significant role to play in understanding the production of the world's refugees, the phenomenon of forced migration and the asylum-migration-community nexus. Based on this understanding and particularly given the refugee crisis in Europe there is an urgent need for dialogue and debate towards the possibilities for a radical democratic future based upon principles of recognition, respect, justice, dignity, and redistribution, that would entail open borders.

At the centre of my work is the importance of renewing methodologies for the work we do in the area of forced migration, humiliation, egalization, and human rights (Lindner 2004) and the usefulness of participatory action research (PAR) methodologies. More specifically, I will talk about the contribution that "ethno-mimesis" (O'Neill 2001) can make under the rubric of PAR.

I developed the concept of ethno-mimesis in the process of imagining a methodological process that might bring together sociology (ethnographic social research) with artistic methods — creative art processes in challenging and changing sexual and social inequalities — towards social justice, inspired by the inter-disciplinary work of Barry Smith who was then leading the Creative Arts Programme at Nottingham Trent University, and the critical theory of Walter Benjamin and Theodor Adorno. Ethno-mimesis (a combination of ethnographic work and artistic re-presentations of the ethnographic developed through participatory action research) is a process and a practice, but it is ultimately rooted in principles of equality, democracy, and freedom, as well as what Jessica Benjamin (1993) describes (drawing on Hegel, Kant, and Adorno) as a dialectic of mutual recognition.

Following Adorno, "mimesis" does not simply mean naive imitation, but rather feeling, sensuousness, and spirit in critical tension to constructive (instrumental) rationality; the "out-there" sense of our being in the world. Mimesis is not to be interpreted as mimicry but rather as relationally deeper — as sensuous knowing. Taussig understands "mimesis as both the faculty of imitation and the deployment of that faculty in sensuous knowing" (1993, 68). Ethno-mimesis is both a practice (a methodology) and a process aimed at illuminating inequalities and injustice through sociocultural research and analysis; but it also seeks to envision and imagine a better future based on dialectic of mutual recognition, congruence, care, and respect for human rights, cultural citizenship, and democratic processes.

I want to highlight here the importance of participatory action research and artistic/visual methodologies for creating a reflective/safe space for dialogue, thinking through issues, and representing the voices of refugees and asylum seekers that speak of loss, mourning, shame, and humiliation as well as mutual recognition and the importance of publicness/public sharing for democratization.

Participatory, creative methodologies also help to counter processes of post emotionalism that Stefan Mestrovic (1997) writes about in his work. Mestrovic writes about how in contemporary "me dominated" (*Western*) society rooted in consumption and commodification our emotions lose their genuineness. We reach a state of "compassion" fatigue and cannot/ or choose not to connect with the pain and suffering of others — we turn over the page or reach for the remote control to switch off the images or words.

Shierry Nicholsen (2002) draws comparisons with post emotionalism (Mestrovic) and normotic illness (Bollas). In her reading of Mestrovic, she says emotions "lose their genuineness and become quasi emotions. The emotional spectrum becomes limited and individual "emotions" blurred." In defining "normotic illness" Shierry states that for the normotic individual subjectivity recedes and the person experiences him/herself more as a commodity object —

describing flatness of emotions and an absence of affective links between people/in relationships. Nicholsen further develops the analysis by drawing on Adorno to argue that normotic illness and post emotionality cannot be understood separately from war.

> Death-dealing violence and social domination are the
> agents of the destruction of experience, and thus inextri-
> cably linked to the phoniness and propaganda quality of
> post emotional society — not the war of the Good Ameri-
> cans a vs Bad Germans, but rather the inextricable presence
> of killing and war-making in the society of domination.
> (2002:11)

For Nicholsen the importance of passion and creativity are crucial to counter the post emotional — and she draws upon Bion and Meltzer as well as Adorno to develop a theory of passion as a form of turbulent emotional experience "that genuine thought can think about…passion provides the fuel for personality development in the sense of the individual's expanding capacity for truth and relation- ship" (2002:15).

To counter post emotionalism and the administered society (in our lived experience but also in building, creating our social worlds) the interrelation between thinking, feeling, and doing is crucial. Moreover, the interplay between critical thought, artistic praxis, and social action is one source of resistance to and transformation of the disempowering and reductive social and psychic processes that Mestrovic (1997) speaks about so clearly in his work. In the process of developing intertextual research with "refugees" and "asylum seekers," I do not aim to or claim to speak for the people I work with, but rather to speak with them, from multiple standpoints, and to open up intellectual and practical spaces for them to speak for themselves. This work as a work in progress, as "micrology," aims to create inter- textual social knowledge as ethno-mimesis (O'Neill 2001; 2004) and can help us avoid accepting reified versions of "reality." It re-presents the complexity of lived experience and lived relations as a counter impulse to "postemotionalism." The research also supports processes of community development (social regeneration, social renewal) and cultural citizenship in collaboration with the individuals and groups. The participants in the research are the co-creators of the research.

In a recent paper O'Neill and Harindranath (2005) argued that PAR/Ethno-mimesis is precisely the methodology that enables such groups to represent themselves, without a cultural or political intermediary talking "on behalf" of them. PAR/Ethno-mimesis transgresses the power relations inherent in traditional ethnography and social research as well as the binaries of subject/object inherent in the research process. For the participants involved in PAR are both objects and subjects (authors) of their own narratives and cultures. PAR/ethno-mimesis is reflexive and phenomenological but also looks to praxis. As previously argued, such renewed methodologies take us "outside of binary thinking and purposefully challenge identitarian thinking…they deal with the contradictions of oppression, and the utter complexity of our lived relations…in ways which counter postemotionalism, valorizing discourses and the reduction of the Other to a cipher of the oppressed/marginalised/exploited" (O'Neill et al 2001:75-6).

The visual examples I brought to the workshop in 2005 were from a project undertaken with Bosnian Muslim Refugees in the East Midlands of the UK. For this project, PAR methodologies were used, and life history narratives were re-presented in photographic form. The life story narratives and photographs re-present three key themes that emerged from the life stories of those involved in the research:

1. Experiences before the war — dislocation marked by post-communist citizenship in "Yugoslavia" that reconstituted "citizenship" on a kinship or community basis; that is, for the Serb leader only Serbs were allowed "citizenship" and the protection of law.

2. Experiences during the war — displaced and abstracted from history, citizenship, and the law, humiliated, separated from families and friends — living in refugee camps, and for some, concentration camps.

3. Experiences of living in the UK — relocating and
   rebuilding lives and diasporic communities

The research is both transgressive and regressive. Working together
with the Bosnians in the Midlands through participatory action
research proved to be transgressive across three levels of praxis.
The first level is textual, performed through documenting their life
stories as testimony to the humiliation, suffering, and genocide they
encountered at the hands of the government, army, police, employers,
hospitals, medics, and former friends and neighbours. The second
level is visual, performed through the production of art forms to
re-present their life stories with the help of freelance artists, saying the
unsayable. The third level combines the visual and textual elements
shared with others — audiences in community spaces, gallery spaces,
civic centres, and universities, and supports and fosters dialogue,
understanding and processes of community development.

Challenging and resisting dominant images and stereotypes of
"refugees" and "asylum seekers" and making this work available to
as wide an audience as possible can also serve to raise awareness, as
well as educate. By both narrativizing and re-presenting/reimagining
history and lived experience the vital importance of opportunities for
social renewal, for creating "citizenship," for re-imagining identities
and communities emerge. The role and purpose of PAR, the vital role
of the arts in processes of social inclusion, the civic role and responsibility of the university, and the vital importance for creating safe
spaces for dialogue that might support processes of restorative justice
and reconciliation were also discussed in the workshop presentation.

There is an urgent need to develop interventionary strategies based
on collective responsibility and what Benhabib (1992) has called a
"civic culture of public participation and the moral quality of enlarged
thought" (1992, 140) in relation to work in the area of humiliation
and dignity. How can ethno-mimesis address this?

The experiences of the people concerned must be listened to and
acknowledged, and advocacy networks developed to facilitate voices,
stories, narratives through participatory action research. Recovering

and retelling people's subjectivities, lives, and experiences is central to attempts to better understand our social worlds with a view to transforming these worlds. Such work reveals the resistances, strengths, and humour of people seeking asylum, as well as knowledge of and a better understanding of the legitimation and rationalization of power, domination, and oppression.

Drawing on Shierry Nicholsen's work, the photographs presented at the workshop have the capacity to arouse our compassion while not letting us forget that what we are seeing is socially constructed meaning. Through re- presenting the unsayable, the images help to "pierce" us, bringing us into contact with reality in ways that we cannot forget — ways that counter the "postemotionalism" of contemporary "me" — dominated society that Mestrovic (1997) details so carefully in his work.

Our work in the UK envisions/imagines a renewed social sphere for asylum seekers and refugees as global citizens. Using the PAR/ ethnomimesis process, our eyes remain firmly fixed on the "becoming" of equality, freedom, and democracy, through processes of social justice, cultural citizenship, egalization, and mutual recognition through renewed social and public policies in the spheres of polity, economy, and culture.

A politics of feeling that emerges through the potential space and the attunement that occurs in and through participatory research projects can counter identity thinking and mis-recognition, de-stabilise regressive discourses, and help us move towards egalization (Lindner 2006, 2007), a recognitive theory of community and social justice. This kind of research runs counter to the kind of messages and images we find in the mainstream media and ultimately feeds into the public imagination.

The HumanDHS global network recognizes the fact that global interdependence forces humankind to face its global challenges, both ecological and social, as a shared responsibility that has to be shouldered jointly. This is reflected in the principles and practices of the network itself. Scholars from around the globe are representative of a world engagement where "recognition" and "understanding" are practiced. The network is founded upon deep respect for the forms in which scholarship and enquiry takes place; and that this is as important as what we study. Hence appreciative enquiry (developed by David Cooperrider at Case Western Reserve University) and appreciative being (developed by Don Klein) are encouraged. Academics, researchers, practitioners make up the membership of the network which grew out of Evelin Lindner's (2006) vision and her relationship and friendship with fellow visionary Linda Hartling (a past associate director of the Jean Baker Miller Institute).

Evelin Lindner (2006) calls for a *Moratorium on Humiliation* to be included into new public policy planning. She encourages us to see the need for new decent institutions and leadership to heal and prevent the dynamics of humiliation, othering, de-humanization, and an examination of governance both nationally and globally. We need to hold on to the ideals of world citizenship and world governance, and the promise of the European Union, because together we are greater than the sum of our parts. The Human Dignity and Humiliation Studies global movement evidences this so very clearly.

References

Adleman, H. (1999). Modernity, globalization, refugees and displacement. In *Refugees: Perspectives on the experience of enforced migration*, ed. A. Ager, 83–110. London: Continuum.

Benhabib, S. (1992). *Situating the Self*. Cambridge: Polity Press

Harrell-Bond, B. (1999). Refugees' experiences as aid recipients. In *Refugees: Perspectives on the experience of enforced migration*, ed. A. Ager, 136–68. London: Continuum.

Lindner, Evelin Gerda (2004). *Humiliation in a Globalizing World: Does Humiliation Become the Most Disruptive Force?* New York, NY: Paper prepared for the "Workshop on Humiliation and Violent Conflict," November 18-19, 2004, at Columbia University.

Lindner, E. (2004). *Humiliation in a Globalizing World: Does Humiliation Become the Most Disruptive Force?* New York, NY: Paper prepared for the "Workshop on Humiliation and Violent Conflict," November 18-19, 2004, at Columbia University.

Lindner, E (2006) *Making Enemies: Humiliation and International Conflict Westport, Connecticut and London: Praeger Security.*

Mestrovic, S. (1997) *Postemotional Society* London and New York: Sage.

Nicholsen, S. (2002). *Adorno's Minima Moralia: On Passion, Psychoanalysis and the Postemotional Dilemma* (from personal communication with the author).

O'Neill, M (2002) Renewed methodologies for social research: ethno-mimesis as performative praxis in *Sociological Review* 50, No 1, Feb 2002.

O'Neill, M and Harindranath, R. (2005) 'Theorising narratives of exile and belonging: the importance of Biography and PAR/ Ethno-mimesis in 'understanding' asylum.' Submitted to *Qualitative Sociology Review* — e journal — thematic issue on 'Biographical Sociology' September 2005.

O'Neill, M (2004). Global Refugees (Human) Rights, Citizenship and the Law in Cheng, S *Law, Justice and Power: Between Reason and Will.* California: Stanford University Press.

Smith, D. (2006) *Globalization. The Hidden Agenda* Cambridge: Polity.

Taussig, Michael (1993). *Mimesis and Alterity: A Particular History of the Senses.* London: Routledge.

Chapter Eight

School Discipline:
A Prosocial Perspective

Philip M. Brown

School discipline policies have been under considerable scrutiny in recent years in the U.S. Policymakers, research scientists and educators alike have shared growing concerns over the negative effects of zero tolerance policies that have aimed to set a high bar for student misconduct and the related inflexible disciplinary practices that have become the norm for many school systems (American Psychological Association Zero Tolerance Task Force, 2008). The evidence has gradually grown that these strictly enforced, rule-bound frameworks and practices have negatively affected the educational prospects of many students, particularly those of color (Mayer, 1995; Fabelo, Thompson, Plotkin, Carmichael, Marchbanks, & Booth, 2011; Balfanz, Byrnes, & Fox, 2013; Morgan, Salomon, Plotkin, & Cohen, 2014). In response to this equity issue, on January 2014, the U.S. Department of Education released a package of resources on school discipline for the purpose of providing guidance designed to help correct discriminatory school discipline practices and address the needs of students with behavior problems.

The underlying issues surrounding school discipline are complex and go beyond any single perspective or measure. There are societal issues that bear on the behavior and misbehavior of children in school such as poverty, child rearing practices, and whether children believe they have a positive role to play in their community and a future in the country's economy. There are also educational governance and human relations issues that can negatively impact the disciplinary environment, such as a lack of social trust among the adults in a school or an authoritarian leadership structure with no opportunities for student or teacher participation in problem solving. Whether the culture and climate of schools fosters a prosocial or antisocial behavioral environment is largely dependent on whether these issues are handled with intelligence and care or neglected out of ignorance or mismanagement.

Discipline: Control and Punishment or Morality and Growth

Most experienced teachers and school administrators know that the meaning and impact of misconduct is mediated by the specific context in which an event occurs and by the individual characteristics of the offender. The same behavior, such as bringing a knife to school, exhibited by different children or children of different ages, does not have the same meaning in different contexts. Context matters: Was the knife provided by mom in the lunch kit of the seven year old, or was it a switchblade brought in by a 15 year-old gang member? So, rules are frequently bent in order to achieve a desired conclusion or remedy a situation that could become worse if not handled adroitly.

For example, a new principal is confronted by an angry mother whose nine-year old child's new shirt had been torn in an altercation with another boy. The parent is seeking retribution and wanted to know how the other boy would be punished. The principal realizes a few minutes into the exchange that a significant part of the parent's anger is due to her inability to buy a new shirt because of the level of poverty the family lived with. He is confronted with the essential question: Is it important to determine who was at fault in the incident and apply the appropriate school rule, or is it important to involve both boys in determining how the shirt would be replaced? Different discipline systems and school administrators would answer this question differently.

Most discipline matters involve this dynamic of interpreting behaviors in the context of desired outcomes. It is important to explore this broad landscape in the context of our history, which has informed generations of American educators regarding their responsibilities in handling school discipline. First things first: Discipline is defined by two eminent sources as:

- Control that is gained by requiring that rules or orders be obeyed and punishing bad behavior; a way of behaving that shows a willingness to obey rules or orders; behavior that is judged by how well it follows a set of rules or orders; control gained by enforcing obedience or order; a rule or system of rules governing conduct or activity; training that corrects, molds, or perfects the mental faculties or moral character; and self-control ("discipline," Merriam-Webster, n.d).

- The practice of training people to obey rules or a code of behavior, using punishment to correct disobedience ("discipline," Oxford Dictionaries, n.d.).

It's interesting to note that both sources indicate that the derivation of the word comes from the Anglo-French and Latin *disciplina*, which means "teaching" and from *discipulus*, or "pupil." The very nature of how we think about discipline is intimately bound up with the teacher-student relationship.

Whether it is a district code of conduct, a classroom rule, or a verbal reprimand, discipline is all about how relationships are conducted and managed for an articulated or assumed purpose. There are then, three themes that constantly interplay when we look at what discipline means and how we are to understand its uses in schools:

1. A set of rules regarding behavior and conduct;

2. The control of student behavior in conformance to these rules; and

3. The training of students in the skills to perfect their moral character and self-control.

Only the third of these three definitions has a basis in values and morality. The lesson here is important: Discipline may be either guided by a moral purpose or framework, or it may be essentially amoral. For example, the Gestapo, the official secret police of Nazi Germany, was a highly disciplined military force with rigorous standards for conduct. Individuals and groups as diverse as Olympic athletes, a jazz quartet, a ballet star, and physicians who work for Doctors Without Borders are all highly disciplined. They all share performance related values such as persistence and creativity, but not necessarily in the service of a moral purpose.

Schools, on the other hand, do have a primary moral purpose: Providing the setting, guidance, and knowledge necessary to help children develop for the good of society. This role that schools play needs to be crafted thoughtfully, based on our growing understanding of human development as well as the core ethical values that represent our social structure. When we don't examine carefully the assumptions and purpose of our disciplinary theory and practices, the outcomes may not be what we want or expect.

Historically, American education has spent much more time and resources on setting rules and being concerned about controlling student behavior to maintain order. Instead, education could invest time and resources in learning how we can educate children to be effective moral agents and ethical citizens. American education could do much more to invest in cultivating the abilities and dispositions that will help children live up to our expectations as mature adults without ignoring lessons from our biological ancestors or recent developmental neuroscience.

Since the 1800s, these two approaches to school discipline and classroom management have defined how educators in America have created social space to teach academics and ethical behavior in the confines of the school walls. The first uses teacher-centered strategies and rules reinforced by either positive or punitive measures to assure conformance. The second focuses on developing self-discipline within students using both student-centered pedagogy and diverse experiential strategies to engender self-control, self-regulation, and character building that centers more on autonomy and social responsibility than on conformity (Bear, 2010).

Prosocial and Our Primate Ancestors

> To educate a man in mind and not in morals is to educate a menace to society.
>
> — Theodore Roosevelt

When we naturally assume that discipline is good for its own sake, we are making the assumption that behaving in conformity to a set of rules is good for the one and good for the many; that by behaving appropriately we are doing so for the greater good of our family, community and society. As social animals some rules enforced by some kind of authority are necessary for our survival. Evolutionary biology offers compelling evidence of the instinctual basis for prosocial behaviors. Primate research demonstrates that key lessons from our nearest ancestors about the importance of sharing scarce resources for the well-being of our tribe, have likely been embedded in our genetic makeup (de Waal, 2006).

Fairness

A sense of fairness in primates may be rooted in the nature of dominance in their group's hierarchy. It is a given that dominant primates will receive a bigger piece of the pie than subordinate primates. The dominant members of the group receive more resources like food and breeding mates compared to the subordinate members. But because the group is so important to everyone's survival, dominant members of a gorilla group make sure that more vulnerable members, such as a nursing mother, receive a share of the food as well.

Membership in this primate group is bountiful for all members (both dominant and subordinate), and the cost of leaving the group is rather high, so membership itself is a desirable resource (de Waal, 2006). This lesson from our ancestors is at the root of our need for belonging, the sense that membership in our profession, union, school, classroom, club, or gang is important to our sense of well-being and meaning in our lives.

Gratitude

Gratitude as well may have deep evolutionary roots and may help us to understand why we are programmed to work together to create a prosocial culture. The bonding and reciprocity promoted by gratitude are the kinds of behaviors that evolutionary biologists see as essential to the survival of the social, mammalian species like us. Frans de Waal of Emory University has found, for example, that chimpanzees remember the individuals who have previously groomed them and return the favor at a later time by sharing food with them (Marsh & Keltner, 2015). De Waal sees this reciprocal altruism as an elementary form of primate gratitude. It is to the primates' advantage to maintain good, cooperative working relationships with others on which they rely and to learn to act in pleasant, kind, and supportive ways. Particularly for primates with little history and a very new dyadic relationship, reciprocity serves an important function. Doing a favor or meeting the request of another can pay off in the future when they have a favor to request. For the primate group, reciprocity and cooperation ensures that everyone is cared for (de Waal, 2003).

Caring

These prosocial exchanges are learned behavior for which we humans are genetically predisposed. We recognize our basic urge to care for one another and feel empathy towards another person. We feel drawn to people who willingly offer help and who support others as we feel called upon to react to situations where we are called upon to help. Any good early childhood teacher knows how to elicit and encourage these caring responses. Nel Noddings (2002) locates the roots of social justice, and therefore the parameters of our discipline system, in our sense of right and wrong behavior, in caring. As she points out, when a caring relationship is not present in schools, "the fault often lies in the structure of classes, rules and evaluations" (Noddings, 2008, p. 163).

For children to care about their place in the school community, they must have had the experience of being cared for and cared about. If a child's early development is in a loving home, transferring the attachment from parent to teacher is not such a difficult task. If not, it is necessary for the teacher to establish that attachment through providing experiences for the child so that he or she knows what it feels like and means to be cared for.

Neuroscience and the Moral Impulse

Recently, neuroscience has had success in locating the precise areas of the brain that relate to empathy and fairness. While the brain finds self-serving behavior emotionally unpleasant, it also finds genuine fairness emotionally uplifting. In other words, the brain works differently when prosocial behavior is exhibited or perceived. The response to situations perceived as fair or unfair is so rapid that the reaction overrules the more deliberate rational mind (Tabibnia, Satpute, & Lieberman, 2008). As three researchers at UCLA put it, faced with a conflict, the brain's default position is to demand a fair deal, thus relying upon one's ability to process empathy and fairness (Association for Psychological Science, 2008).

As adults we have an ethical obligation to provide environments that foster full development and the potential for a fulfilling and meaningful life, not just an economically productive one. Brown, Corrigan, and D'Alessandro (2012) use prosocial education as an umbrella term that encompasses the philosophy and programs that guide society's goal to foster positive youth development. A biological metaphor of a helix is an apt visualization to describe the interrela-tionship of the strands that comprise prosocial education. Consider prosocial education as a helix with strands that include prosocial behavior constructs, the principles of social–emotional, moral, and civic education, as well as academic learning.

Prosocial Development

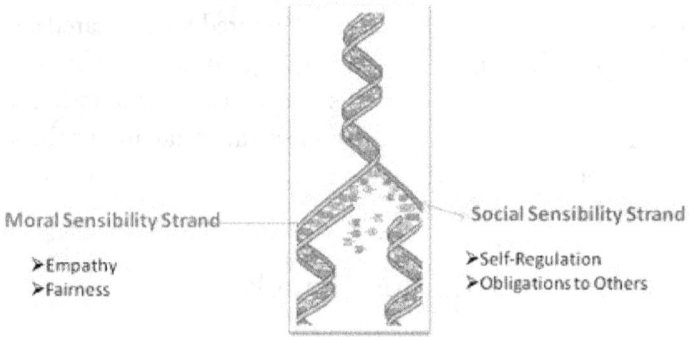

Moral Sensibility Strand   Social Sensibility Strand

➤Empathy   ➤Self-Regulation
➤Fairness   ➤Obligations to Others

Figure 1: Brown, Philip M. (2016). *Student Discipline: A Prosocial Perspective.* Lanham, MD: Roman & Littlefield, p. 7.

The constructs of empathy and fairness each have become sources of explanation in building theory supportive of prosocial behavior. In our visual model, these serve as core activating strands for the development of other behaviors and skills. There is currently a considerable amount of neuroscience as well as cognitive and developmental psychology research under way to learn more about the biological and developmental underpinnings of prosocial attitudes and behavior.

It is important to understand that prosocial education is not just about encouraging educators to implement programs and strategies that contribute to building prosocial behavior conducive to learning, socialization, and development. Prosocial education also asks us to consider how this emerging knowledge helps us better understand how humans think, learn, and act in a social context. For example, what have we learned from neuroscience about empathy that makes it a critical concept for understanding the importance of prosocial behavior and prosocial education?

First, empathy has been demonstrated to occur in the first years of life, implying that it may have a genetic basis (Zahn-Waxler, Robinson, & Emde, 1992). Second, both neuroscience research on the mirror neuron system and developmental theorists commonly ascribe empathy as the mechanism behind understanding self–other differentiation (Jeannerod & Anquetil, 2008) and the exhibition of caring behaviors in response to signs of distress or need in others (Hoffman, 2001). Third, empathy involves both perception and cognition of the emotional states of others, and genetics has been shown to account for the systematic change and relative continuity of empathy over time (Knafo, Zahn-Waxler, Hulle, Robinson, & Rhee, 2008).

As with many human skills, awareness of the genetic basis of empathy is important because it offers us a basis for understanding what we have in common in order to foster personal growth, cohesion, and cooperation. There are two different aspects of empathy: the ability to see the world from the perspective of another and the ability to imagine what another person is feeling and to care about their pain or suffering.

While the empathic tendency may not be evenly distributed among all of us, both aspects of empathy can be learned. However, it may take some children longer than others, however. Children on the autism spectrum, for example, may have problems reading the cues signaling distress or have trouble imagining themselves in someone else's shoes, yet be very sensitive to other's pain (Szalavitz, 2013). Armed with this knowledge, as well as the kind of approaches and programs represented in this volume, educators have far better methods for developing children's moral sense and social connectedness, approaches that work far better than implementing zero tolerance policies for misbehavior.

One contribution that neurobiology can make to school discipline is helping educators to better understand the impact that early caregiving and stressful conditions — at home and in school — can have on students' behavior. If secure attachment to a caregiver is not achieved when a child is very young, the child's response to perceived or real threats is compromised (Narvaez, 2014). It is more difficult for them to restore a sense of calm and to develop a repertoire of adaptive responses, such as realizing that something that might be scary (e.g., a loud noise) is usually not a threat, or realizing that a cut finger can be cared for and the pain will be temporary.

For a child with an insecure attachment to caregivers, a habitual mode of impaired functioning may result, which is focused on self-protection. Insecure relationships with caregivers can lead to impaired socioemotional processing as well, affecting the child's capacity to learn to interpret the behavior of others and to modulate and control basic feelings such as excitement, rage, and panic and hopelessness (Narvaez, 2014; Schore, 2003). Likewise, stressful conditions can also impede learning to respond and adapt to one's social environment. Children who grow up in high-stress homes or neighborhoods may have deficiencies in the natural human ability to feel empathy. They may overreact to situations that are not dangerous, or they may ignore real danger.

With an unbalanced stress response, a child will find it more difficult to self-regulate and may more easily slip into out-of-control mode. When this becomes a child's dominant experience, the child will find it "hard to feel compassion or behave in a prosocial manner" (Narvaez, 2014, p. 143). The good news is that early intervention in combination with skill-based training and a supportive social climate can help to rewire the empathy system and help most children recover their prosocial orientation and behaviors.

Self-Regulation

The single most important ability we learn that impacts student and school discipline as we grow up is self-regulation. Self-regulation involves multiple areas of neuroanatomy; there are emotional, cognitive, and behavior components governed by different, interrelated parts of the heart-brain system (McCraty, R., Atkinson, M., Tomasino, D. & Bradley R.T., 2006). The social aspects of functioning are learned as the brain and experience develop together. Self-regulation is a construct that describes how we learn to manage both our thoughts and feeling to enable us to achieve our goals. In order to accomplish this we need to learn to control our impulses and be able to organize and direct our behavior as we face immediate challenges and long-range problems.

The connection between self-regulation and discipline is easy to see. Social competence and positive, prosocial behavior are rooted in a child's growing ability to self-regulate attention, emotion, and behavior. Self-regulation involves the ability to inhibit the expression of behavior and emotion and to focus attention. It facilitates the ability to express emotion in constructive ways. (Derryberry & Rothbart, 1997; Eisenberg & Fabes, 1992; Murray & Kochanska, 2002). This connection is important enough that the Administration for Children and Families of the U.S. Department of Health and Human Services has begun a research project (Murray, Rosanbalm, Christopoulos, & Hamoudi, 2015) examining the relationship between self-regulation and toxic stress, the kind of stress that is linked to poverty, inadequate early childhood development, and children living under stressful family conditions. Below are seven key principles from the first report of this work that summarize our current understanding of self-regulation development in context:

1. **Self-regulation serves as the foundation for lifelong functioning** across a wide range of domains, from mental health and emotional well-being to academic achievement, physical health, and socio-economic success. It has also proven responsive to intervention, making it a powerful target for change.

2. **Self-regulation is defined from an applied perspective as the act of managing cognition** and emotion to enable goal-directed actions such as organizing behavior, controlling impulses, and solving problems constructively.

3. **Self-regulation enactment is influenced by a combination of individual and external factors** including biology, skills, motivation, caregiver support, and environmental context. These factors interact with one another to support self-regulation and create opportunity for intervention.

4. **Self-regulation can be strengthened and taught like literacy,** with focused attention, support, and practice opportunities provided across contexts. Skills that are not developed early on can be acquired later, with multiple opportunities for intervention.

5. **Development of self-regulation is dependent on "co-regulation" provided by parents or other caregiving adults** through warm and responsive interactions in which support, coaching, and modeling are provided to facilitate a child's ability to understand, express, and modulate their thoughts, feelings, and behavior.

6. **Self-regulation can be disrupted by prolonged or pronounced stress and adversity including poverty and trauma experiences.** Although manageable stress may build coping skills, stress that overwhelms children's skills or support can create toxic effects that negatively impact development and produce long-term changes in neurobiology.

7. **Self-regulation develops over an extended period from birth through young adulthood** (and beyond). There are two clear developmental periods where self-regulation skills increase dramatically due to underlying neurobiological changes — early childhood and adolescence — suggesting particular opportunities for intervention. (Murray et al., 2014, p. 3)

Much of what we know about how to teach self-regulation and create learning environments conducive to learning self-regulation has emerged over the past 20 years as social-emotional learning and school climate improvement.

Social-Emotional Learning

Social–emotional learning (SEL) is one of the codeterminants of disciplined, moral behavior, along with individual neurobiology, cultural norms, and the social climate. An individual's moral sense emerges from early experience with caregiving and contributes to long-term well-being. But, as Darcia Narvaez puts it so well,

> …on a moment-to-moment basis, an individual's morality is a shifting landscape. We move in and out of different ethics based on the social context, our mood, filters, stress response, ideals, goals of the moment, and so on…The trick for most wise behavior is to maintain emotional presence-in-the-moment. Our capacity to spend more time in a prosocial-egalitarian mindset is reliant on well-functioning emotion systems (Narvaez, 2014, ppxxv11-xxviii).

What is social and emotional learning? Social and emotional learning is the process of acquiring the competencies to recognize and manage emotions, develop caring and concern for others, establish positive relationships, make responsible decisions, and handle challenging situations effectively (Osher et al., 2008; Weissberg, Payton, O'Brien, & Munro, 2007). That is, SEL teaches the personal and interpersonal skills we all need to handle ourselves, our relationships, and our work effectively and ethically. Accordingly, SEL is aimed at helping children, and even adults, develop fundamental skills for success in school and life.

SEL builds from the assumption that educational interventions can be designed to foster children's social and emotional strengths and resiliency. It has been informed by work in child development, classroom management, and public health prevention, as well as the growing understanding of the role of the brain in self-awareness, empathy, and social-cognitive growth (e.g., Best & Miller, 2010; Carter, Diamond & Lee, 2011; Goleman, 2006; Greenberg, 2006). SEL focuses on the skills that allow children to calm themselves when angry, make friends, resolve conflicts respectfully, and make ethical and safe choices (Schonert-Reichl & O'Brien, 2012). SEL offers educators, families, and communities relevant strategies and practices to better prepare students for "the tests of life, not a life of tests" (Elias, 2001).

SEL is grounded in research findings that suggest social and emotional skills can be taught, that SEL promotes developmental assets and reduces problem behaviors, and that SEL will improve children's academic performance, citizenship, and health-related behaviors (e.g., Durlak, Weissberg, Dymnicki, Taylor, & Schellinger, 2011). SEL has been used both as an organizing framework and infused in commercial programs guiding a wide variety of efforts to prevent drug and alcohol use, reduce conflict, and combat bullying as well as in positive youth development (Devaney, O'Brien, Resnick, Keister, & Weissberg, 2006; Elias et al., 1997).

Table 1: Dimensions of social and emotional learning and related skills (Schonert-Reichl & O'Brien, 2012, p. 316).

SEL Dimension	Description
Self awareness	Accurately assessing one's feelings, interests, values, and strengths; maintaining a well-grounded sense of self-confidence.
Social awareness	Being able to take the perspective of and empathize with others; recognizing and appreciating individual and group similarities and differences; recognizing and using family, school, and community resources.
Self-management	Regulating one's emotions to handle stress, control impulses, and persevere in overcoming obstacles; setting and monitoring progress toward personal and academic goals; expressing emotions appropriately.
Relationship skills	Establishing and maintaining healthy and rewarding relationships based on cooperation; resisting inappropriate social pressure; preventing, managing, and resolving interpersonal conflict; seeking help when needed.

SEL Dimension	Description
Responsible decision-making	Making decisions based on consideration of ethical standards, safety concerns, appropriate social norms, respect for others, and likely consequences of various actions; applying decision- making kills to academic and social situations; contributing to the well-being of one's school and community.

Figure 2. A framework identifying the relations among classroom and school contexts, social and emotional competencies, and outcomes. Safe and Sound: An Educational Leader's Guide to Evidence-Based Social and Emotional Learning (SEL) Programs (CASEL, 2003).

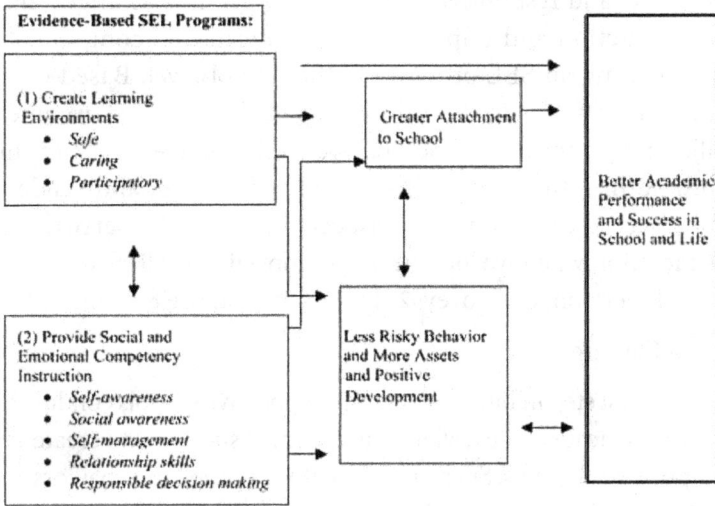

As illustrated in this model developed by the Collaborative for Academic, Social, and Emotional Learning (CASEL), SEL includes both an environmental focus and a person-centered focus (Zins et al., 2004). A person-centered emphasizes that social and emotional education involves teaching children and adolescents to be self and socially aware, competent self-managers and able to successfully build relationships and make responsible decisions.

SEL instruction is most effective when it is integrated into the school's curriculum and other programs, such as sports and other extracurricular programs, and when it includes meaningful partnerships of schools, families, and communities. Some SEL programs encourage students to use SEL skills to set academic goals and improve their study habits. Other SEL programs infuse SEL skills into academic subject matter, by providing literature activities that require using social awareness to understand a protagonist's motivations and actions (Schonert-Reichl & O'Brien, 2012).

In addition to focusing on specific instruction in social and emotional skills, SEL occurs in the context of a school culture, and therefore, creates a school and classroom community that is caring, supportive, and responsive to students needs. It is as important as skill instruction and important as an interrelated component in implementing an SEL program at the school level. Based on the research that points to the importance of classroom environments (Milkie & Warner, 2011) and positive teacher-student relationships in promoting students' positive social, emotional, and academic competence, the environmental aspect of the model deserves special consideration when we look next at school climate (Brackett, Reyes, Rivers, Elbertson, & Salovey, 2011; Jerome, Hamre,& Pianta, 2009).

School Climate

> The first step in building safe and supportive schools conducive to academic excellence and student success is to create positive climates. Such climates prevent problem behaviors before they occur and reduce the need for disciplinary interventions that can interfere with student learning. (U.S. Department of Education, 2014, p. 5)

Over the past few decades, there has been a growing body of empirical research confirming that school climate matters. Positive and sustained school climate is associated with increased academic achievement, positive youth development, effective risk prevention, health promotion efforts, and teacher satisfaction and retention. (Adelman & Taylor, 2005; Bryk et al., 2010; Centers for Disease Control and Prevention, 2009; Cohen, 2012).

School Climate Defined

School climate refers to the quality and character of school life. Here is how the National School Climate Council defines the concept:

> School climate is based on patterns of people's experience of school life; it reflects the norms, goals, values, interpersonal relationships, teaching, learning, leadership practices, and organizational structures that comprise school life. (National School Climate Council, 2011, p. 2)

A prosocial school climate embraces the school's mission to create safe, caring, and participatory learning environments. A sustainable, positive school climate fosters the youth development and learning necessary for a productive, engaged, and satisfying life in a democratic society. This climate includes:

- Norms, values, and expectations that support people feeling socially, emotionally, and physically safe.

- People are engaged and respected.

- Students, families, and educators work together to develop, live, and contribute to a shared school vision.

- Educators model and nurture an attitude that emphasizes the benefits and satisfaction from learning.

- Each person contributes to the operations of the school and the care of the physical environment. (National School Climate Council, 2007, p. 5)

With this in mind, here is my reworking of the central components of a robust school climate as defined by the National School Climate Center (Cohen, 2012).

1. *School climate is an organizing concept.* A core concept in school climate improvement is the importance of recognizing the essential social, emotional, ethical, civic, and intellectual aspects of learning.

2. *A prosocial school climate supports shared leadership and learning.* A growing body of research and practice calls for education leaders — teachers, principals, and superintendents — to become more transparent about their goals and to ensure that all education stakeholders participate in building a high-quality learning environment. (National Middle School Association [NMSA], 2003). Measuring and improving school climate supports transparent, democratically informed leadership and learning (Deal & Peterson, 2009; Kokolis, 2007).

3. *A responsive school climate promotes school–family–community partnerships.* Comprehensive school climate improvement practices should include "the whole village." This means actively seeking meaningful ways of involving parents and other community members in planning and decision-making processes, as well as using the school as a center for community activities and services.

4. *A robust school climate promotes student engagement.* There is a growing body of research that underscores the notion that when students are engaged in meaningful learning and work (for example, in service-learning), the result is that achievement, positive youth development, and school connectedness are all enhanced. When students become involved in the process of developing, implementing, and understanding projects that grow out of their analysis of school and community needs, we are promoting the skills and dispositions that support engaged citizenry and student engagement in particular. (Cohen, 2006; Kohlberg & Higgins, 1987; Reed, 2008)

5. *School climate improvement is an ongoing process.* Schools are not static institutions. Students and staff are continually changing, as are the demands on public education and the socio–economic conditions that influence school politics, challenges, and resources. School climate improvement requires a set of reflective steps that include use of a valid assessment, stakeholder involvement in reviewing climate data from multiple sources, and planning for programs and services in response to those data and student needs. Policy makers need to become more aware of school climate research and the importance of a positive school climate in determining academic success. There are compelling reasons why K–12 schools need to evaluate school climate in scientifically sound ways and use these findings to create a climate for learning.

For example, prosocial school climate can significantly impact graduation rates. A large study of 276 Virginia high schools found that a school climate characterized by lower rates of bullying and teasing was predictive of higher graduation rates four years later. Even more impressive was the study's finding that having a problematic school climate was as much an important factor related to children failing to graduate from high school as was student poverty (Cornell, Gregory, Huang, & Fan, 2013).

National, state and local district policies on school climate should:

1. Define school climate in ways that are aligned with recent research;

2. Recommend that schools routinely evaluate school climate comprehensively, recognizing student, parent, and school personnel "voice" and assess all of the major dimensions that shape school climate (e.g., safety, relationships, teaching and learning, and the environment);

3. Consider adopting or adapting the National School Climate Standards (http://schoolclimate.org/climate/

standards.php) that reflect and suggest norms and values that support democratically informed learning, teaching, and school improvement efforts;

4. Use school climate assessment as a measure of accountability;

5. Ensure that credential options maintain high-quality school climate-related standards for educators and school-based mental health professionals in general, and administrators in particular

6. Encourage teacher preparation programs that give teachers and administrators the tools to evaluate classroom and school climate and take steps to use these findings to promote a climate for learning and development in our schools; and

7. Increase support for research on the evaluation and improvement of school climate.

School Climate Policy Example

The Westbrook, Connecticut Board of Education (2014) adopted a school climate policy based on the NSCC standards. It includes the legal context for the standards, a rich set of definitions, and specific guidelines for district-wide and school-level implementation of a rigorous process of continuous school climate improvement. The following section of the policy delineates the planning process that pulls together the roles and responsibilities of all the players in the school community who have a stake in creating a prosocial school climate, as well as the actions that the school board believes will create a foundation for continued improvement:

VII. School Improvement Plans
    A. In collaboration with the [district] Coordinator, each [school] Specialist shall develop and/or update an Improve-

ment Plan based on the findings of the School Climate Survey.

1. The Specialist and the Committee shall develop and/or update the Improvement Plan using the School Climate Improvement Plan template (Appendix C), taking into consideration the needs of all key stakeholders, with sensitivity to equity and diversity

2. The Improvement Plan shall support the actualization of the following five Standards:

   Standard 1: Develop a shared vision and plan for promoting, enhancing, and sustaining a positive school climate.

   Standard 2: Develop policies that promote social, emotional, ethical, civic, and intellectual learning as well as systems that address barriers to learning

   Standard 3: Implement practices that promote the learning and positive social, emotional, ethical, and civic development of students and that promote student engagement while addressing barriers to learning.

   Standard 4: Create an environment where all members are welcomed, supported, and feel safe in school: socially, emotionally, intellectually, and physically.

   Standard 5: Develop meaningful and engaging practices, activities and norms that promote social and civic responsibilities and a commitment to social justice.

3. Each Improvement Plan shall be submitted to the Coordinator for approval and implementation no later than mid-September of each school year. The Coordinator may provide feedback to the Committee with respect to amendments to the Improvement Plan (Westbrook, Connecticut, 2014, p. 8).

Five Things You Should Know About School Discipline

A recent issue of *Child Trends* (Darling-Churchill, 2014) provides a useful overview of the key points emphasized throughout this book at the core of the movement to reform disciplinary policy and practices:

1. *School discipline actions should be considered as learning opportunities rather than measures to keep order and enable academics to proceed.* Though often viewed through a negative lens as managing student behavior, school personnel, families, and other student support services can work together to use disciplinary matters to support positive child and youth development and ensure school success.

2. *Student behavior problems may be about more than the behavior itself.* Student disciplinary infractions may reflect students' struggles with increasingly rigorous academic expectations, or circumstances affecting them outside of school. While behavior issues, absenteeism, and violence in schools undeniably impact academic instruction, policies and disciplinary actions that fail to consider the range of student backgrounds and contexts are missing an opportunity to identify needed supports for at-risk and struggling students.

3. *Research shows a strong link between disciplinary policies and actions and a host of negative outcomes.* Suspension in ninth grade doubles a student's likelihood of dropping out, from sixteen percent to thirty-two percent for those suspended just once, and students with a history of disciplinary issues are at risk of ending up entangled in the criminal justice system. Nonpunitive responses to negative behaviors (such as targeted behavioral supports) have shown promise in reducing violent behavior in school.

4. *Recent federal guidance supports efforts to ensure that discipline practices are fair and equitable.* In response to evidence of the uneven application of school discipline

practices based on race, ethnicity, gender, or other characteristics — known as "disproportionality" — the Department of Education is encouraging schools and districts
to develop research-based, locally-tailored approaches to
discipline that strive to circumvent exclusionary discipline,
especially for minor misbehaviors. Many school systems
are embracing this opportunity to showcase and/or accel-
erate their progress in this area.

5. *Schools set the tone for the disciplinary climate.* Thought-
fully-designed and administered school discipline policies
can serve to maintain safety and order, while also providing
supports for students. Encouraging positive relationships
between students and adults, promoting students' sense of
belonging, having student supports available, and training
staff on classroom management are at the core of positive
school climates and solution-focused disciplinary environments, and can minimize the need to resort to harsher
school discipline.

Summing Up

The foundation for a safe school rests on the creation of a healthy
school climate, a caring community where students feel safe and
secure. There are two main conditions which facilitate and support
safety and security:

1. An orderly, predictable environment where school staff
provide consistent, reliable supervision and discipline in
the context of a culture where prosocial values are articulated and lived, and

2. A school climate where students feel connected to the
school and respected and supported by their teachers and
other school staff.

A balance of structure and support is essential, and requires an organized, school-wide approach that is practiced by all school personnel (Brown et al., 2012; Sugai & Horner, 2008; Mayer, 1995). Being a somebody, having an identity in school, means being accepted as part of a group in the classroom and with other students. This is why social belonging is such a key feature of programs highlighted in this volume. Strategies and approaches such as social-emotional learning and restorative justice have shown success in building positive school climates where children spend their energy contributing to the greater good rather, than defending themselves from bullying and other forms of aggression and violence.

The effectiveness of the rules and sanctions that form the public outline of discipline policies are mediated by both the actual interactions of all of the school community members and how they are perceived. Beyond teaching the five core SEL competencies, efforts to create a prosocial school climate must also include a focus on adult relationships and an emphasis on adult modeling of appropriate behaviors. The quality of interactions between all members of the school community constitute a "hidden curriculum" that defines the moral fiber of a school. School discipline rests in the web of this hidden curriculum.

References

Adelman, H., & Taylor, L. (2005). *The implementation guide to student learning supports in the classroom and school wide: New directions for addressing barriers to learning.* Thousand Oaks, CA: Corwin Press.

American Psychological Association Zero Tolerance Task Force (2008). Are zero tolerance policies effective in the schools? An evidentiary review and recommendations. *American Psychologist,* 63(9), 852–862.

Association for Psychological Science. (2008, April 16). Are humans hardwired for fairness? *Science Daily.* Retrieved December 2, 2011, from http://www.sciencedaily.com/releases/2008/04/080416140918.htm

Balfanz, R., Byrnes, V., and Fox J. (2012, December 21). *Sent home and put off-track: The antecedents, disproportionalities, and consequences of being suspended in the ninth grade.* Retrieved from http://civilrightsproject.ucla.edu/resources/projects/center-for- civil-rights-remedies/school-to-prison-folder/state-reports/sent-home-and-put-off-track-the-antecedents-disproportionalities-and-consequences-of-being-suspended-in-the-ninth-grade/balfanz-sent-home-ccrr-conf-2013.pdf

Bear, G. G. (2010). *School discipline and self-discipline: A practical guide to promoting prosocial student behavior.* New York, NY: The Guilford Press.

Best, J. R., & Miller, P. H. (2010). A developmental perspective on executive function. *Child Development,* 81, 1641–1660.

Brackett, M. A., Reyes, M. R., Rivers, S. E., Elbertson, N., & Salovey, P. (2011). Classroom emotional climate, teacher affiliation, and student conduct. *Journal of Classroom Interaction,* 46, 27–36.

Brown, P. (2016). *Student Discipline: A Prosocial Perspective.* Lanham, MD: Roman & Littlefield.

Brown, P., Corrigan, M., & D'Alessandro, A. (2012). *Handbook of prosocial education.* Lanham, MD: Rowman & Littlefield.

Bryk, A. S., Sebring, P. B., Allensworth, E., Luppescu, S., & Easton, J. Q. (2010). *Organizing schools for improvement: Lessons from Chicago.* Chicago: University of Chicago Press.

Carter, D. S., Harris, J., & Porges, S. W. (2009). Neural and evolutionary perspectives on empathy. In J. Decety & W. J. Ickes (Eds.), *Social neuroscience of empathy* (pp. 169–182). Cambridge, MA: MIT Press.

Centers for Disease Control and Prevention. (2009). *School connectedness: Strategies for increasing protective factors among youth.* Atlanta, GA: Author. Retrieved January 30, 2012. Retrieved from http://www.cdc.gov/healthyyouth/adolescenthealth/pdf/connectedness.pdf

Cohen, J. (2006, Summer). Social, emotional, ethical and academic education: Creating a climate for learning, participation in democracy and well-being. *Harvard Educational Review,* 76(2), 201–237.

Cohen, J., & Pickeral, T. (2009). *The school climate implementation road map: Promoting democratically informed school communities and the continuous process of school climate improvement* (1st ed.). New York: National School Climate Center.

Cohen, J. (2012). School climate and culture improvement: A prosocial strategy that recognizes, educates and supports the whole child and the whole school community. In P. Brown, M. Corrigan, & A. D'Alessandro, *Handbook of prosocial education* (pp. 227-252). Lanham, MD: Rowman & Littlefield.

Cornell, D., Gregory, A., Huang, F., & Fan, X. (2013). Perceived prevalence of teasing and bullying predicts high school dropout rates. *Journal of Educational Psychology*, 105(1), 138-49.

Darling-Churchill, K. (2014, March 19). *Five things to know about school discipline*. Retrieved from http://www.childtrends.org/wp-content/uploads/2014/03/2014-12CT5SchoolDiscipline2.pdf

Deal, T. E., & Peterson, K. D. (2009). *Shaping school culture: Pitfalls, paradoxes, & promises* (2nd ed.). San Francisco: Jossey-Bass.

Derryberry, D., & Rothbart, M. K. (1997). Reactive and effortful processes in the organization of temperament. *Development and Psychopathology*, 55 (4), 633-52.

Devaney, E., O'Brien, M. U., Resnik, H., Keister, S., & Weissberg, R. P. (2006). *Sustainable schoolwide social and emotional learning (SEL): Implementation guide and toolkit*. Chicago: Collaborative for Academic, Social, and Emotional Learning.

De Waal, F. B. (2003, November). *Morality and the social instincts: Continuity with the other primates*. The Tanner Lectures on Human Values presented at Princeton University, Princeton, NJ.

De Waal, F. B. (2009). *Primates and philosophers: How morality evolved*. Princeton, NJ: Princeton University Press.

Diamond, A., & Lee, K. (2011). Interventions shown to aid executive function development in children 4 to 12 years old. *Science*, 333, 959–964.

discipline. n.d. In *Merriam-Webster.com*. Retrieved from http:// www.merriam-webster.com/dictionary/discipline

discipline. n.d. In *OxfordDictionaries.com*. Retrieved from http://www.oxforddictionaries.com/us/definition/american_english/discipline

Durlak, J. A., Weissberg, R. P., Dymnicki, A. B., Taylor, R. D., & Schellinger, K. B. (2011). Enhancing students' social and emotional development promotes success in school: Results of a meta-analysis. *Child Development, 82*, 474–501.

Eisenberg, N., & Fabes, R. A. (1992). Emotion, regulation, and the development of social competence. In M. S. Clark (Ed.), *Emotion and social behavior: The review of personality and social psychology* (119-50). Thousand Oaks, CA: SAGE Publications, Inc.

Elias, M. J., Zins, J. E., Weissberg, K. S., Greenberg, M. T., Haynes, N. M., Kessler, R., et al. (1997). *Promoting social and emotional learning: Guidelines for educators.* Alexandria, VA: Association for Supervision and Curriculum Development.

Elias, M. J. (2001). Prepare children for the tests of life, not a life of tests. *Education Week, 21*(4), 40.

Fabelo, T., Thompson, M. D., Plotkin, M., Carmichael, D., Marchbanks, M. P., & Booth, E. A. (2011, July). *Breaking schools' rules: A statewide study of how school discipline relates to students' success and juvenile justice involvement.* Retrieved from http://csgjusticecenter.org/wp- content/uploads/2012/08/Breaking_Schools_Rules_Report_Final.pdf

Greenberg, M. T. (2006, December). Promoting resilience in children and youth: Preventive interventions and their interface with neuroscience. *Annals of the New York Academy of Sciences, 1094*, 139–150. doi:10.1196/annals.1376.013

Hoffman, M. L. (2001). *Empathy and moral development: Implications for caring and justice.* Cambridge, UK: Cambridge University Press.

Jeannerod, M., & Anquetil, T. (2008). Putting oneself in the perspective of the other: A framework for self-other differentiation. *Social Neuroscience, 3*(4), 356–367.

Jerome, E., Hamre, B. K., & Pianta, R. C. (2009). Teacher-child relationships from kindergarten to sixth grade: Early childhood predictors of teacher-perceived conflict and closeness. *Social Development*, 18, 915–945.

Knafo, A., Zahn-Waxler, C., Hulle, C. V., Robinson, J. L., & Rhee, S. H. (2008). The developmental origins of a disposition toward empathy: Genetic and environmental contributions. *Emotion*, 8(6), 737–752.

Kohlberg, L., & Higgins, A. (1987). School democracy and social interaction. In J. Gewirtz & W. Kurtines (Eds.), *Social development and social interaction* (pp. 246–278). New York: Wiley Interscience.

Kokolis, L. L. (2007). Teaming was a catalyst for better climate and improved achievement. *Middle School Journal*, 39(1), 9–15.

Losen, D. J., & Gillespie, J. (2012, August). *Opportunities suspended: The disparate impact of disciplinary exclusion from school.* Retrieved from http://files.eric.ed.gov/fulltext/ED534178.pdf

Marchbanks, M. P., Blake, J. J., Booth, E. A., Carmichael, D., Seibert, A. L., & Fabelo, T. (2013, April 6). *The economic effects of exclusionary discipline on grade retention and high school dropout.* Retrieved from http://civilrightsproject.ucla.edu/resources/projects/center-for-civil-rights-remedies/school-to-prison-folder/state-reports/the-economic-effects-of-exclusionary-discipline-on-grade-retention-and-high-school-dropout/marchbanks-exclusionary-discipline-ccrr-conf.pdf

Marsh, J., & Keltner, D. (2015, April 9). How gratitude beats materialism. *DailyGood.* Retrieved from http://www.dailygood.org/story/1010/how-gratitude-beats-materialismjason-marsh-dacher-keltner/

Mayer, G. R. (1995). Preventing antisocial behavior in the schools. *J Appl Behav Anal*, 28(4), 467-78.

McCraty, R., Atkinson, M., Tomasino, D. & Bradley R.T. (2006). The coherent heart: Heart-brain interactions, psychophysiological coherence, and the emergence of system-wide. *Integral Review*, December 2009, Vol. 5, No. 2.

Milkie, M. A., & Warner, C. H. (2011). Classroom learning
    environments and the mental health of first grade chil-
    dren. *Journal of Health and Social Behavior,* 52, 4–22.
    doi:10.1177/0022146510394952
Morgan, E., Salomon, N., Plotkin, M., & Cohen, R. (2014). *The
    school discipline consensus report: Strategies from the field to
    keep students engaged in school and out of the juvenile justice
    system.* Retrieved from http://csgjusticecenter.org/wp-c
    ontent/uploads/2014/06/The_School_Discipline_Consensus_
    Report.pdf
Murray, D. W., Rosanbalm, K., Christopoulos, C., & Hamoudi,
    A. (2015). *Self-regulation and toxic stress: Foundations for
    understanding self-regulation from an applied developmental
    perspective* [OPRE Report #2015-21]. Washington, DC: Office
    of Planning, Research and Evaluation, Administration for
    Children and Families, U.S. Department of Health and Human
    Services.
Murray, K. T., & Kochanska, G. (2002). Effortful control: Factor
    structure and relation to externalizing and internalizing
    behaviors. *J Abnorm Child Psychol,* 30(5): 503-14.
Narvaez, D. (2014). *Neurobiology and the development of human
    morality.* New York, NY: W. W. Norton & Company, Inc.
National Middle School Association. (2003). *This we believe:
    Successful schools for young adolescents.* Westerville, OH:
    Author.
National School Climate Council. (2007). *The school climate chal-
    lenge: Narrowing the gap between school climate research and
    school climate policy, practice guidelines and teacher education
    policy.* New York: Author. Retrieved January 29, 2012, from
    http://www.schoolclimate.org/climate/documents/policy/
    school-climate-challenge-web.pdf
National School Climate Council. (2011). *National school climate
    standards: Benchmarks to promote effective teaching, learning
    and comprehensive school improvement.* Retrieved from http://
    www.schoolclimate.org/climate/documents/school-climate-
    standards-csee.pdf

Noddings, N. (2002). *Educating moral people.* New York: Teachers College Press.

Noddings, N. (2008). Caring and moral education. In L. Nucci & D. Narvaez (Eds.), *Handbook of moral and character education* (pp. 161-174). New York, NY: Routledge.

Osher, D., Sprague, J., Weissberg, R. P., Axelrod, J., Keenan, S., Kendziora, K., et al. (2008). A comprehensive approach to promoting social, emotional, and academic growth in contemporary schools. In A. Thomas & J. Grimes (Eds.), B*est practices in school psychology V* (Vol. 4, pp. 1263–1278). Bethesda, MD: National Association of School Psychologists.

Reed, B. (2008, Spring–Summer). Student engagement gains ground: A research brief. *Northwest Education,* 13(3), 37–38. Retrieved August 14, 2009, from http://educationnorthwest. org/webfm_send/434

Schonert-Reichl, K.A. & O'Brien, M.U. (2012). Social and emotional learning and prosocial education: Theory, research, and programs. In P. Brown, M. Corrigan, & A. D'Alessandro, *Handbook of prosocial education* (pp. 311-346). Lanham, MD: Rowman & Littlefield.

Schore, A. N. (2003). *Affect regulation and the repair of the self.* New York, NY: W. W. Norton & Company.

Sugai, G., & Horner, R. l. (2008). What we know and nerd to know about preventing problem behavior in schools. *Exceptionality,* 16, 67-77.

Szalavitz, M. (2013, November 16). *Theory finds that individuals with Asperger's Syndrome don't lack empathy — in fact if anything they empathize too much.* Retrieved from https:// seventhvoice.wordpress.com/2013/11/16/new-study-finds- that-individuals-with-aspergers-syndrome-dont-lack- empathy-in-fact-if-anything-they-empathize-too-much/

Tabibnia, G., Satpute, A. B., & Lieberman, M. D. (2008). The sunny side of fairness: Preference for fairness activates reward circuitry (and disregarding unfairness activates self-control circuitry). *Psychological Science,* 19(4), 339–347.

Westbrook, Connecticut School Climate Policy #5131.914 (2014): Author U.S. Department of Education, (2014). *Guiding Principles: A Resource Guide for Improving School Climate and Discipline.* Washington, D.C.: Author.

Weissberg, R. P., Payton, J. W., O'Brien, M. U., & Munro, S. (2007). Social and emotional learning. In F. C. Power, R. J. Nuzzi, D. Narvaez, D. K. Lapsley, & T. C. Hunt (Eds.), *Moral education: A handbook,* Vol. 2, M–Z (pp. 417–418). Westport, CT: Greenwood Press.

Zahn-Waxler, C., Robinson, J. L., & Emde, R. N. (1992). The development of empathy in twins. *Developmental Psychology,* 28(6), 1038–1047.

Zins, J., Weissberg, R. W., Wang, M. C., & Walberg, H. (Eds.). (2004). *Building school success on social emotional learning: What does the research say?* New York: Teachers College Press.

Chapter Nine

Mindfulness, the Reawakening of Black Dharma, and Mastering the Art of Policing

Tony Gaskew

> Every Black birth in America is political. With each new birth comes a potential challenge to the existing order. Each new generation brings forth untested militancy.
>
> — Jamil Abdullah Al-Amin (H. Rap Brown)[1]

During my *vipassanā*[2] within the criminal justice system, which includes working as a police detective at M.P.D., assigned as a member of the Department of Justice's Organized Crime Drug Enforcement Task Force, and currently as a tenured associate professor of criminal justice and founding director of a nationally recognized prison education program at the University of Pittsburgh (Bradford), there is very little that I have not seen, heard, or done in the construct of crime and justice. I relied upon mindfulness to navigate through the pain and suffering of thousands of arrests, convictions, and prison sentences, including death penalty cases, as a *Bodhisattva* of justice.[3] My mindfulness permitted me to bring W.E.B. Du Bois to every arrest, James Baldwin to every court proceeding, and Ralph Ellison to every sentencing. There was never a moment throughout my career as a Black American criminal justice professional immersed within the policing culture, that Jamil Abdullah Al-Amin, Kwame Ture, and El-Hajj Malik El-Shabazz were not with me.

You see, mindfulness provided me with the wisdom, morality, and awareness to walk the path of truthfulness, fearlessness, and compassion as a police officer, academician, activist, and more importantly, as a living being, to provide the *right view*[4] of my collectively lived Black American experiences, and to confront the pain and suffering of Black spaces within the constructs of crime and justice.[5] The synergy of direct and structural violence aimed at Black American diaspora by the criminal justice system is much more complex and destructive than it sounds. Over the past 400 years, the criminal justice system, specifically the policing culture, has been used to create a fictional narrative of Blackness under a multi-layered set of systemic humiliations.[6]

These systemic humiliations incorporate what is referred to as the *wrong view.*[7] Harmony in any true community, depends on a shared commitment to ethical conduct and a shared commitment to virtue. Systemic humiliations use the poisons of greed, hatred, and delusion to destroy communities under the poisons of shame, self-segregation, and transgenerational learned helplessness.[8] It attempts to intentionally strip away any level of dignity and respect and sets into motion a climate void of the universal language of love, empathy, compassion, mercy, and humility. Its recipients have always been America's indigenous populations, and none greater than its native sons, Black America. By way of the policing culture, systemic pain and suffering have been applied to generations through the likes of the Black Codes, Jim Crow, and mass incarceration[9] with the sole intent to destroy the three treasures of cultural Blackness in America: teachers, teachings, and community.[10] However, speaking the language of a social scientist, systemic humiliations are not the root *cause* of this failed attempt at cultural genocide but the insidious *side-effect* of an invisible history of micro and macro-sufferings against Blackness. Born from the womb of our nation's *original sin* of chattel enslavement and the Black American Holocaust, the mental illness of *white supremacy* is the fundamental "cause" of human pain and suffering, and continues to sit at the core of how Black spaces are "effected" through institutionally controlled and constructed forms of oppression, marginalization, and humiliation. The policing culture, by way of the original stop-and-frisk enforcers — slave patrols — was nourished and grew inside the womb of white supremacy. The four-centuries-old illusion of white superiority and Black inferiority has saturated the poisons of greed, anger, and ignorance[11] into the hearts, minds, and souls of tens of millions of people willing to embrace its ugly distortion of self-preservation without moral accountability.[12] [13]

Given the disproportionate use of direct and structural violence inflicted on Black spaces under the constructs of crime and justice, there is very little doubt the policing culture has weaponized the psychic violence of white supremacy. Today, despite making up less than five percent of the adult population, Black men occupy nearly forty percent of our nation's prison cells.[14] Black American bodies are more likely to be stopped, more likely to be arrested, and more likely to be incarcerated. As a result, today a police officer can walk into any maternity ward in America, and with an almost statistical certainty, place handcuffs on one out of every three nameless newborn Black American male infants.[15] You see, crime is a constructed humiliation designed to displace the true richness, beauty, and essence of Blackness in America.

The misery caused by the policing culture on Black bodies are metaphysical in nature, scope, and understanding, thus, it's only logical that a Black ontological lens be used to uncover a path of liberation. In the brief space of this chapter, I will attempt to synergize thirty years of my *vipassanā* into my chosen livelihood, crime and justice, and examine how mindfulness can lead down a path of reawakened Black consciousness, a *Black Dharma,* where it can be used to challenge, destabilize, and reframe the existing policing cultural narrative. A mindfulness that will apply the essence of fearlessness to unfriend the fictional narrative the policing culture has spread of Black lives.

Thus, as part of this metaphysical path to liberation that engulfs Black resistance to all forms and shapes of white supremacy, in every page of this essay, I capitalize the *B* in *Black* while leaving the *w* in *white* in lowercase as a display of fierce compassion. You see, what I've discovered in my sometimes uncomfortable journey to a path of well-being and happiness is that it's okay to sometimes feel uncomfortable. At the deepest levels of human growth and potential, is our collectively shared fear of being inferior, that is, the pain and suffering associated with our unwillingness to understand that all living beings are connected and that all of our actions and deeds are reciprocal in nature. Using all of our senses, the constructs of supremacy and the wrong view, rooted in fear and anger, must be exposed, destabilized, and reframed. It is at this point that the doors of compassion are fully opened. Tiptoeing around racism, and the differences guided by its self-preserving constructs is unhealthy and only leads down a path of systemic pain, suffering, and humiliation.

However, I cannot overemphasize that every word in this essay is spoken under the universal language of an earthy, karmic, and collective love. Love that confronts, love that changes, love that forgives, love that heals, and love that liberates. *Our love.* Unraveling the messy entanglement that white supremacy and it's many tentacles have had on the thoughts, feelings, dreams, and humanity of all people, will require a radical dharma.[16] *Our dharma.* It will take the virtues of wisdom, morality, and awareness to produce justice. *Our justice.* It will take right understanding and right thought. Right speech, action, and livelihood. Right effort, engagement, and concentration. *Our righteousness.* It will take a warrior's spirit to save all beings, to balance all desires, to master all truths, and to liberate all sufferings. *Our Bodhisattva.* Finally, it will take personal transformation. A transformation that begins with embracing humility, ethical self-discipline, and cultivation of the mind.[17] A transformation that acknowledges the good of generosity over greed, patience over anger, and *sangha* over ignorance. *Our transformation.*

The Reawakening of Black Dharma

James Baldwin believed that Black Americans are the conscience of America, and to be Black and conscious in America is to be in a constant state of mindfulness.[18] You see, the search for a strong and vibrant Black consciousness defined my own sense of *Zen*. Black consciousness is at the forefront of mitigating the uncontrolled desires of greed, anger, and ignorance. Black consciousness is the physical, psychological, and spiritual heartbeat of redemption, forgiveness, and healing. Black consciousness is the voice for the voiceless. Black consciousness serves as the vanguard dark matter for social movements around the world searching for answers to human pain and suffering. As a Black American man born in the early 1960s, I saw first-hand the incredible life force of Black consciousness with the awakening of the Black Power Movement, giving birth to a generation of *Bodhisattvas*, who immersed themselves in the collective goals echoed by Karenga:[19] to solve pressing problems within the Black American community; and to continue the revolutionary struggle being waged to end white supremacy, racism, and oppression against Black spaces.

Today, Black consciousness needs a reawakening. A reawakening I initially described as *Black Cultural Privilege* (BCP) in my book, *Rethinking Prison Reentry: Transforming Humiliation into Humility*. Black Cultural Privilege is the physical, mental, and spiritual awareness that connects the rich diverse history of an African past with the ever-evolving journey into the legacy of the collective lived Black American experience. It's an unconscious bond that exists amongst a people whose roots share an indestructible cultural DNA that has only been strengthened by 400 years of direct and structural violence, enslavement, the Black Codes, and Jim Crow. BCP defines the essence of Blackness in America.[20] However, what I discovered over the last few years is that the most radical aspect of Black consciousness is its evolutionary state-of-*shamatha*.[21] Black Cultural Privilege was only a part of the *dharmachakra*[22] and the ongoing reawakening towards human liberation.

Without a doubt, we, as an entire universe of living beings, are one. Everything in it, around it, and shaped by it is alive, always in motion, and interconnected to everything else. We know this for a fact because our common senses are designed for the sole purpose of this synergy. When the sun shines, the wind blows, or the rain falls, it brings with it the same window of life to all living beings. Nothing in the universe is spared. The human connection with the universe began in the rich cultural *sangha* [23] of Africa. Black bodies were the first human students of the universe and Black Americans are their *samsāra*.[24] Black bodies were the first human voices, created the first human languages, and the first human civilizations. Black bodies were the first human beings to be taught the gifts of *dharma*, humility, and forgiveness; that we all share the same duty of preserving life; that we are all connected under the universal principle that if one living being suffers, all living beings suffer; we were the first to absorb the life lessons of compassion, mercy, pride, empathy, righteousness, courage, unity, compromise, and love; the first to apply the gift of the *fourth eye*. Black bodies were the first scholars of metaphysics, the ethnosphere, spirituality, enlightenment, faith, and karma;[25] [26] the first to apply justice, under the philosophical concepts of awareness, morality, and wisdom;[27] the first to be taught about the poisons of greed, anger, and ignorance;[28] the first to use the family building blocks of teachers, teachings, and communities;[29] the first to understand the law of causation, that pain and happiness, along with life and death, are all part of the interconnected cycle of life. Black bodies were the first to apply the principles of fearlessness[30] as a life road map; the first to recognize the duty of not contributing to evil, doing good, and doing good for others.[31] The universe taught the world's first human beings, Black people, *the art of life*.[32]

Just to be clear, this evolutionary reawakening is not just another layer of Afrocentricity.[33] Black Americans are no longer negotiating from a position of social, political, or economic weakness. Those days are over. We have the resources to frame and define the constructs of crime and justice. Kwame Ture once noted that "confusion is the greatest enemy of the revolution."[34] There is no longer any confusion in our revolution. We know exactly what to do. We now simply have to do it. This reawakening is the natural evolution of the Black American consciousness. I would describe this higher level of consciousness as *Black Dharma*.[35]

Black Dharma is a radical metaphysical force that filters, deconstructs, and eliminates the by-products of shame, self-segregation,
and transgenerational learned helplessness[36] inherited by 400 years
of white supremacy. It liberates Black spaces in the ideological war
against white superiority and Black inferiority. It produces a cultural
fearlessness that challenges the legitimacy of any construct in America
that attempts to criminalize Blackness. It confronts the systemic actors
of direct and structural violence that use the mask of law and order to
conspire against the Black American diaspora. It compels transpar-
ency and accountability, holding institutional stakeholders responsible
for maintaining justice to standards established and owned by Black
American voices. As the founders of humanity, Black people must
take responsibility for their own liberation. Black Americans must
make peace with their own historical legacy. Black Americans must
take ownership of either transforming or disposing of the current
criminal justice system and policing culture. Black Americans must
wake up each morning and take full responsibility for the changes that
we want to make in our lives and in *our* world.[37] The reawakening of
a twenty-first century Black Dharma will end the *samsāra* of white
supremacy and place the moral compass back into the hands of the
universes first human beings. At the core of Black Dharma sits four
interconnected strategies designed to liberate ourselves from pain and
suffering, and to mastering the art of policing: *mindfulness, accountability, empowerment,* and *healing.*[38] [39]

Mindfulness

This first dharma Black America must master is the art of *mindfulness* regarding the criminal justice system and the policing culture.
As a people, we need to stop lying to ourselves. We don't have either
a good or bad relationship with the justice system. We simply don't
have a relationship. The criminal justice system is not part of the
organic connective bond that living beings have within the universe.
The criminal justice system does not recognize the cultural legacy of
the first humans on the planet. The actors whose livelihood depends

on the criminal justice system do not recognize their duty to not spread evil, to do good, and to do good for others. Its inner core is based on the foundational poisons of greed, anger, and ignorance, all directed at the dehumanization of the Black experience in America. Thus, as Black Americans we must first decide whether creating a relationship with the criminal justice system and its gatekeepers, the policing culture, is even worth the effort. Is the system even worth reforming or saving? The construct that started off as slave patrols, conducting stop-and-frisks on Black bodies for over three centuries, has never morphed into anything other than a weaponized tool of white superiority and Black inferiority. I ask again, is reforming the criminal justice system and its policing culture even worth the cosmic energy of the founders of humanity?

Additionally, there are two cultural truths about the criminal justice system that Black America should consider before moving forward. First, white supremacy will always be embedded within the policing culture and the criminal justice system. Regardless of the sincerity of any reform efforts, the social institutions of policing, courts, and corrections were made by white Americans, are controlled by white Americans, only to serve and benefit white Americans, and to dehumanize Black Americans. The criminal justice system in America is the *Great White Shark*,[40] a corporately constructed twenty-four-hours-a-day, seven-days-a-week eating machine and multi-trillion-dollar-a-year business [41] with the sole purpose of morally destroying Black bodies, Black culture, and Black potential.[42] It will never willingly surrender its cultural influence to inflict systemic pain and suffering against Black spaces. Its influence must be weakened and its culture humbled.

Second, only a complete state of Black American hopelessness in the justice apparatus will usher in the opportunity for systemic reform, and we are not there yet. There is much more pain and suffering that needs to be absorbed. Please keep in mind, a nation that was founded on the universal evils of greed, anger, and ignorance [43] has a created a very high threshold for Black violence, which, by the way, does not bode well for the policing culture karmically. Over the last four centuries, the mental illness of white supremacy has very effectively enslaved a segment of the Black American population, convincing them that their Black lives, the lives of their Black families, and the lives of their Black communities are worthless and inferior, while at the same time, convincing them that white lives, the lives of white families, and the lives of white communities are valuable and superior. Black inferiority and white superiority has resulted in the killings of Black bodies at the hands of other Black bodies, as well as the attempted extermination of Black culture and Black potential through the holocaust of mass incarceration. For the most part, the policing actors who maintain its culture from the original sins of this nation, the colonization and criminalization of Black bodies, have escaped the cosmic wrath of their actions. However, those days are coming to an end. The metaphysics of violence has shifted. Black voices — whether they are framed by scholarship or clergy, that white fragility historically counted on to pacify young Black rage against state-sponsored violence — are now silent. You see, over the past several hundred years, the policing culture has demanded two basic needs from Black America: *respect* and *fear*. Black America never respected the policing culture and never will. It is impossible to respect any living being that does not understand the oneness of humanity. However, some Black American communities provided the policing culture the fear they demanded. There are literally generations of Black American bodies who have been corporately conditioned not to make eye contact with the police; to treat them as overseers on a plantation; to run and hide at the very mention of the police, for little or no justification. In fact, an argument can be made that the transgenerational trauma of *police fear* is regenerated every time Black parents have the legendary "talk" with Black sons or Black daughters about how to survive a police encounter.

The universal dilemma facing the policing culture today is that slowly but surely, Black souls are being woken. The illusion of justice is being exposed and the primary tool of fear used to enslave Black people is quickly losing its effectiveness — to many unlawful stops, arrests, and shootings — too many excuses, lies, and cover-ups — too much greed, anger, and ignorance — too much death and indifference - too much evil. Black America has reawakened to the reality that there is nothing else the criminal justice system can inflict on their lives, that has not already been tried to void their entire human condition: oppression, marginalization, alienation, subjugation, enslavement, incarceration, and even extermination. Economic, employment, medical, housing, and educational sanctions. Basic human rights denied. All modes of evil tried and failed. Now, fearlessness is beginning to take hold among Black spaces. The same Black spaces who once saw no value or worth in their own Black lives is beginning to see no value or worth in police lives. The same Black spaces who once saw themselves as active peacemakers are now sitting back and waiting for the universe to correct itself. Violence begets violence and the policing culture will no longer be bystanders to karma, the law of moral causation, which insures that good and bad deeds eventually produce their appropriate fruits.[44] The policing culture will never be safe from pain and suffering as long as Black America is not safe.[45]

Accountability

The second dharma Black America must master is the art of *accountability*. As Fanon suggested regarding the process of decolonization, "to tell the truth, the proof of success lies in a whole social structure being changed from the bottom up."[46] If Black America decides it is worth their human investment to decolonize the criminal justice system and the policing culture, then their full and unwavering commitment of their *sangha* is required. There will no longer be a moral middle ground on issues of Black humanity. It's either all or nothing and Black America must be prepared to hold the criminal justice system fully accountable. Black America must be willing to *unfriend* the gatekeepers of justice, the policing culture. Unfriending the policing culture becomes a logical choice for Black America once we awaken to the right understanding of friendship. Strong communities depend on the personal relations between their members, and the most basic relation between people outside their family connections is that of friendship. One's choice of friends have a profound influence one one's individual development as well as on the creation of a harmonious and ethically upright community. Friendship is essential not only because it benefits us in times of trouble, satisfies our social instincts, and enlarges our sphere of concern from the self to others. More importantly, friendship plants the seeds that help us develop a sense of discretion, the ability to distinguish between good and bad, right and wrong, and to choose the honorable over the expedient.[47] Using this as a new map towards understanding happiness and well-being, the policing culture has never had a friendship with Black America.

The policing culture in America has been tasked with one of the most sacred duties in the universe, serving as the gatekeepers to *justice*, providing the roots of the wholesome: wisdom, morality, and awareness. However, since its inception over 400 years ago, the policing culture has succumbed to the evils of white supremacy, embracing the roots of the *unwholesome*: greed, hatred, and ignorance, with no living beings harmed more for the policing cultures *wrong view* than Black America.[48]

Unfriending involves a great deal of tough love, and is no different than managing the lifestyle changes of someone who is suffering from an addiction, Black America must stop enabling the policing culture — that is, eliminate all *Black funding, Black patronage,* and *Black empathy* for the policing culture. First, Black America must withdraw all economic support for the policing culture, which includes opposing any and all efforts that increase the monetary coffers of policing. New pay raises, new equipment, or new training should never receive Black support; oppose the hiring of any new officers or police staff; and vote anyone out of office that supports any of these efforts. In any case of alleged police misconduct, Black America must levy federal civil litigation against the city, the agency, and the officers involved. Black America must file official complaints on every police contact. This includes any police encounter, whether a traffic stop, a pedestrian stop, and any level of verbal or physical force used by the police. Black America must make every single Black American contact with the police cost the justice system. Second, Black America must entirely withdraw their community support for the policing culture. Do not participate in police–community relations meetings, volunteer police academies, or the police athletic league; oppose any effort to establish community-oriented policing in Black neighborhoods; and do not support the use of school resource officers in any educational setting that serves Black students. Additionally, Black America must actively withdraw any future employment participation within the policing career field. Although Black Americans serving as police officers nationwide have always been sparse,[49] the policing culture does not deserve the human potential and moral sacrifice of one more young, dignified, and talented Black American body among its rank and file. Black American police will no longer be caught in the crossfire between *Black and Blue.*

Third, and finally, Black America must abandon all of its emotional support for the policing culture. The biggest advantage of being from a family of Black American police officers with over seventy years of combined participant observation experience is that you are completely immersed in the emotional make-up of the policing culture. Without a doubt, the absolute worst and most seductive vice the policing culture has ever inherited from Black communities across the nation is their emotional permission of *perceived entitlement.* Since the twilight years of the Black Power Movement, Black inferiority and white superiority in policing has successfully framed a narrative of good and bad Black America. The rules are simple. If you unquestionably believe the American system of justice is fair, equitable, and color blind; if you openly support the policing culture; and, most importantly, if you publicly criticize and degrade Black spaces, you are considered a good Black American. If not, you are a bad Black American. As noted in *Rethinking Prison Reentry,*[50] there is a segment of Black America that is very comfortable with this narrative because it allows them a metaphysical window to escape the weight of 400 years of dehumanization. Thus, good Black Americans have given the policing culture emotional carte blanche to police bad Black Americans — that is, the emotional permission to basically do whatever the policing culture wants, whenever the policing culture wants, and to whomever the policing culture wants, as long as they don't *incarcerate* good Black Americans; the emotional permission to do no wrong and to never admit guilt, fault, or weakness about anything, anywhere, or anytime, as long as they don't *humiliate* good Black Americans; the emotional permission to embrace a pseudo-warrior mentality, where the policing culture is given hero-like status, have funeral processions reserved for mythical royalty, and openly rewarded for acts of direct and structural violence, as long as they don't *terrorize* good Black Americans; and the emotional permission that has allowed police chiefs from Baltimore, Chicago, and New York to look right into the eyes of good Black Americans and successfully frame the narrative that Black-on-Black crime is the fault of bad Black Americans. Perhaps even more telling, the emotional permission that granted the policing culture unfiltered permission to unlawfully stop, search, arrest, and kill Black bodies and to know with a degree of absolute certainty that they will never be held accountable by good Black Americans. Thus, the manufactured narrative of two opposing Black Americas must be exposed, confronted, and fused, and the emotional support for policing must be culturally rescinded by all of Black America.

Black America must allow the policing culture to fail; to take back the gift of Black forgiveness; to withdraw Black empathy; and to remove Black mercy and compassion. No more Black righteousness, or wisdom. Black America must stop apologizing for and protecting the policing culture from Black America; to let white supremacy, permeate and suffocate whatever good remains of the policing culture; to admit that the policing culture has spread evil; to allow the universal poisons of greed, anger, and ignorance to completely consume the policing culture; to welcome the onset of fear and mortality within the policing culture; to concede that pain and suffering are universal truths that the policing culture must also face. Black America must get out of the way of karma. Police cultural fragility is the best kept secret in the business of crime and justice.[51]

Empowerment

The third dharma Black America must master is the art of *empowerment*. The Black American experience must define and frame the policing culture. Black community-controlled policing, from bottom to top, must project its own sense of justice into the policing role, purpose, and culture. Black voices must approve the hiring of every single new police officer across the nation. No pay raises, promotions, or union perks will go unchecked without Black oversight. Black Americans will create and chair community-controlled committees to manage policing. The process of all citizen-initiated complaints regarding police misconduct towards Black bodies, and all subsequent internal investigations, will be managed by Black people. Black community-controlled policing will require every single police officer in the nation to retake their oaths and rededicate their allegiance to serve and protect under the tenets of generosity, mercy, and compassion. The purpose of policing will no longer be to serve the best interests of their fellow officers, their agency, or the corporate greed of the criminal justice system. Black community-controlled policing will shift the narrative of the policing culture. First, there are no *good* or *bad* cops, just people doing good or bad deeds and actions. There are *righteous, rotten,* or *riddled* people, all who happen to have badges and guns. Those who are righteous, the *Bodhisattvas'* of justice, simply try *to do the right thing.* Those who are rotten, the corruptors of justice, simply try to do evil. And those who are riddled, the cowards of justice, simply *try to do nothing.* Second, the overwhelming majority of police officers today and the true enemy of Black America live comfortably within the riddled spectrum of the policing culture. These are the police officers, both Black and white, that witness the daily pain and suffering projected on Black bodies under the rule of law and use the power of their silence to protect the policing culture from the law of causation. Their cowardice must be exposed and punished. And third, more Black bodies must be willing to sacrifice and share their Black essence by serving as *Bodhisattvas'* of justice. A reawakened Black Dharma will usher in an ultra-professional Black American police officer. These Bodhisattvas' of justice will understand the right view of friendship with the Black community: one that is helpful and serves as a refuge for the Black community; one that restrains from evil, does good, and does good for the Black community; and one that shares in both the happiness and suffering of the Black community, guarding its dignity and protecting its humanity, even if that requires sacrificing his own life. These *Bodhisattvas'* of justice will not be seduced by the cultural offerings of greed (money, power, and sex), anger (punishing Blackness), or ignorance (assimilating to white supremacy). The blue wall of silence will fade to black, and the policing culture as we know it will either assimilate or become extinct. However, a reawakened Black consciousness without a sense of *healing* only sows the seeds of shame, self-subjugation, and transgenerational learned helplessness. That realm of metaphysical violence will no longer be accepted. Black Dharma also requires the policing culture to publicly confess and to publicly accept culpability for its *crimes against Black humanity.*[52]

Healing

The last dharma Black America must master is the art of *healing*. Truth and accountability panels must be held across the nation, where police officers, police agencies, and the policing culture publicly admit the destruction they have intentionally inflicted upon Black lives. These actors of pain and suffering must admit their deeds against Black humanity, and accept full accountability for their actions. Without exception, every policing agency in America must submit to actively participating in this process of systemic healing. Second, every single Black body that has suffered at the hands of the policing culture will be made whole again by investing in their human potential. Every single Black body that has been jailed or imprisoned will be compensated. Every single Black body that has come under the control of community corrections will be compensated. Every single Black child whose parent has been subjected to pain and suffering, will be compensated. Every single police officer in America will understand the consequences of the wrong view: when they make a decision to harm a Black body under the tenets of white superiority and Black inferiority, a compensatory price will be paid. Third and finally, the policing culture will be the source of the compensation. Every single dollar obtained through civil asset forfeiture, court fines, and associated fees nationwide will be used to make Black bodies whole again. According to the National Institute for Justice, since 2001 nearly $30 billion has been seized through civil asset forfeiture and sits in the drug war chest of the policing culture.[53] This number grows exponentially each year by $4 billion. Unfortunately, there is a dearth of research on the exact dollar amount collected by each of our 35,000 municipalities regarding the criminal court costs associated with the enslavement of Black bodies. But, if a town the size of Ferguson, Missouri, with a population of roughly 22,000, can issue nearly 33,000 warrants and collect $2.6 million in revenue during a single year, can you just imagine the hundreds of billions of dollars being generated annually by the policing culture from Black bodies?[54] Can you imagine the trillions of dollars that the policing culture has pilfered by dehumanizing Black bodies, Black culture, and Black potential since the inception of slave patrols? The time has come for Black America to demand payment on a 400-year-old debt.[55]

Final Thoughts

Liberation is not an end, but a means to an end. It's a roadmap in the art of life. It's the universe's GPS system to the path of happiness. Liberation is an awakening that acknowledges that the lives of every living being is interconnected, and that the laws of moral causation, retributive consequences that reflect the actions from which they spring, are just part of our shared journey. Generosity triumphs over greed and empathy is a natural extension of love. Good deeds, the right view, produces well-being and bad deeds, the wrong view, produces misery. Every single human being who was ever been inspired by any higher power in the universe, has shared this exact same message to mankind throughout humanity. We must begin to invest in humility.

The policing culture in America has been tasked with one of the most sacred duties in the universe, serving as the gatekeepers to justice, and provided with the roots of the wholesome: wisdom, morality, and awareness. However, since its inception, the policing culture has succumbed to the evils of white supremacy, embracing the roots of greed, hatred, and ignorance, with no living beings harmed more than Black America. We, as living beings, must begin to come to terms with the reality that the policing culture is a white supremacist institution that carries out white supremacist mandates, one being the destruction of Black lives.[56] Under the mask of friendship, the policing culture has weaponized the universal virtue of justice, using it as moral precept to pacify any response against their brutality against Black American bodies. Compassion involves embracing these realities; however, not with anger and hate, but with right understanding, right thought, right speech, right action, right livelihood, right effort, right engagement, and right concentration.

As the founders of humanity, Black people must take responsibility for liberation, because our liberation is your liberation. Black Americans must begin to take ownership to end their own pain and suffering caused by the policing culture. A reawakening, a *Black Dharma,* is required. A metaphysical road map that filters, deconstructs, and eliminates the by-products of shame, self-segregation, and transgenerational learned helplessness[57] inherited by 400 years of white supremacy. One that produces a cultural fearlessness that challenges the legitimacy of any construct in America that attempts to criminalize Blackness. One that incorporates mindfulness, accountability, empowerment, and healing to restore a balance between good and bad, right from wrong, and the honorable over the expedient. One that inspires *Bodhisattvas'* of justice. Those who will understand the right view of friendship with the Black community. Those who will serve as a refuge for the Black community. Those who will do good for the Black community. Those who will guard the dignity and protect the humanity of the Black community, even if that requires sacrificing their own lives. Liberation demands it.[58]

Notes

1. H. Rap Brown [Jamil Abdullah Al-Amin]. *Die Nigger Die: A Political Autobiography*. (Chicago: Ill. Lawrence Hill Books, 1969), 1.
2. Bhikkhu Bodhi. *The Buddha's Teachings on Social and Communal Harmony: An Anthology of Discourses from the Pali Canon*. (Sommerville: MA: Wisdom Publications 2016).
3. Gaskew, *Rethinking Prison Reentry: Transforming Humiliation into Humility*. (Lanham, MD: Lexington Books, 2014).
4. Bodhi, *The Buddha's Teachings on Social and Communal Harmony*, 5.
5. Gaskew, "The Policing of the Black American Male: Transforming Humiliation into Humility in Pursuit of Truth and Reconciliation."
6. Gaskew, "Do I want be a 30 Percenter or 70 Percenter?"; "Unfriending the Policing Culture: The Reawakened Black Consciousness"; "Transforming the Systemic Humiliation of Crime and Justice: Reawakening Black Consciousness."
7. Bodhi, *The Buddha's Teachings on Social and Communal Harmony*,12.
8. Ibid.
9. Derrick Bell, *Faces at the Bottom of the Well*. (New York, NY: Basic Books, 1992).
10. Angel Williams, *Being Black: Zen and the Art of Living with Fearlessness and Grace*. (New York, NY: Penguin Compass Press, 2000), 32-35.
11. Williams, *Being Black*.
12. Salathiel Thompson and Connor Stevens. The United States of America vs. The United States of America [Lecture Notes]https://courseweb.pitt.edu/webapps/blackboard/content/listContentEditable.jsp?content_ id=_20249473 1&course_id=_320452_1&mode=reset
13. Salathiel Thompson, Anthony Boyd and Chris Colon. Just Mercy: A Transformative Criminal Justice Journey to Expose and Uproot White Supremacy [Lecture Notes] https://courseweb.pitt.edu/webapps/blackboard/content/list.
14. ContentEditable.jsp?content_id=_21479986_1&course_id=_352616_1&mode=reset.
15. "The Sentencing Project." Black Lives Matter: Eliminating Racial Inequity in the Criminal Justice System. http://sentencingproject.org/wp-content/uploads/2015/11/Black-Lives-Matter.pdf
16. Bureau of Justice Statistics. Prevalence of Imprisonment in the U.S. Population, 1974-2001. http://www.bjs.gov/content/pub/pdf/piusp01.pdf
17. Angel Kyodo Williams, Rod Owens & Jasmine Syedullah in *Radical Dharma: Talking Race, Love, and Liberation* (Berkley, CA: North Atlantic Book, 2016), 191.
18. Bodhi, *The Buddha's Teachings on Social and Communal Harmony*, 5.
19. James Baldwin. "Negro Leaders on Violence," (Time, 86, 1965), 17-21.
20. Maulana Karenga, *Introduction to Black Studies*, (Los Angeles, CA: University of Sankore Press,2010).
21. Gaskew, *Rethinking Prison Reentry*.
22. Williams, Owens & Syedullah, *Radical Dharma: Talking Race, Love, and*

Liberation, 207.

23. Bodhi, T*he Buddha's Teachings on Social and Communal Harmony,* 147-150.

24. Ibid., 207.

25. Ibid., 207.

26. Karenga, *Introduction to Black Studies.*

27. Williams, *Being Black.* Ibid., 40.

28. Ibid., 46.

29. Ibid., 33-35.

30. Ibid., 166.

31. Ibid., 91.

32. Ibid., 7.

33. Molefi Asante, *Afrocentricity: The Theory of Social Change.* (Souk Village, IL: African American

34. Images, 2003).

35. Kwame Ture, *Black Power: The Politics of Liberation.* (New York, NY: Vintage Books, 1967), viii.

36. Williams, Owens, & Syedullah, *Radical Dharma: Talking Race, Love, and Liberation,* 206.

37. Gaskew, *Rethinking Prison Reentry.*

38. Williams, *Being Black,* 178.

39. Gaskew, "Unfriending the Policing Culture."

40. Gaskew, "Do I want be a 30 Percenter or 70 Percenter."

41. Gaskew, *Rethinking Prison Reentry.*

42. Ibid., 65.

43. Karenga, *Introduction to Black Studies.*

44. Williams, *Being Black.*

45. Bodhi, *The Buddha's Teachings on Social and Communal Harmony,*13.

46. Gaskew, "Unfriending the Policing Culture."

47. Franz Fanon, *The Wretched of the Earth.* (London: Penguin, 1967), 35.

48. Bodhi, *The Buddha's Teachings on Social and Communal Harmony,*85.

49. Ibid., 17.

50. "Bureau of Justice Statistics." Employment and Expenditure. http://www.bjs.gov/.

51. Gaskew, *Rethinking Prison Reentry.*

52. Gaskew, "Unfriending the Policing Culture."

53. Ibid., 10.

54. "The National Institute for Justice." Policing for Profit. http://ij.org/report/policing-for-profit/executive-summary/

55. "The United States Department of Justice." Investigation of the Ferguson Police Department.

56. https://www.justice.gov/sites/default/files/opa/press-eleases/attach-ments/2015/03/04/ferguson_police_department_ report.pdf

57. Gaskew, "Unfriending the Policing Culture."

58. Williams, Owens & Syedullah, *Radical Dharma: Talking Race, Love, and Liberation,* xxvi.

59. Gaskew, *Rethinking Prison Reentry.*
60. Gaskew, "Unfriending the Policing Culture."

References

Asante, Molefi. *Afrocentricity: The Theory of Social Change.* Souk Village, IL: African American Images, 2003.

Baldwin. James. *Negro Leaders on Violence*, Time, 86, 17-21, 1965.

Bell, Derrick. Faces at the Bottom of the Well. New York, NY: Basic Books, 1992.

Bodhi, Bhikkhu. (Ed.). *The Buddha's Teachings on Social and Communal Harmony: An Anthology of Discourses from the Pali Canon.* Sommerville: MA: Wisdom Publications, 2016.

Brown, Rap H. [Jamil Abdullah Al-Amin]. *Die Nigger Die: A Political Autobiography.* Chicago: Ill. Lawrence Hill Books, 1969).

"Bureau of Justice Statistics." Employment and Expenditure. Accessed September 16, 2016 http://www.bjs.gov/

____. *"Prevalence of Imprisonment in the U.S. Population, 1974-2001."* Accessed September 16, 2016. http://www.bjs.gov/content/pub/pdf/piusp01.pdf

Du Bois, W.E.B. *The Souls of Black Folk.* Mineola, NY: Dover Publications, 1994.

Fanon, Franz. *The Wretched of the Earth.* London: Penguin, 1967.

Gaskew, Tony. *Rethinking Prison Reentry: Transforming Humiliation into Humility.* Lanham, MD: Lexington Books, 2014.

____. "The Policing of the Black American Male: Transforming Humiliation into Humility in Pursuit of Truth and Reconciliation." In I. Michelle Scott, *Crimes Against Humanity in the Land of the Free: Can a Truth and Reconciliation Process Heal Racial Conflict in America?* Santa Barbara, CA: ABC-CLIO Publishing, 2014.

____. "Do I want be a 30 Percenter or 70 Percenter?: Black Cultural Privilege." *Race, Education, and Reintegrating Formerly Incarcerated Citizens: Counter Stories and Counter Spaces.* Edited by Joni Schwartz and John Chaney. Lanham, MD: Lexington Books, 2017.

___. "Unfriending the Policing Culture: The Reawakened Black Consciousness." In *Policing Black and Brown Bodies: Policing in the Age of Black Lives Matter.* Edited by Sandra E. Weissinger and Dwayne Mack. Lanham, MD: Lexington Books, 2017.

___. "Transforming the Systemic Humiliation of Crime and Justice: Reawakening Black Consciousness." In Daniel Rothbart (Ed.). *Power, Humiliation, and Suffering in America.* New York, NY: Palgrave Macmillan, 2017.

Karenga, Maulana. *Introduction to Black Studies.* Los Angeles, CA: University of Sankore Press, 2010.

"The National Institute for Justice," *Policing for Profit.* Accessed September 16, 2016. http://ij.org/report/policing-for-profit/executive-summary/

"The Sentencing Project." *Black Lives Matter: Eliminating Racial Inequity in the Criminal Justice System.* Accessed September 16, 2016. http://sentencingproject.org/wp-content/uploads/2015/11/Black-Lives-Matter.pdf

"The United States Department of Justice." *Investigation of the Ferguson Police Department.* Accessed September 16, 2016. https://www.justice.gov/sites/default/files/opa/press-eleases/attachments/2015/03/04/ferguson_police_department_report.pdf

Thompson, Salathiel and Connor Stevens. *The United States of America vs. The United States of America* [Lecture Notes] (2015) https://courseweb.pitt.edu/webapps/blackboard / content/listContentEditable.jsp?content_id=_20249473 1&course id=_320452_ 1&mode=reset

Thompson, Salathiel, Anthony Boyd and Chris Colon. *Just Mercy: A Transformative Criminal Justice Journey to Expose and Uproot White Supremacy* [Lecture Notes] (2016) https://courseweb.pitt.edu/webapps/blackboard/content/list-ContentEditable.jsp?content_ id=_21479986_1&course_id=_352616_1&mode=reset

Ture, Kwame. *Black Power: The Politics of Liberation.* New York, NY: Vintage Books, 1967.

Williams, Angel. *Being Black: Zen and the Art of Living with Fearlessness and Grace.* New York, NY: Penguin Compass Press, 2000.

Williams, Angel, Lama Rod Owens and Jasmine Syedullah. *Radical Dharma: Talking Race, Love, and Liberation.* Berkley, CA: North Atlantic Books, 2016.

Chapter Ten

Suspension Bridge Mental Health Networkfor Human Dignity*

Michelle Jones

> Unless we address those who are leaving prisons, we can't begin to repair the damage of mass incarceration and make our communities whole and healthy once again.[1]
>
> — Susan Burton

Introduction

In 2014, one in six incarcerated men and women had a mental illness.[2] Today, 1.2 million people across the country, nearly half of all people currently incarcerated have a mental illness.[3] Women in this population are increasingly vulnerable, with some researchers reporting that ninety percent of women in prison have a history of

---

*This article is dedicated to the women of the Indiana Women's Prison, rwho are suffering from the lack of decent mental and physical health care. In this article, I privilege my experiences as a formerly incarcerated woman who lived and worked within the Indiana Women's Prison for over twenty years.

trauma.[4][†] In my personal experience, factors like early childhood trauma, familial and community violence, and substance use disorders increase the number of people in prison, length of stay and the number of those who are mentally ill in prison.[5] As a recent *New York Times* article describes, "[a]s the country tries to shrink its aging prison population, the inmates being released after years locked away often have mental illnesses and addictions that can land them back in prison if untreated."[6]

What follows comes from my twenty years of living in prison in Indiana and from dealing with my own trauma. I watched women with severe mental health issues cycle in and out of prison during today's era of privatized and for-profit mental health services that too often intensify illnesses and increase trauma. Providing for-profit mental and physical health services to a marginalized and vulnerable population is illogical, primarily because this model is built on incentives to keep overhead costs low, while charging as much as possible for those services. The way health care contractors execute this model is by denying treatment and care, which creates perpetual patients whom contractors can use to demand price increases over time while looking like they are currently keeping overhead costs low. For those they do treat, contractors charge the state exorbitant amounts of money, which motivates facility administrators to deny care because the costs are too high. In the end, it is incarcerated individuals who suffer.

I, like many others, am trying to come up with viable solutions to this disheartening situation.[7] In the quest for human dignity, I offer one solution. In an ideal world, people with mental illnesses would not be sent to prison. In a better world, there would be a continuity

---

† Trauma – Individual trauma results from an event, series of events, or set of circumstances that is experienced by an individual as physically or emotionally harmful or life threatening and that has lasting adverse effects on the individual's functioning and mental, physical, social, emotional, and spiritual well-being. (*SAMHSA's Concept of Trauma and Guidance for a Trauma-Informed Approach. Substance Abuse and Mental Health Services Administration. U.S. Department of Health and Human Services, July 2014.*)

of quality services, all the way from arrest to incarceration to release. But the reality is this: privatized mental health care and "cost cutting" hinder continuity of care and wellness for many incarcerated men and women. When the call of "med line" rings loudly on every housing unit in the prison, and the multitudes line up to receive their often contraindicated doses of medicinal social control, you can't but see that a great injustice is occurring. This is not new. Medicating incarcerated people in order to subdue them has a long history.[8] Prisons are not sites for holistic healing. Actually, any restoration that an individual ekes out in those places is more of a testament to the individual and her fellow captives, rather than an indication of the quality care the individual received in the prison.

Consequently, I offer an approach that is not the ideal but comes from my personal observations over the years and from my deep hope for a better future. The *Suspension Bridge* approach that I propose here would be a net — as in "safety net" and a "network" — to help incarcerated women and men receive continuity of care and support that is critical to self-sufficiency and sustainability. Let's begin with a little contextualization of mental health care in Indiana that I personally witnessed.

Privatization of Mental Health in Indiana

I was incarcerated at the Indiana Women's Prison (IWP) from 1990–2017. Currently, if you are sent to IWP having committed a serious crime, you are basically on your own. But this wasn't always true. Due to budget cuts, the privatization of services (provided by for-profit corporations), the increasingly punitive attitudes towards prisoners in general, and female prisoners in particular, it is nearly impossible for people at IWP (and most other prisons) today to receive adequate physical/psychiatric health care. Gone are the mental health teams I knew when I was first incarcerated that helped women deal with the things they have done and/or the things that had happened to them. Today at my prison, there are only two psychologists, one of whom exclusively serves the Special Needs Unit (unit housing women diagnosed with mental health issues). For the rest of the population — perhaps 600 women — to be referred to the other available psychologist or social worker you must have a diagnosis, a mental health classification, and/or be on medication. Otherwise, you are out of luck, whether you desperately need individual or group therapy or not. Moreover, constant turnover of the privatized staff means there is no continuity of mental health care, even for those who get regular appointments as they are always starting over with the next practitioner.

Most women in prison have experienced childhood or adult abuse — even those who only sold or took drugs — and most of them have hurt others and/or themselves. Abuses upon the mind, body, and spirit leave deep wounds and cultivate distrust. Without continuity of mental health care via a stable program and staff, women do not break through the wall of distrust and deal honestly with their trauma. Processing that trauma is critical to becoming a new person with a new life. Today, more than ever, incarcerated women are having very different experiences than I did nearly twenty years ago. It is nearly impossible for incarcerated persons to receive adequate physical/psychiatric health care from a private contractor because there is an incentive to do less, thereby saving the corporation money on supplies, surgeries, medications, etc. Typically, health care — mental or physical — only degrades over time. This is why it is vastly counterproductive for this service to be privatized. Under these conditions, mental health care positions are treated as revolving doors. Within the prison community, in my opinion, health care providers are not invested in the prisoner's livability and sustainability, nor invested in the prisoner's efforts to piece together a supportive community.

To appreciate the magnitude of the climate inside most prisons, as well as the changes that privatization has wrought, consider a prisoner not so different from me, whom I shall call "Rebecca." Rebecca suffers from the effects of serious trauma and a substance use disorder.[9] Rebecca is easily agitated and angered, and is especially incited by slights of any kind. Her responses are always highly verbal, and she is known to "cuss out" officers and staff in a heartbeat. Rebecca can be sweet and generous, almost child-like, but is also extremely violent and suicidal.

Rebecca has received so many conduct reports that her conduct history reads like a criminal rap sheet on *Chicago PD*.[10] How do I know? I know because she and I were incarcerated together for several years. I've watched her cycle from solitary confinement to the behavioral modification unit, which attempts to help women "stair-step" back into the open population.[11] Committing any infraction while on that unit, no matter how small, can result in a conduct report, which results in more time on the unit *or a return to solitary*. Each new conduct report can lead to the loss of "good time," in effect lengthening one's sentence. Rebecca has cycled between solitary confinement and the behavior modification unit so many times I worry that she'll never get out of prison. Worse, over the time I've known her, I've watched her slowly begin to lose her mind. But because she isn't classified as a special needs offender and is high functioning intellectually, she can't get help. They expect her to somehow fix herself. Speaking from my firsthand observations, this seems very unlikely. What is Rebecca to do?

The mental health care team — comprised of a housing unit counselor for each unit (who had time to interact with residents), three to four psychologists, and two psychiatrists — is a thing of the past. Luckily, women at Rebecca's prison still have the good fortune to have plethora of awesome volunteers who come in weekly to provide much needed programming, much of it religious. There are also 12-step, educational, and recreational programs that are making space for women — women not located on the GRACE (Guided Response Action Creates Empowerment) unit — to help them eke out a degree of livability and sustainability.

These volunteers are filling the gap left by professional psychological therapy that had been available prior to budget cuts and privatization. Volunteers have become lay psychologists, helping some women navigate and marginally heal their lives through whatever religious or secular lens that particular group of volunteers advocate. There is also a contingent of incarcerated women who offer to help fellow women start to heal their lives using whatever lens helped them become mentally and emotionally stable, be it religious, self-help, or creative writing.

The sad irony is that women like Rebecca, who are in desperate need of help, are not permitted to attend these groups and not permitted to attend educational or vocational programming. And, help from a fellow resident on the behavioral modification unit may not be what the doctor ordered.[12] Actually, what the doctor orders may not be what is needed either. I observed that some women, especially gender non-conforming women on that unit are dispensed anti-depressants and anti-psychotic drugs often without psychotherapy and even when contraindicated. For women like Rebecca, paths to wholeness are blocked by inadequate mental health care that is increasingly privatized. Furthermore, these paths are blocked by the tendency of prison officials to address mental health care issues as behavioral issues requiring punitive responses.

After a brief stint in open population marred by yet another conduct report, I heard Rebecca taunt her adjudicators, "Come on and let's just get this over with. It doesn't matter, nobody cares, and nobody gives a damn." What scares me is how much of what she said is the truth.

Why does this matter? There are hundreds of thousands of mentally ill men and women suffering in prisons and jails.[13] What kind of woman is Rebecca becoming? What kind of mother or citizen will she be when she is finally released? How much does her lack of mental health literally ensure her re-incarceration in the future? These are questions that should be at the forefront when administrators decide what care they will or will not provide incarcerated humans, especially if "rehabilitation" is to remain a key tenet of corrections. Therefore, departments of correction across this country need to proactively assess the needs of women and men like Rebecca and provide additional services while they are incarcerated so that they can obtain mental and emotional stability. Then they should provide the essential services needed at the time of their release, so formerly incarerated individuals can eventually obtain a degree of livability and sustainability. If not, these people will likely return to prison, further fragmenting families and communities. The solution that follows is a clarion call for human dignity. The incarcerated and formerly incarcerated simply deserve better. Notice that I am not making a differentiation between the mentally ill who are incarcerated and everyone else in prison. While there are women like Rebecca in every prison, nearly all women inside prison were traumatized before incarceration, and they quickly discover that incarceration itself is its own trauma-inducing entity. Most people don't realize that the cost of inadequate mental health care inflicts a profound human cost that is often hidden behind tons of cinder block. What follows is but one solution. It represents a quest for human dignity for all traumatized incarcerated people everywhere. It is called the *Suspension Bridge Mental Health Network.*

What is Suspension Bridge?

My proposed Suspension Bridge Mental Health Network would be a not-for-profit intervention organization that uses a "trauma-informed approach"‡ to connect formerly incarcerated men and women to licensed professional psychologists and social workers in order to provide counseling and therapeutic mental health care to the newly released.[14] The Suspension Bridge would be a continuously updated website to be used by re-entry coordinators, case managers, and/or parole-probation officers as a resource to help them create and oversee exit plans for released men and women in departments of correction across the United States. All data on individuals and organizations providing mental health services would be centrally located in one place. The Suspension Bridge would connect existing mental health care providers directly to those in critical need.

---

‡ Trauma-Informed Approach — A program, organization, or system that is trauma-informed realizes the widespread impact of trauma and understands potential paths for recovery; recognizes the signs and symptoms of trauma in clients, families, staff, and other involved with the system; and responds by fully integrating knowledge about trauma into policies, procedures, and practices, and seeks to actively resist re-traumatization. (Ibid.)

Why the Term "Suspension Bridge?"

A suspension bridge is not as rigid as standard bridges. They are suspended by extremely strong support cables above the bridge deck. Most importantly, a suspension bridge "can better withstand outside forces, such as earthquakes." [15] This network is named for an engineering marvel because the network mirrors it in many ways. First, the network is designed with several strong supports that start while the person is incarcerated and continues throughout the release and re-entry process. It is designed to assist the formerly incarcerated in navigating and weathering the challenges of everyday life upon release. Finally, the network is strong because, as you will see, it builds support from within its ranks, which means it is sustainable over time, just like a suspension bridge.

Issues in Mental Health Care

Men and women in prison are often misdiagnosed and prescribed medications as a means of controlling behavior rather than as a form of treatment, and with no individualized counseling or other therapies. Growing prison populations of diagnosed and non-diagnosed trauma sufferers, men and women, are receiving subpar/reduced mental health care and treatment because of budget cuts and privatization. Those receiving treatment represent less than half of all trauma sufferers in prison, leaving a large neglected population of trauma sufferers currently incarcerated without treatment. These people are then returning to communities without sustainable treatment plans, counseling, or medication if needed, which increases the potential for re-incarceration.

Most re-entry coordinators and case managers are not trained in the trauma-informed approach and do not have a cohesive or efficient way to connect people exiting the system to mental health counseling and therapy. Therefore, the diagnosed and medicated are often relegated to group counseling (if they receive counseling at all) where the taint of criminality and mental illness prevent healing and wellness. In Indiana, only incarcerated men and women with

DOC mental health code classifications receive a scheduled doctor's
appointment upon release for mental health care follow up. This leaves
thousands of men and women (non-diagnosed trauma sufferers),
those who could benefit from counseling and therapy, without any
treatment or care.[16] Further, trauma survivors are more likely to
have difficulty in employment and family relations. Men and women
leaving prison often have no one in whom they can confide and trust
who will provide therapy and counseling to aid them in becoming
self-sufficient. Re-entry for the formerly incarcerated is already hard
enough due to the taint of criminality, limited access to resources,
distressed familial relationships, and limited housing and employment opportunities.

Goals of Suspension Bridge

- To create a mental health network for the formerly incarcerated,
  in order to reduce recidivism and promote sustainability for
  newly-released men and women. Each year 700,000 people are
  released from prisons across the country and nearly half of them
  have mental health problems. Suspension Bridge would potentially connect 350,000 people to needed mental health care.[17]

- To provide diagnosed and undiagnosed formerly incarcerated
  men and women with counseling and therapy. This service is
  especially for those undiagnosed trauma sufferers who did not
  receive any counseling, treatment, or medication while incarcerated due to factors such as poor assessment, reduced mental
  health care services, or failure to promote trauma recovery for
  those persons without a DOC mental health code classification.

- To ensure that diagnosed and undiagnosed men and women
  have completed necessary health care paperwork before leaving
  prison.

- To provide re-entry coordinators and/or case managers with
  a ready resource to help locate and connect individual mental

health professionals with re-entering women and men.

- To create a mental health care network that would be comprised of private psychologists, licensed social workers, and advanced practicum students in social work and psychology programs in local universities throughout the state

- To connect that network with newly-released persons needing therapeutic and psychiatric one-on-one counseling and other mental health services.

- To provide a professional, safe environment where the formerly incarcerated can work through past trauma and current challenges, thus greatly improving their chances for self-sufficiency and sustainability.

- To retrain re-entry coordinators, case managers, and/or probation-parole officers in the trauma-informed approach to help them develop a real sensitivity to all survivors of trauma, not just those identified by the DOC as needing mental health care or those needing medication.

- To develop a trauma-informed screening and assessment procedure that would identify more men and women who could benefit from counseling and therapy services.

- To work to empower clients and encourage consistent participation in the mental health care to which Suspension Bridge has connected them.

Mental Health Care Providers

The large number of trauma sufferers (diagnosed and undiagnosed) needing care will require the help of people within the mental health profession. There are three primary sources of mental health care providers. The first is the *Professional Track*, which includes licensed social workers and psychologists. Just as law firms allocate a certain number of pro bono hours allotted in service of clients unable to pay, which becomes a charitable/philanthropic component of their work, Suspension Bridge would mobilize professional social workers and psychologists by encouraging them to offer fee-free hours providing mental health care to newly-released men and women within ten miles of their geographic location. The licensing bodies of these professions could offer incentives to providers donate their mental health care services to the formerly incarcerated.

The second track is the *Advanced Student track*, which would involve engaging area colleges and universities with social work and psychology programs. Advanced practicum students in local universities throughout the state would be encouraged to provide formerly incarcerated men and women with counseling and general mental health care. Where possible, students would receive credit for their assistance toward any practicum or clinical requirements

The third track would be engaging other *Licensed Professionals* within local county health departments to help individuals re-entering their communities after incarceration. Where applicable, this track would also help connect clients with substance use treatment resources in their communities.

How Would It Start?

The Suspension Bridge would contact all the professionals listed above in order to create a database for the website that could be searched by location. We would work with each state's Department of Corrections to establish a common taxonomy of mental health care. Our staff would advocate trauma-informed training for departments of correction, universities, and mental healthcare providers. In addition, it would train re-entry coordinators and case managers in the trauma-informed approach and train them to respond to gender-based needs of our clients. Once the network was in place, Suspension Bridge would coordinate and rollout the website, presenting it to Departments of Corrections by hosting informational and training meetings for re-entry coordinators, case managers, and/

or probation/parole officers. Suspension Bridge would become the central site through which professional and advanced post-graduate students would be able to receive basic information on individuals needing counseling.

How Would It Work?

Simple. When preparing exit plans for former prisoners, re-entry coordinators, case managers, and/or probation-parole officers would log onto the site, enter the city and county into the search field, and find a list of participating professional counselors, therapists, and advanced students. The site would describe these professionals' areas of specialization and the number of clients each professional is able to receive. Coordinators, case managers, and/or probation-parole officers would then complete an information page about each new client on an intake form and submit it to Suspension Bridge. Suspension Bridge would coordinate with the specific mental health care provider, schedule the appointment, and send a confirmation back to the re-entry coordinator, case managers, and/or probation-parole officers. In support of this process, one study concluded that direct referral and assessment resulted in the formerly incarcerated actively seeking treatment, which reduced recidivism rates.[18]

While Suspension Bridge is an electronic website, there would be staff members available to answer client questions and to log and manage any client complaints. Suspension Bridge would provide its own staff with training in trauma and trauma-informed approach, especially focused on skills for communicating with clients released from prison. It would also encourage feedback from clients, licensed professionals, advanced post-graduate students, and partner agencies.

Medications

People leaving prison, at least in Indiana, are usually signed up for Medicaid prior to release. Typically, medicated persons leaving prison are given a standard appointment and a few days' dosage of medication. Suspension Bridge mental health care providers would be able to give accurate information about their clients and would be able to help correct any misdiagnoses and prescriptions.

Time Frame

Suspension Bridge would suggest a cap of two years on one-on-one counseling, leaving the option for persons in the Professional Track and Advanced Student Track to continue at their own discretion.

Sustainability

Though Suspension Bridge emphasizes one-on-one counseling, it would work with local county health departments to create a formerly-incarcerated, peer-facilitated group counseling component for those people interested in the group format. The goal is to cultivate peer-facilitated group counseling, wherein those who have success-fully completed the program support newcomers as they begin their journey toward mental health. The group counseling would remain connected to the network for crises and in-group facilitation.

Funding Mental Health Care

According to the U.S. Department of Health and Human Services, Substance Abuse and Mental Health Services Administration, provisions for these types of services were in place via the Affordable Care Act. These funds could cover the costs of providing mental health care to the formerly incarcerated in states that adopted it.[19] [20] However, since the Trump administration took over the White House, efforts to repeal the Affordable Care Act may result in thousands of formerly incarcerated people losing critical mental health support.[21]

In states that did not adopt the Affordable Care Act, Suspension Bridge would emphasize the pro bono spirit of the program, rein-forcing the idea that we are all in community with one another. Failing to care for the mental health needs of the formerly incarcerated is an enormous mistake. It will show up in the recidivism-related costs of a former prisoner's unfortunate next arrest, trial, and incarceration.[22] It will show up in the costs of caring for their children in state institutions, the disintegration of families, and the possible incarceration of their children a generation later. Currently, 5.7 million children — one in twelve — have, or have had, a parent incarcerated during their lives. The stress and trauma of an incarcerated parent manifests in behavioral issues, anxiety, depression, and possible incarceration.[23] It should be clear that the stakes are too high for society to fail to equip the newly released with the resources they need to be successful.

Human Dignity for the Incarcerated and Formerly Incarcerated and Their Families

We cannot and should not fail in our duty as human citizens to be a part of the solution. The consequences of doing nothing will continue to ripple throughout our collective consciousness and create a world that we don't want. *Those of us who are, or who have been, in prison are people.* We are deserving of decent mental and physical health care in and out of prison. If prisons must exist at all, we are deserving of a community that recognizes that the time spent in those tombs represents a debt to society that has been paid. Further punishment beyond the cell disrupts the entire purpose of prisons and makes the sufferings of millions meaningless.

We are human. Humans err. Sometimes badly. To legally, socially, and permanently exile humans and their children to a captive system, called the *carceral state*, says more about the degradation of our collective consciousness and interconnectedness than anything else.[24] The carceral state is a system encompassing state, federal, and financial entities that empower their agents to dictate punitive norms. The carceral state "naturalizes" the legal power to punish, as it "legalizes" the technical power to discipline."[25] In fact, our carceral system necessitates certain groups remain in a perpetual criminalized status because it has become the primary apparatus whereby surplus and disposable populations are surveilled, cordoned off, and judged.[26] Most importantly, it is a tool for social control because people in the carceral state are denied legal recourse to contest the laws that have trapped them and are "denied both the political legitimacy and moral credibility necessary to question them."[27] Therefore, the incarcerated and formerly incarcerated are left without critical resources for self-sufficiency and sustainability, such as equitable mental and physical healthcare.

Michelle Alexander, author of *The New Jim Crow: Mass Incarceration the Age of Colorblindness* said, "[a]s a society, our decision to heap shame and contempt upon those who struggle and fail in a system designed to keep them locked up and locked out says far more about ourselves than it does about them."[28] As a human family, we must do better. We must take care of our own.

Notes

1.   Burton, Susan. "Susan Burton Quotes." BrainyQuote.com. Xplore Inc, 2018. Accessed 23 May 2018. https://www.brainyquote.com/quotes/susan_burton_897828
2.   "Crisis in Correctional Care: Mental Illness." April 8, 2014.
3.   Cassibry, Kathryn. "Access to Mental Health Care and Incarceration." *Mental Health America.* 14 Nov. 2017. www.mentalhealthamerica.net/issues/access-mental-health-care-and-incarceration.
4.   Benedict, Alyssa. "Using Trauma-Informed Practices to Enhance Safety and Security in Women's Correctional Facilities." National Resource Center on Justice Involved Women.
5.   Kim, KiDeuk, Miriam Becker-Cohen and Maria Serakos. "The Processing and Treatment of Mentally Ill Persons in the Criminal Justice System." The Urban Institute. March 2015: v, 1-3; 8-9.
6.   Brown, Patricia Leigh. "They're Out of Prison. Can They Stay Out of the Hospital?" *The New York Times.* 29 May, 2018. Accessed 31 May 2018. https://www.nytimes.com/2018/05/29/health/ex-prisoners-health-california.html
7.   Collins, Sam. P.K. "How to Break the Cycle of Imprisonment for Mentally Ill Americans." Online. 5 February 2015. Accessed 21 May 2018. https://thinkprogress.org/how-to-break-the-cycle-of-imprisonment-for-mentally-ill-americans-9489d34d4978/; Ono, Nadine. "Report: New Thinking Needed to Break Cycle of Incarceration of Mentally Ill Populations." CA Fwd. 9 March 2016. Accessed 21 May 2018. http://cafwd.org/reporting/entry/report-new-thinking-needed-to-break-cycle-of-incarceration-of-mentally-ill.
8.   Kauffman, Kelsey. *Prison Guards and Their World.* Cambridge: Harvard University Press, 1988: 60.

9. "The Burden of Mental Illness Behind Bars." Vera Institute of Justice. Accessed 24 May 2018. https://www.vera.org/...mental-health.../the-burden-of-mental-illness-behind-bars

10. "Today, nearly 68 percent of people in jail overall and more than 50 percent of those in state prisons have a diagnosable substance use disorder, compared to nine percent of the general population. Moreover, most people who have a serious mental illness also have a co-occurring substance-use diagnosis. For instance, in jails an estimated 72 percent of people with a serious mental illness also have a substance use disorder."

11. A class A, B or C conduct can send a person to solitary confinement. Five class C conduct reports result in a Habitual Offender conduct report and will automatically send the person to lock for up to 90 days with a loss of 90 days of earned credit time, a drop-in credit class and 30 days of restricted activities.

12. The (Guided Responsible Action Creates Empowerment) GRACE unit is a behavioral modification unit that is supposed to stair step a person back into open population via a phase system.

13. The GRACE unit is completely segregated from the rest of the "open" population. Women on this unit are forbidden to talk to or otherwise communicate with any person outside that unit. They are locked inside in their cells 18-20 hours a day. Even though the cells are for two people, they exist in a semi-solitary confinement state that continue indefinitely. Therefore, the stress and strain that this unit can bring to bear upon an individual can be such that all of the people are suffering and may not possess coping skills.

14. Pope, Leah G., Kim Hopper, Chelsea Davis, and David Cloud. "First Episode Incarceration." Vera Institute of Justice. January 2016. Accessed 24 May 2018. https://storage.googleapis.com/vera-web-assets/downloads/Publications/first-episode-incarceration-creating-a-recovery-informed-framework-for-integrated-mental-health-and-criminal-justice-responses/legacy_downloads/first-episode-incarceration-integrated-mental-health-criminal-justice-responses.pdf

15. Benedict, 4-5.

16. Snilsberg, Thor. "Feel the Forces of a Suspension Bridge." *Scientific American –* Online. October 13, 2011. Accessed 21 May 2018. https://www.scientificamerican.com/article/bring-science-home-suspension-bridge/

17. Kim, KiDeuk, et al., 10.

18. Bryon, Robert. "Criminals Need Mental Health Care" *Scientific American –* Online. 1 March 2014: 2-3.

19. Kim, KiDeuk, et al., 33.

20. Substance Abuse and Mental Health Services Administration. "Establishing and Maintaining Medicaid Eligibility upon Release from Public Institutions." HHS Publication No. (SMA) 10-4545. Rockville, MD: Center for Mental Health Services. Substance Abuse and Mental Health Services Administration, 2010: 3-6; 63-65.

21. Phillips, Susan D. "The Affordable Care Act: Implications for Public Safety and Corrections Populations." *The Sentencing Project.* September 2012: 3-4.

22. Brown, *The New York Times*. "The expansion of Medicaid in 32 states under the Affordable Care Act has been what many in the field consider a criminal justice milestone, making low income men and women who are single and childless potentially eligible for free health care for the first time."
23. Kim, KiDeuk, et al., 11.
24. Gotsch, Kara. "Families and Mass Incarceration." 24 April 2018. *The Sentencing Project*. Accessed 23 May 2018. http://www.sentencingproject.org/publications/6148/
25. Cacho, Lisa Marie. *Social Death: Racialized Rightlessness and the Criminalization of the Unprotected*. NJ: Princeton University Press, 2012: 8.
26. Foucault, Michel. *Discipline and Punishment: The Birth of the Prison*. First Vintage Book, 1979: 303.
27. Cacho, 6, 64.
28. Alexander, Michelle. *The New Jim Crow: Mass Incarceration in the Age of Colorblindness*. Revised Edition. NY: The New Press, 2011: 176.

Chapter Eleven

Human Dignity and Human Rights Terms in Transition

Zaynab El Bernoussi

The terms *human dignity* and *human rights,* having circulated in Europe for some time, remain quite new in many other parts of the world, making their entry into the cultures and countries of our planet in different ways. In some, both terms have arrived together, in others, one has become known and then the other, while elsewhere one is seized on as salient and the other means little. In addition, whether the terms are seen as linked, and which precedes or serves as the foundation for the other, differs from place to place. There is no universal consensus about the meaning of these terms across all cultures. What we are witness to is the negotiation of the ways these terms may be relevant and meaningful at this moment in historical time, in very particular places, a stage that necessarily precedes wider agreement on what the words shall mean in practice. This is to be expected, given that what is really being negotiated in each case is the nature of social structure, social change, and cultural life, which is particular to each culture. This chapter provides a review of what people in various places are making of these words in relation to their culture at this time.

Background

In more ancient philosophical concerns for dignity in the European world, the works of Cicero and Giovanni Pico della Mirandola (who was cited in my interviews with Egyptian protesters regarding their demand for dignity for his work on Islam) viewed dignity as universal to all human beings, holding all human beings to be equal. Philosopher Jean-Jacques Rousseau did not talk directly about dignity, but he talked about an *amour-propre* (meaning "self-love") and an *amour de soi* (meaning "love of self"), two different concepts not to be confused with the meaning of ego which has a negative connotation. For Rousseau, the *amour de soi* can be dangerous as it could inflate the ego; on the other hand, the *amour-propre* that he associated with *dignité* ("dignity") was positive and desirable because individuals needed to love themselves in order to thrive in their societies. Rousseau's practical definition of dignity stressed that individuals conscious of their worth can be more productive than those who are not.

Moving from these early reflections on the individual's worth in relation with a prosperous society, more recent attempts to view human dignity as part of a human rights framework reinforces the interdependent relation between individuals and the state. It is in the interest of states to recognize the worth of individuals so that they are empowered actors in the development of these states. However, with the prevalence of neoliberal economic development models in which income inequality is often inherent to profit maximization, the state is faced with a dilemma: continue its recognition of the centrality of human rights and jeopardize the optimal expansion of a capitalist economic model, or sacrifice capitalist development to stay faithful to its need to empower all its citizens equally. The ongoing, overriding concern with economy seems to jeopardize respect for human rights and human dignity, yet the protection of human rights is vital to the well-functioning of democracies despite any economic costs. It should be noted that this is a utilitarian approach to human rights and conflicts with the view that both are intrinsic and unconditional in character. Within what we now call Western Civilization, this seems to be the state of the two terms at present. What about in the rest of the world?

A Postcolonial Overview

The independence process in colonized territories of the 20th century involved a claim for the full rights of natives. As globalist Diana Brydon puts it, the history of postcolonialism is first the history of human rights.[1] While there may be disagreements with this broad statement, it is important to recognize the centrality of demands for human rights in formerly colonized societies since the process of human discrimination was deepened by foreign occupation and became two-dimensional (from within and from outside). Given the violence-ridden aftermath of independence in postcolonial societies, many scholars in postcolonial studies have expressed an overall concern that there has been a failure of the human rights discourse in these societies. On the one hand, these failures are sometimes credited to historical silencing reflecting a subordination of the human rights struggles in societies of the Global South to other agendas. As a result, some scholars suggest getting these historical accounts not only from history textbooks but also from different locals' narratives. On the other hand, an alternative worth exploring is whether the discourse of human rights in postcolonial societies has reactively benefitted from this silencing by becoming a stronger demand for human rights (El Bernoussi, 2015). This could also serve a pragmatic use of the concept of human dignity to empower political agency (Kateb, 2011).

Historian Michel-Rolph Trouillot sheds light on the important process of subverting the past as a mechanism of epistemic violence against a population: dispensing of people's histories as an act of violence. In his book *Silencing the Past* (1995), Trouillot presented the case of the Haitian Revolution as a "non-event," meaning a historical moment that did not get appraisal as a historical event. However, the actual events that shook Saint-Domingue (renamed Haiti) from 1791 to 1804 were very symbolic of a claim of human rights as slaves successfully led a revolution against their "masters." The Haitians could be said to have spoken a claim to human rights in the language of action. This giant event in the history of humanity was dismissed from major historical accounts (for instance in school curricula). One can recognize there was an interest in sabotaging such a giant event when the slave trade was still profitable to capitalist expansion.

The question of legality of equal rights for all individuals was clearly at stake, not only in Haiti, but also in the process of modern capitalist expansion in general, and here Joseph Slaughter proposed that "the gap between what everyone knows and what everyone should know poses human rights as a question of both literacy and legislation, as much matters of literature as of law."[2]

Slaughter was among those, in postcolonial studies, who led the trend to explore narratives in dealing with the question of human rights in societies of the Global South (2009). Yet, it is important in such critiques to be aware of the pitfalls of narratives of victimization that oppose the "them" to the "us." This binary is even more problematic in the contemporary context of hybridization in globalization, in which one sees increasing feelings of transnationalism and supranationalism that unify people and causes beyond borders (Scholte, 2005). In his call for a more humane global society, Jan Scholte proposes to "subordinate all transplanetary governance to human rights standards" and calls for developing "a legally binding and enforced transplanetary bill of rights" (2005, p. 396). Here we see the wide span in the embrace of "human rights" as a concept, from narrative silence regarding the revolution in Haiti to claims of human rights as transplanetary.

In the absence of such ambitious plans as proposed by Scholte, other critical scholars preferred to go back to history to evaluate the failures of the human rights discourse in societies of the Global South instead of projecting a plan for the future. One issue revealed is a tendency of human rights movements in postcolonial societies to target only local repression and dismiss connections with external hegemonic powers. By contrast, the case of Burma/Myanmar with the struggle of activist Aung San Suu Kyi for human rights and democracy is an alternative and to some extent a model for postcolonial human rights action because the parallel between the local and the global was made (Chowdhry and Nair, 2002). At the same time, critical theorist Sheila Nair who also looked at the Burmese model noted that, in the field's literature, there is "a neglect of the impact of economic globalization on the creation and maintenance of an effective human rights framework" (2002, p. 257).

Pheng Cheah's work filled the gaps created by the neglect in dealing with the impact of the neoliberal development model on postcolonial societies. In *Inhuman Conditions, Cosmopolitanism, and Human Rights,* Cheah shows that individuals are shaped by their specific context, which challenges the ambition of the new cosmopolitanism, as proposed by Scholte: operating communally under intergovernmental institutions. Cheah adds that global capitalism is the context for most people; capitalist globalization constitutes a context for human rights in which the inhuman, defined as the imposition of limits on an individual's being what she or he aspires to be, battles the human for the sake of money and power (2006). This critique stresses the centrality of economic inequalities inherent to the capitalist model that not only concern actors within a market but also communities and states within an integrated world economy. The need for a dignity approach in the management of the economy becomes even more vital to the planet (Lindner, 2012).

In *Fictions of Dignity* (2012), critical theorist Elizabeth Anker goes back to the need for looking at narratives to understand the question of human rights in societies of the Global South. Anker enumerates several novels that represent such narratives and among them there is *Woman at Point Zero* (1975) by Egyptian feminist Nawal El Saadawi. Anker explains that a mismatch between the fiction of human dignity and bodily restrictions enforced by modern legal structures create an anxiety surrounding human rights discourse in the Global South, as seen with the case of feminism in Egypt in El Saadawi's novel for instance (2012).

Anthropologist Partha Chatterjee's message concerning rights in postcolonial societies is, by contrast, somewhat hopeful because he suggests that economic adversity might present opportunities for democratization. While postcolonialist Gayatri Spivak famously asked in her notorious essay (1988), "[Can] the subaltern speak?" Chatterjee's work on political society (2011) seems to retort that, in some way, the subaltern has found subversive ways to create democratic processes for a society of rights and so become empowered. This postcolonial society, as defined by Chatterjee, is opposed to a civil society and operates outside a political system to influence the regime. This political society is like a fringe society who does not use civism but rather bargains for its survival outside of the legal space of state actions (for instance, by being bribed by the state or enjoying state tolerance even in illegality, as with squatting). One might wonder if insistence and bargain are sufficient for the subaltern to "speak," but it could be, at least, a step forward in order for her to be heard. Nonetheless, one should remember that postcolonial societies inherited a system of "free use of violence" in which this bargaining can be cut short due to oppressive postcolonial regimes that brutalize individuals' rights and liberties (Bayart, 1993; Crowder, 1984 [1976]; Mamdani, 1996).

In addition, Chatterjee's suggestion concerning the divide between two societies in postcolonial India finds similarities with postcolonial Egypt, where struggles and attempts for democratic negotiations were notoriously repressed. Indeed, comparative political scientists Alfred Stepan and Graeme Robertson investigated the dearth of democracy in many Arab societies and argued that it was not caused by the dominance of Islam in these societies, since other Muslim societies in Southeast Asia performed better in democracy indicators (Stepan and Robertson, 2003). It was, therefore, the peculiarity of the Arab context and the problem with the local identity that seemed better leads in the Stepan and Robertson's study on democratic problems in the region.

Postcolonial literature has repeatedly pointed out the issues of human rights discourses in the Global South, but if we take into account the dynamic nature of societies molding themselves to changing needs, it seems that alternative spaces can present ways for systems of rights to operate in these societies. In the case of Egypt, human rights are an ongoing concern since the birth of the new postcolonial state. The regional context is also similar in this concern and is challenged by several forces in the case of Egypt as an Arab state; this could in turn challenge the creation of a stable identitarian context for human rights.

In short, once the focus shifts from Western Civilization proper to the postcolonial world, we find the concept *human rights* being given meaning in relation to multiple frameworks, frequently at the same time: the postcolonial situation, specific countries and local cultures, and the context of globalizing capitalism. The meanings and place of the term in society, and the tensions and conflicts surrounding it, differ in each context, as do the practices (for example, silencing, "speaking" through action, bargaining outside of legal space, declarations of transplanatery value status).

In all of this we have been discussing the term *human rights,* but a second term has come into the discourse as well, that of *human dignity* and with it the question of the relationship between the two concepts.

Dignity as a Human Right in Egypt

In the case of human rights in Egypt, Saad Eddin Ibrahim, a human rights activist and academic, has been vocal about democracy; his virulent criticism toward Mubarak's government cost him several legal trials. In 2003, he was acquitted after being condemned for "undermining the dignity of the state and tarnishing its reputation."[3] This is an interesting case of endowing a nonhuman entity, in this case the State, with a seemingly human characteristic, namely dignity. Ibrahim stressed the need to respect human rights in Egypt; for him, protection of human rights is vital for a genuine democratic establishment. Ibrahim has also called the U.S. Congress to condition its military aid to Egypt on improvements in the country's human rights records. Moreover, he has called for the conditioning of U.S. aid on freeing civilian political prisoners who were still facing trial in military courts under martial law during Mubarak's regime.

It is important to note that human rights activism in Egypt aims to attain legislative reform to establish institutions and laws for the protection of human rights and to fight corrupted structures and mechanisms that facilitate the mistreatment of citizens by the state. For instance, a major concern in this reformatory movement aims to separate the dignity of the state and the dignity of the individual. Indeed, the 1971 Egyptian Constitution, which was amended in 2007 (in the most recent case before the uprisings), declared: "Man's dignity is a natural reflection of the nation's dignity, now that the individual is the cornerstone in the edifice of the homeland, the land that derives its strength and prestige from the value of man and his education" (Proclamation, Section Four). This discussion could be seen as problematic because relating national dignity to individual dignity undermines the concept of human dignity as self-worth and as an independent notion from any form of national consideration. Dignity also may become the state's "property," in which case an individual cannot embody her or his own dignity.

An important episode of human rights violations and the problematization of human dignity in contemporary Egypt can be seen in the case of the arrest of the fifty-two men caught in a floating gay nightclub called the Queen Boat on May 11, 2001, in Cairo. In this arrest, fifty men were charged with "habitual debauchery" and "obscene behavior," under Article 9c of the Law Number 10 of 1961 on the Combat of Prostitution.[4] The other two men were charged with "contempt of religion," under Article 98f of the Penal Code. All of the men pleaded innocent.[5]

The Queen Boat trial, also known as Cairo 52, presented a case in which the lack of clear condemnation for the activities in the gay nightclub led to the use of proxy condemnations that punish debauchery and obscenity and led to infringements of human rights. At the time, many critics of the government denounced the media's political use of this trial to justify the state's arbitrariness in using proxy condemnations, instead of making efforts to address the case in a more just manner.

Cairo 52 is a case of gay rights violation as accounted for by several international organizations for human rights; however, in countries where gay rights are not recognized, the case was perceived as a defensive circumstance for the state. In a completely different case, but also one of proxy condemnations, to protect what is seemingly morally correct, could be an infringement of the rights of the individual. This case happened in France in the Morsang-sur-Orge's dwarf-tossing issue in 1995, in which the local mayor, in the name of the dwarves' *dignity*, prohibited the tossing contest. After appealing in different levels of administrative courts, the concerned plaintiff reached the French Council of State that acts both as a legal adviser to the executive branch and as the supreme court for administrative justice. Despite strong controversy about the judge's dismissal of the plaintiff's calls for the freedom of action and the freedom of expression, the mayor won the case and succeeded in prohibiting the contest in the name of human dignity (Rosen, 2012). This shows the ability of the state to actually bestow and enforce dignity even if it acts against the protection of freedom of action.

In this French case, or in Cairo 52, it seems that protecting human morals by enforcing rights and laws may lead to overwhelming state intervention in an individual's social life, leading to a decreased agency. Therefore, we can imagine that the enforcement of such legislation may even create feelings of assault on one's dignity, in the name of a communitarian sense of dignity that is safeguarded by the state.

Clearly, meanings assigned to human dignity not only differ at times, but are also, at times, in conflict with one another, as witness the tension between individual dignity and the perceived dignity of the community or state. At other times they are linked, as when human dignity is perceived not only as desirable but as itself a human right.

Expressions of Dignity as a Human Right in 2011

In the early events of the Arab Spring, acts of self-immolation were poignant symbols of self-inflicted harm to denounce state humiliation. In the case of Egypt, one of the early revolutionary slogans was "Bread...freedom...human dignity." It is interesting here to stop at the choice of the wording "human dignity" ("*karama insaniyya*") instead of simply "dignity." One possibility, and this is only speculation, is to ask whether the use of "human" is related to the discourse of "human development" and "human rights." The reference to "human" can also serve the attempt to establish an individual dignity distinct from a national dignity. Such relationships would make sense to a certain extent of the incongruous choice of saying *"karma insaniyya"* over simply *"karama"* (i.e., "dignity"). At the same time, referring to human rights in the slogan served the need to denounce state humiliation and torture, which were targeted by protesters in the Arab Spring uprisings.

A major figure of these uprisings in Egypt was Wael Ghonim, a Google employee who created a Facebook page called "We Are All Khaled Saeed" to denounce the brutal torture and killing of the young cyber activist, Khaled Saeed, by Egyptian police on June 6, 2010, due to his release of sensitive information on corruption cases in Egypt. Saeed's killing had a more significant impact on larger segments of the Egyptian society because this time the young cyber activist was more of a normal citizen (rather than a marginal). Sympathy with the case of Saeed and of Ghonim was, therefore, greater. Ghonim was imprisoned, but his popularity led to an important outcry against his arrest, which consequently led to his freeing. After being freed from jail, Ghonim's first words included the need to restore the "dignity" of all Egyptians.[6]

On Dignity as a Human Right

Is dignity one among several human rights, and so protected by a commitment to the framework of human rights? Or is the framework of human rights anchored in human dignity, with human rights protected by a commitment to a sense of intrinsic human dignity? There is no single answer today, the relationship between the two being still in contention. The answer depends very much on who is answering it, and where.

After World War II, the 1948 United Nations Universal Declaration of Human Rights, which Egypt ratified, had been an instrument to monitor peace in societies and used human dignity as a foundation for those rights (Ishay, 2008; Lawler, 2009). Indeed, dignity is part of the larger institutionalization of human rights, an important gain in the history of humanity that provided a framework for more equality between different ethnic factions. However, is dignity itself a clearly protected right? The answer varies among countries: law may not always protect dignity. Freedom of speech, freedom of religion, freedom of assembly and freedom to petition for redress of grievances, are, on the other hand, cases of rights for which an individual can expect protection from governmental intrusion in a more forthright manner. By contrast, some perceive *dignity* as something that an individual earns by hard work and accomplishment, assuming of course the government does not get in the way. In that view, protecting such dignity can be achieved if the right to pursue dignity is protected, but this is not the same as an inherent right to dignity that applies to all, earned or not. Many post-independence regimes in the Middle East and North Africa do not even prioritize human rights protection and make use of discourses of dignity without treating people with dignity.[7] Indeed, in such regimes, there is a dichotomy between a political discourse that promises protection of dignity while accounts of human rights violations are not addressed.[8] It seems that these political discourses of dignity focus more on urgent needs of recognition or just plain demagoguery to shift blame for governance issues onto external enemies (perhaps foreign powers, perhaps perceived internal threats, as with the government opposition), rather than embodying genuinely ethical behavior by treating people with dignity.

The concept of human dignity is, in theory, ingrained in philosophies of human rights. However, the abstract nature of human rights philosophies seems to omit any convincing understanding of human dignity; most detractors of the concept of dignity view it as nothing but a catch phrase. In contrast, Charles Beitz (2013) examined this lack of "texture" in the human dignity discourse and proposed to formalize human dignity within the concrete structure of bioethics. Beitz noted that the current *human rights* discourse bases all of human rights (civil, economic, social, and political) on the principle of recognizing human dignity.[9] This framework is particularly present in the case of the German Constitution in which dignity is the source of all rights. To Beitz such statements undermine a clear and independent understanding of human dignity. What then is dignity? He proposes to frame the answer in a context of rights derived from bioethical considerations. This way, human dignity would be determined by specific cultural conditions that concern the bioethical considerations of different religious and ethnic groups and also sexual minorities. Again the question: is human dignity a universal or not?

Complicating the matter further, the modern Universalist claim in human rights discourses has often been undermined by the reality of economic development led by a national or local elite in power, which is the case in societies such as Egypt. The theme of dignity as a human right is consequently problematic in the context of significant economic inequalities between states and within states. This could prompt us to look for something more "basic" than dignity conceived as a human right and more in line with dignity as an intrinsic need for survival and recognition. This intrinsic nature of dignity as a demand for recognition is also particularly useful to consider when negotiating conflict resolution among warring parties (Hicks, 201). As it stands today in many countries, it seems that dignity as a human right does serve primarily as a catch phrase used to join a global project of universalism rather than something to abide by. Nonetheless despite the apparent illusion of human rights protections in societies of the Global South, the models provided by success in the struggle for rights by globally marginalized groups (such as LGBT communities, for instance) encourage a strategic political use of both human rights and human dignity concepts as bargaining processes for empowerment.

However, this too is contentious. When the United States Supreme Court ruled in favor of same-sex marriage, the majority opinion celebrated the recognition of the dignity of all the people and particularly their dignity in their sexual orientation. Yet, in a minority opinion, Federal Justice Clarence Thomas argued that there is a misunderstanding, in the United States, of human dignity as a constitutional right when, in reality, there is not a single mention of dignity in the U.S. Constitution. Justice Thomas added that, even without a constitutional right to dignity, people should not feel that they are in a reduced mode of being. Justice Thomas stated: "Slaves did not lose their dignity (any more than they lost their humanity) because the government allowed them to be enslaved."[10] For Justice Thomas, the problem of claiming that human dignity is assaulted, or not granted, is a way of implying that the people who suffered injustices in human history did not have dignity. Justice Thomas continued:

> Those held in internment camps did not lose their dignity because the government confined them. And those denied governmental benefits certainly do not lose their dignity because the government denies them those benefits. The government cannot bestow dignity and it cannot take it away.[11]

Justice Thomas also argued that people seem to expect a state intervention by which human rights and human dignity are bestowed, a position he rejects. In his view, human dignity is inherent and independent of how a person is or isn't treated by the state. A great many people, however, view a government policy used to subjugate people as a way to humiliate those people, served as a way to make them feel that they have in fact lost their dignity. To give one example from the current refugee crisis: A Danish policy approving seizure of valuables from refugees is being viewed as an assault on their dignity.

In contrast to Justice Thomas's views, the state is often targeted by dignity demands, as seen with the protesters of Tahrir square in 2011 who called for a state that respects and protects the *karma insaniyya* (human dignity) of the Egyptian people (this was also one of the main slogans of the uprisings). From the uprisings' slogan of human dignity, it seems that the state is held responsible for human rights protection and protection of human dignity, and that it had failed in this task. In the context of state and individuals' contention over rights, Martha Nussbaum stressed that contention between agency and victimhood is a fertile terrain for the development of human rights discourses for marginalized groups (2003). The recognition of victimhood is particularly important as a recognition of otherness, which is often missing in Universalist human rights discourses that minimize or dismiss otherness.

In the case of Egypt, human rights seemed to be less central in the political discourse of Nasser, which was more concerned with national dignity (Hopwood, 1993). Sadat, on the other hand, used a discourse of political freedoms to first ally with the regime's opposition, the Muslim Brotherhood, against factions in the regime that resisted him (Waterbury, 2014). Sadat's propaganda, which used a language of freedom for political ends, was, however, inconsistent with his ongoing use of systems of torture of the opposition, in the style of the Eastern German state security commonly known as Stasi, inherited from Nasser's era and enhanced with the establishment of the Central Security Forces (CSF) (which were particularly targeted in the 2011 protests). After the assassination of Sadat, Mubarak came to power and played with opposing factions to consolidate his rule, but also continued with repressive methods (McDermott, 2012). Unlike Nasser's socialist context, both Sadat and Mubarak favored a context of economic liberalization but one in which the benefits were limited to a small elite. Again in these two liberal economic contexts before the Arab Spring, it was hard to picture a prosperous environment for the development of a society of rights or recognition of dignity in Egypt, both of which were demanded in the 2011 uprisings. Such difficulties were not uncommon around the planet

Summary

At this time, the understandings of human rights and human dignity remain in flux, varying widely depending on the country, the culture, the vantage point (global, universalist vs. local, particular). The terms may be used as catchphrases covering over abuses or as tactics in consolidating power. Joining with the global universalist project may serve the interests of power while subverting those of the marginalized, or may be used by the marginalized to develop empowerment at the expense of the state. Both terms embody deep and widespread aspirations for a better life, but their acceptance and application in practice are still very much embedded in the actual struggles over power, victimization, and wealth across the planet. Both concepts, however imperfectly committed to today, side with a desire for less humiliation, less exploitation, better life circumstances, and greater dignity for all human beings, the wish enshrined in the United Nations' Universal Declaration of Human Rights.

Notes

1. Diana Brydon's lecture on "Postcolonial and Global Approaches to Human Rights" delivered at the University of Manitoba on September 1, 2012.
2. Ibid.
3. American Sociological Association, announcement. "Egyptian Sociologist Ibrahim Is Acquitted", April 2003.
4. "Egypt: Egyptian Justice on Trial — The Case of the Cairo 52". *OutRight Action International.* October 15, 2001.
5. Ibid.
6. *The Crunch,* 2011. "Wael Ghonim's First Interview after Jail Release" by Alexia Tsotsis, February 7, 2011.
7. Freedom in the World 2014: The Annual Survey of Political Rights and Civil Liberties. Rowman & Littlefield, 2014.
8. Ibid.
9. The Helsinki Act of 1975, an act that marked the success of peace discussions during the Cold War, is an example in which it was agreed that the human dignity predetermined all human rights.
10. Raw Story, 2015. "Clarence Thomas holds some pretty horrifying views on human dignity," by Travis Gettys, June 26, 2015.
11. Ibid.

References

Anker, Elizabeth S. *Fictions of Dignity: Embodying Human Rights in World Literature.* Cornell University Press, 2012.

Beitz, Charles R. "Human Dignity in the Theory of Human Rights: Nothing But a Phrase?" *Philosophy and Public Affairs* 41.3: 259–290, 2013.

Chatterjee, Partha. *Lineages of Political Society: Studies in Postcolonial Democracy.* Columbia University Press, 2011.

Cheah, Pheng. *Inhuman Conditions: On Cosmopolitanism and Human Rights*. Harvard University Press, 2006.

Chowdhry, Geeta, and Nair, Sheila. *Introduction: Power in a Postcolonial World: Race, Gender and Class in International Relations*. London: Routledge, 2002.

Crowder, Michael. *The Cambridge History of Africa*. Volume 8. Cambridge University Press, 1984.

El Bernoussi, Zaynab. "The Postcolonial Politics of Dignity: From the 1956 Suez Nationalization to the 2011 Revolution in Egypt." *International Sociology* 30.4: 367–382, 2015.

El Saadawi, Nawal. *Woman at Point Zero*. Zed Books, 2007.

Hicks, Donna. *Dignity: The Essential Role It Plays in Resolving Conflict*. Yale University Press, 2011.

Hopwood, Derek. *Egypt, Politics and Society, 1945–1990*. Psychology Press, 1993.

Ibrahim, Saad Eddin. *New Arab Social Order: A Study of the Social Impact of Oil Wealth*. Westview Press, 1982.

Ishay, Micheline R. *The History of Human Rights: From Ancient Times to the Globalization Era*. University of California Press, 2008.

Kateb, George. *Human Dignity*. Harvard University Press, 2011.

Lawler, Peter. "The Human Dignity Conspiracy." The Intercollegiate Review, 2009.

Lindner, Evelin. *A Dignity Economy: Creating an Economy that Serves Human Dignity and Preserves our Planet*. Dignity Press, 2012.

Mamdani, Mahmood. *Citizen and Subject*. Cambridge: Cambridge University Press, 1996.

McDermott, Anthony. *Egypt from Nasser to Mubarak: A Flawed Revolution*. Vol. 3. Routledge, 2012.

Nussbaum, Martha C. *Upheavals of Thought: The Intelligence of Emotions*. Cambridge University Press, 2003.

Rosen, Michael. *Dignity: Its History and Meaning*. Harvard University Press, 2012.

Scholte, Jan Aart. *Globalization: A Critical Introduction*. Palgrave Macmillan, 2005.

Slaughter, Joseph. *Human rights, Inc.: The World Novel, Narrative Form, and International Law*. Fordham University Press, 2009.

Spivak, Gayatri Chakravorty. "Can the Subaltern Speak?" In *Colonial Discourse and Post-Colonial Theory: A Reader*, edited by Patrick Williams and Laura Chrisman. Originally published in 1988. Hertfordshire: Harvester and Wheatsheaf, 1994.

Stepan, Alfred C., and Graeme B. Robertson. "An 'Arab' More Than a 'Muslim' Democracy Gap." *Journal of Democracy* 14.3: 30–44, 2003.

Trouillot, Michel-Rolph. *Silencing the Past: Power and the Production of History.* Beacon Press, 1995.

Waterbury, John. *The Egypt of Nasser and Sadat: The Political Economy of Two Regimes.* Princeton University Press, 2014.

Chapter Twelve

On the Problem of Evil and Violations of Human Dignity: A Moral Approach to Transforming Humiliating and Degrading Treatment of Person

Kebadu Mekonnen Gebremariam

> Throughout history, it has been the inaction of those who could have acted; the indifference of those who should have known better; the silence of the voice of justice when it mattered most, that has made it possible for evil to triumph.
>
> — Haile Selassie I

Introduction: The Moral Urgency for Revisiting the Problem of Evil

The problem of evil has attracted sparse academic interest in recent philosophical discourse given the post-enlightenment secular framework within which moral concepts are generally conceptualized. History is replete with examples of the terrible acts of cruelty and evil that humanity is capable of perpetrating on one another. However, the intellectual discourse largely struggles to catch up with the harsh reality of life in which encountering acts of evil has hardly been a rare sight. There is a theoretical case to be made relating to the nature of evil and the critical challenge it poses on the basic moral fabric of society. Despite a body of work dedicated to the understanding of evil, we are far from establishing a compelling account of the nature of evil, to say nothing about an overarching systematic approach on how we can overcome or at least minimize acts of evil in the world.

A number of mutually intertwined reasons may account for the general neglect of the problem of evil in mainstream academic discourse. Whereas some of the most detailed analysis of good and evil can be found in intellectual traditions that are not strictly within the boundaries of the academic moral discourse, for the most part the problem of evil is principally considered as an existential question relating to the fundamental nature of reality, rather than as a question of principal concern to normative moral theory. One has to do with the obvious association of ideas of good and evil with religious or metaphysical conceptions of the absolute nature of reality. The notion of evil is thus conceived as a strange topic for academic pursuit, as the prevailing approach to moral philosophy tends to be more analytic than speculative while the study of evil presumably consists in the analysis of the essential nature of existence, of which religious belief and mythology attempt to give an explanatory account.

However, an overwhelming number of philosophers no longer consider a religious basis for morality as a compelling intellectual option. Immanuel Kant dismisses the idea of a moral law external to us as baseless. Similarly, Nietzsche saw in western societies a crisis in the authority of morality due to the erosion of the belief in God and with it the collapse of metaphysical polarities such as the idea of good and evil. He wrote of the death of God as a terrible tragedy brought by Christianity at the hands of its own, with catastrophic implications the depth of which we cannot fathom. Nietzsche went a step further than merely providing a historical analysis of how the Judeo-Christian moral value system, in the particular form and content in which it manifested, collapsed under its own weight. He insists that such value system only makes manifest the opposite of what it intends to bring forth: instead of guiding the struggle to overcome evil and malevolence, it serves to keep the weak and vulnerable in perpetual servitude.

His objection is that a religious basis for morality paints a very bleak portrait of the nature of moral values and the grip they have on us. If the only thing that keeps a person decent and morally virtuous is the expectation of divine reward or escape from divine retribution, the value of morality is then rendered derivative and hence its authority compromised. It is precisely in that alleged metaphysical basis of the nature of morality that nihilism is rooted.

Furthermore, Nietzsche critiqued what he saw as a morality of "resist no evil" (i.e., the meek shall inherit the earth through forgiveness of the cruel and the tyrannical) as a Trojan horse disguising weakness as moral virtue, a morality whose poisonous effect accounts for the value system's gradual loss of authority in society. Although many people share Nietzsche's critique of a religious basis for morality, some struggle to endorse his most devastating claim to the effect that the prevailing Western moral value system does not have the wherewithal to guide us in overcoming evil and malevolence. He attributed that to what he saw as its fatal connection with Judeo-Christian value systems. The solution to this, he opines, is a "revaluation of all values" based on the understanding of the nature of "man" in his totality ("against the separation of reason, sensuality, feeling, will")[1], and a new morality underpinned by such understanding.

This is not to promote a blanket endorsement on my part of all the extraordinary claims about the nature of morality made by Nietzsche across his vast literary work. For instance, I do not agree with the common belief shared amongst his most passionate followers that Nietzsche is harmless. For it was no sheer coincidence that some of his ideas inspired the Nazis, who appropriated very selected and distorted versions of his work to a devastating effect. Some of the dangerous and destructive elements of his theoretical framework notwithstanding, we ought to take seriously the fact that Nietzsche

---

1 Friedrich Nietzsche *Twilight of the Idols*, Part Nine, Section 49

described the weakest link in the foundation of Western moral value systems with extraordinary perception. Two points are worth noting. One is that he successfully debunked the notion that religious morality has the authority it claims to have, and secondly he challenged the received historical account of the Genealogy of Morals.

He believed that, if correctly harnessed, the destruction of the Judeo-Christian morality could be a fertilizer for cultivating something better. The extraordinary moral challenges humanity is facing today across the globe are not much different in substance from what we find in the historical records of the twentieth century. It is thus imperative that we take seriously the fact that our moral arsenal needs fundamental retooling. We can begin by recognizing that Nietzsche's challenge is still pertinent today: for it is far too common to find an odd mixture of nihilism and totalitarianism masquerading as religious, nationalist, or otherwise tribal Puritanism which sharing this common thread and are often the driving force for violent conflicts across the world.

Many people perceive in modern societies the decline in grip religious authority used to have as a testament to the collapse in the moral order of things, and consequently seek to fill the void left by the waning of religious authority either with Marxist inspired totalitarianism or with some revitalized notion of "the absolute." Recent history indicated that both attempts at replacing the religious basis of morality brought forth terrible consequences. Turning a few pages inside a history book, and encountering a few reminders of the Gulags, concentration camps, and all manner of mass atrocities we are capable of inflicting on one another, provides sufficient evidence for the boundless moral corruption of our recent history, the highlights of which is brilliantly chronicled in Jonathan Glover's seminal book, *Humanity: A Moral History of the Twentieth Century.*[2]

---

2 Jonathan Glover. *Humanity: A Moral History of the Twentieth Century* (New Haven: Yale University Press, 2000)
   Another equally dangerous intellectual tradition of late Twentieth century, whose only persuasion is owing to its fashionable association with recent pop culture, comes in the form of the post-modernist inspired idea of nihilistic amoralism. I leave a full exploration of the role of post/modernist amoralism in "making it possible for evil to triumph" for another occasion.

Evidently neither religious belief nor political ideology seem to insulate us from humanity's darkest drives and impulses, while in some cases a belief in the supernatural order or in some other form of essentialism seems to provide the necessary fuel for the monsters within us to emerge with vengeance. Religion-inspired atrocities, hatred and bigotry are commonplace today as epitomized by the rise of the so called ISIS or Daesh and other extremist groups (of diverse metaphysical creeds and ideologies). A religious, nationalist, or tribal zealot is often unhinged in his disgust towards the idea of the world that is not organized according to the strict dictums of his comprehensive metaphysical, religious, or ideological framework.

The question then is, what ought we to do about it? The beginning of solving any moral problem is fostering better understanding of its nature and root cause.[3] Certainly, the problem of evil presents a unique challenge that is of great moral magnitude. It must therefore be studied with fervent care, acute analytical pedantry coupled with a strong imaginative insight.

Clarifying the Distinction between Tragedy and Evil

The root cause of the difficulty in solving the problem of evil is partly due to the failure to conceptually distinguish between tragedy and evil. Many tragic events are considered evil simply due to the severity of their consequences to humanity; the more devastating to human life they are, the quicker we are to brand them as evil. But evil and malevolence have peculiar characteristics that not every tragic event has, although both intersect at times. Tragedy occurs as the result of the intrinsic vulnerability that characterizes our existence. Human vulnerability is tragic and that seems to be the price we pay for being. There can be no being without limitation, and such finitude

---

3   This is not to suggest that adequate understanding is an absolute prerequisite for solving every practical everyday problem at the personal level. I do not need to know the root cause of two people fighting to immediately intervene to stop the violence, especially if both are complete strangers less likely to cross each others' paths.

on which tragedy rests is simply an essential condition of existence. The tragedy of sickness, suffering and death, accidents, calamity and natural disasters are realities into which we are born. All of this recalls the First Noble Truth in the teachings of the Buddha that "life is suffering." Ancient Romans created a goddess of fortune out of a similar idea, which they called Fortuna; she is the personification of luck and destiny, the dictates of which no soul can escape or is exempted from. The correct moral response may then be to ask ourselves if there is a way to conduct our lives in such a way that the inherent vulnerability that characterizes our existence is rendered not only tolerable but desirable. The quest for meaning in our otherwise tragic existence is the ultimate driving force behind any worthwhile intellectual pursuit, epitomized by that age old poignant question "what is the meaning of life?"

Tragedy itself, which is merely the revelation of our vulnerability, cannot be regarded as evil. It is thus necessary to distinguish the tragic conditions of existence from evil and malevolence, as there are certain categories of human action that lie outside the parameters of mere tragedy. Defined in simpler terms, evil is an act of cruelty committed for its own sake. In contrast to tragedy, voluntarism and lack of necessity distinctively characterize acts of evil. What is more, evil deeds are usually accompanied by a partial or complete denial to victims of their moral identity, often resulting in the degrading and humiliating treatment of those victims as persons. Let me expand on that.

As noted earlier in the previous section, the received view contrasts good and evil as metaphysical polarities. One significant implication of such characterization is that their existence is considered necessary. But elevating notions of good and evil to the intelligible world of absolutes brings forth a disturbing consequence that fundamentally challenges the foundation of moral responsibility. If an act of evil is determined to be a necessary occurrence, then the voluntary nature of the motive to act by the moral agent shall carry no moral weight in that determination. One does not have to necessarily question the agent's volition in order to believe that his act is necessary or fated. Homer's Iliad, for example, tells of the legend of Achilles from both points of view, as someone whose destiny is predefined by the gods before he was born and yet lived the life of a true hero and a libertine. However, in the grand scheme of things Achilles who according to Greek prophesy was born for the Trojan war was not to account for the countless soldiers he slayed, except for the life of one man — Hector, for Achilles is fated to die young if he kills Hector. Such a dramatic interplay between fate and free-will reflects the brilliance of Greek Tragedy whose role in shaping Western civilization and culture has proved to be enormous several centuries after. Be that as it may, unfortunately, we do not live in an alternate reality that is shrouded by legends of quarrels between gods and goddesses to which we are mere pawns. Good and evil do exist; they are not metaphors personified by warring gods but are acts committed mostly by ordinary people.

As we've seen, the identification of good and evil as metaphysical polarities distorts the nature of moral judgment potentially resulting in the exoneration of moral agents who committed acts of evil — most of whom historically happened to be ordinary people from moral culpability. In *A Report on the Banality of Evil*, Hannah Arendt challenged the widespread conviction that judgments of personal responsibility can sometimes justifiably be withheld during times of extraordinary crisis affecting the foundation of the basic fabric of society as a result of which large scale atrocities are committed. The reason for that conviction is that it is impossible to withstand temptations of any kind under totalitarian dictatorship, which was Adolf Eichmann's defense during his trial in Jerusalem where he insisted that only a person who has been in his situation can attest to whether his predicament was surmountable, not, as it were, by people whose judgment was merely guided by legends borne of hindsight or hypothetical reasoning about what could have been. His defense was centered on the notion that he was fated to follow orders as soon as he was tied by the bounds of duty, and there was nothing he could have changed without sacrificing his own life. In response, Arendt asserts that "while a temptation where one's life is at stake may be a legal excuse for a crime, it certainly is not a moral justification."[4] Eichmann, however, poses a very peculiar problem to morality as

---

4 Hannah Arendt, *Responsibility and Judgment* Edited and with an Introduction by Gerome Kohn (New York: Schocken Books, 2003), 18

well as to legal responsibility. Most people associate evil acts typically with diabolical monsters with exceptional appetite for pure malice and cruelty, particularly true of people like Amon Göth, Reinhard Heydrich, the Saddam brothers, and countless enthusiastic floggers in torture chambers. However, Eichmann's trial reveals something uniquely profound that had escaped popular perceptions of evil, which is that evil acts are committed for the most part by half-wits who are unable to think for themselves. That speaks of the propriety of the phrase—the Banality of Evil.

At this point I think it would be proper to discuss the distinction between moral responsibility and legal responsibility as a way of explaining away the excuse often given by people in public office who participated in acts of evil under the excuse that it is impossible to resist official commands under totalitarian systems. According to this line of reasoning, moral responsibility for crimes committed under totalitarian systems must be borne collectively. If anything, it is not individuals but the collective entity such as the Nazis, Bolsheviks, the Interahamwe, the German people, or all of humanity that stands accused of the respective historical crimes. But, the retreat into the collective rather than healing the wounds of history instead aggravates it. There can be no scenario in which a crime is committed for which no one in particular can be held to account. What is more, it is absurd to attribute moral responsibility (guilt in particular) to a group of people en masse. One is morally responsible only to the extent of one's participation in a criminal act, and the fact of multiple agents involved in the crime is only incidental but not constitutive to its moral condemnation.

Clearly, there is such a thing as collective responsibility for moral wrongs committed in the name of certain identifiable groups of people. The nature of such responsibility has not been clearly articulated, and controversy often arises as to the normative grip it has on individual members of a given society. It is however worthwhile to delineate the notion of collective responsibility from "collective guilt," for it would be flawed to think that moral culpability can be held collectively. When we concern ourselves with collective responsibility in which a member of a community is held vicariously responsible for things she did not participate in but which were done in her name, one suggestive way to think is in terms of 'remedial responsibility' — the responsibility to set things right, which is principally a political, not a moral, consideration. Non-participation carries no moral weight, but the collective nature of the act does not excuse from moral culpability a person who did in fact participate in the act. The following passage from Arendt succinctly captures the point: "[i]n the center of moral considerations of human conduct stands the self; in the center of political considerations of conduct stands the world."[5]

In ancient Greek and Rome, morality holds a different connotation than its modern use, and moral virtues were conceived as an integral part of politics — as customs and manners proper to the citizen. According to that frame of understanding, morals are meant for cultivating virtuous citizens who are then capable of functioning well in the world in which they live. The center of interest was the integrity of the polity, not the integrity of the individual except in reference to the first. The modern notion, however, connotes something different. It detaches morals from the political world in which the individual lives. So in the same way, in a seminal piece Benjamin Constant presents a contrast between two different connotations of the word "liberty," precisely between the liberty of ancients and that of the moderns.[6] Ancient Athenian and Roman societies conceive of and exercise their liberty collectively through direct participation in the affairs of the state, whereas the modern notion of liberty connotes individual self-determination and normative control over essential spheres of one's life. In his historical analysis, he points to Rousseau who mistook in his writings the ancients' liberty for that of the moderns and inadvertently inspired what he called the "evil beginnings" of the "happy revolution." He was of course referring to the so called "rein of terror" that immediately followed the heydays

---

5   Hannah Arendt, *Responsibility and Judgment*, 153

6   Benjamin Constant, "The Liberty of Ancients Compared with that of Moderns" (1816)

of the French Revolution.

One of the defining features of that particular evil beginning was the summary execution of the entire French nobility, not for the crimes they may have committed that could be established under due process of law, but due to their perceived guilt by association. During that period the notion of collective responsibility was central to what led to the determination of their trial by guillotine. One can say that the refusal to recognize the self as the kernel of moral responsibility is precisely what made it possible for evil to take root in society.

Now that we have outlined the social and psychological fault-lines that account for the prevalence of evil in the world, we must now proceed to ask what, if anything, we can do about it. Alan Watts is right in saying that one "does not eliminate poisons by knowing their names."[7] The following questions suggest themselves. What shall we do about it? In shielding humanity from the poisons of evil, which moral resources can we draw from?

For overcoming evil and further drain the social breeding grounds that make it possible for evil to grow, we have two moral resources at our disposal. One relates to the morality of respect for the humanity in every person. Our humanity founded on the notion of basic moral equality of every person confers one crucial moral resource to combat evil, and yet it will remain mechanical unless supplemented with adequate moral psychology informed by the knowledge about what governs human action and behavior. That brings us to the second moral source we can tap into for combating evil and malevolence, which is the virtue-ethical conception that morality can only be preserved by individuals who aspire to cultivate the highest virtue in themselves, not often by those who take an impersonal duty-based approach to moral responsibilities. If history be of any guidance, hard men with a strong sense of duty are more likely to drive other people into despicable acts or commit such acts themselves than those who are more prone to cultivate a personalized sense of moral identity.

---

7   Alan Watts, *The Wisdom of Insecurity: A Message for an Age of Anxiety* (New York: Vintage Books, 2nd Vintage Books Edition, 2011), 93

On the flip side, the latter are more likely to resist temptations for acquiescing to evil on conscientious grounds; they tend to internalize circumstances of choice by probing it against the question whether they will be able to live with themselves were they to choose one way instead of another. That question becomes the guiding mantra for individual who are deeply concerned with cultivating an unshakable moral integrity. The most significant take-away from this may be that the most promising shield from evil and malevolence is ultimately the moral integrity of individuals.

Respect for the Dignity of Persons

Identity-conferring human relationships such as belonging to a community or a nation may strengthen fraternal feelings and with that comes a sense of sympathy and cooperation, and consequently such relationships lead to a display of self-restraint, care, and concern for the well-being of others. However, these sources of human fellowship, if left unchecked, tend to entrench a sense of apathy and indifference towards the plight of others that are defined outside the parameters of the identifiable "us." National identity, ethnic and social kinship, and membership in a belief system do serve as bases for inclusion and could to that extent be forces for good; but they also serve as the basis for exclusion on equal measure. The tendency that conceptions of "us" are usually defined in reference and stark contrast to some iden-tifiable "others" makes it natural for people to display objectionable forms of partiality and all other works of inequity. Reactions to others who do not share our national identity and social value systems may range from mere apathy and indifference to disgust, then ultimately transformed into hatred that often leads to malicious intent and an outright passion for cruelty and violence. Passionate demonization of and lust to annihilate "the other" can thus be born out of the familiar, narrow but benign sense of community and fellowship.

We are not at a loss though. Our distinctively psychological responses to the good or bad fortunes of people with whom we share distinctive identities can be harnessed in such a way that we can embrace human fellowship in the broader sense of the term.

In relation to the broadening up of identity conferring human relationships, we can look at two moral resources. Both relate to what might be called "human responses" encompassing proactive as well as reactive attitudes. "One is the tendency to respond to people with certain kinds of respect. This may be bound up with ideas about their dignity…just as fellow human beings."[8] This idea of common humanity has been around for ages, inspiring the disposition to show respect for people. The attitude of respect is much richer than the disposition to protect the weakest amongst us or the sensationalism of moral outrage and disgust at someone's humiliation. Appeal to respect for human dignity is a powerful restraint on cruelty and barbarism, precisely because dignity symbolizes the equal moral standing had by all individuals without which no moral relation is possible. Immanuel Kant advanced a very influential account of human dignity. Describing dignity as a "worth that has no price," Kant asserted that "a human being regarded as a person…possesses a dignity…by which he exacts respect for himself from all other rational beings in the world." He emphasized that respect is a fitting response to dignity in the same way that esteem or appraisal is for merit, desire for the desirable, and appreciation for beauty. But in exactly what sort of treatment does respect for the dignity of persons manifest? According to Kant, respect for dignity is a way of valuing every person intrinsically:

> Humanity itself is a dignity; for a man cannot be used merely as a means by any man…but must always be used at the same time as an end. It is just in this that his dignity (personality) consists…[so in the same way] he is under obligation to acknowledge, in a practical way, the dignity of humanity in every other man.[9]

Sometimes cruelty is practiced as a means to an end, such as to

---

8   Jonathan Glover, *Humanity: A Moral History of the Twentieth Century,* 23

9   Immanuel Kant, *The Metaphysics of Morals,* trans. Mary Gregor (Cambridge. 1991), p. 255.

intimidate and silence political opponents or to exercise overwhelming power over victims so as to extract valuable information. Without denying the proven fact that these attempts are rather counterproductive, and that treating persons as a means to an end violates the principle their dignity, what interest us here is a category of cruel treatment that is committed for its own sake. It is precisely that category of cruelty which uniquely characterizes acts of evil.

There is something that usually precedes premeditated acts of evil. The will to humiliate does not spring overnight; there was first a systematic dehumanization of a certain group of people to give all sort of excuses for perpetrators of horrible crimes to bask in the pleasure of cruelty. It all begins with systematically installing a narrative of inferiority about "the other" and, as time progressed to be replaced with an outright denial of the group's humanity. In connection to that, Kant speaks of three specific vices that typically violate the duty of respect: arrogance, defamation, and ridicule. Committing one of these three vices involves arrogating to oneself, and the likes of oneself, greater "self-esteem" simply by demanding that others "think little of themselves in comparison with [one's self]." Holding others in contempt (arrogance or self-conceit) or disseminating information about others that induces public disrepute (defamation) for the purpose of pure gloating at their disgrace while rendering them objects of mockery and derision (ridicule), for Kant, constitute paradigmatic modes of disrespect to their dignity. Many instances of degrading and humiliating treatments, for example, showcase familiar ways of committing these three vices. To humiliate or degrade the humanity in a person means to deny him the moral standing that he is in some fundamental sense the moral equal of anyone (and everyone).

Mockery and derision are strongest when expressed through the cold joke. Scornful parading of prisoners before jeering crowds in Abu Ghraib and Guantanamo prisons, and the subsequent taking of pride and gloating at their humiliation are prime examples of it. The cold joke emerges when their public humiliation is described with cynical humor as the "successful exploitation of the internees." When a guard is sent with instructions to that effect, it often meant a prisoner should be met with punitive measures such as having dogs sent on him, or to be subjected to some public sexual humiliation. In that context, "cold joking" becomes common. For instance, "telephoning," "the submarine," "the aeroplane ride," and "playing the radio" were some of the nicknames for specific types of torture employed by torturers under Apartheid South Africa. During the civil war in the 1980s, the military regime in Ethiopia used to assassinate what it called "counter-revolutionaries" and left their bodies to rot in the streets of Addis Ababa. In some instances the military security would go to the victims' families and serve their cruel jokes cold by demanding that the families pay up for the bullets "wasted." Saddam Hussein's security henchmen used to sneeringly call the tank of battery acid into which their victims are thrown to their deaths as " the swimming pool." In addition to mocking the victims, the cold joke serves as a psychological ploy at anesthetizing the human response, suggesting that the deliberate jamming of empathy requires strenuous effort.

Acts of cruelty arouse our moral revulsion, and justifiably so. During war times reports of torture, humiliation, mass rapes and mutilations are more commonplace than is generally known by those outside the warring parties. Reports of unspeakable cruelty are met with total disbelief and shame at belonging to a species "that inflicts pain for the pleasure of doing it." That often makes one wonder what especially inspires the love of cruelty in times of war. Moral psychology might explain it through a gradual loss of inhibition instigated by continued involvement in war: routine participation in violence tends to dull critical thinking and moral sensibilities. Perhaps men pushed beyond their limits experience cracks in their soul that can slowly erode their moral identity and slide them into the abyss of darkness. But none of that can explain or justify the willful acts of barbarism, and the urge to humiliate, torture, and dehumanize civilians and the defenseless who have the misfortune to find themselves under the complete mercy of their abusers.

We know too well the festivals of cruelty reported to have taken place in concentration camps and countless torture chambers. The story of Jews ordered to scrub pavements on their knees in the streets of Vienna, Albanian women raped in front of their spouses and children by Serb militants, "rape squads" holding women under sexual slavery during the Rwandan genocide, horrendous reports about mutilated bodies left for animals to scavenge on, these are in fact watered down wartime narratives the veracity of which has been established. The victims are gone, but their cries echo from the banks of the Congo river, from the valleys surrounding the Musa Dagn mountains in Armenia, and from the jungles of Cambodia. These examples of treating human beings as if they are not worthy of human dignity involve one or both of the following: "treating humans as non-human, rejection [of a human being from the human commonwealth], and acts intended to lead to lack of control or to highlight one's [perceived] lack of control [attested by the victim's total subordination and loss of self-respect in his own eyes]."[10]

A loss in one's sense of self-worth that characteristically figure in the minds of victims of humiliation highlights the extent of damage to the human psyche caused by inhumane treatment of persons. It is also said that dignity is inherent to the human person, meaning that it cannot be lost or forfeited or diminished over time. However, just because inhumane treatments results in victims losing access to their sense of dignity and self-worth does not mean dignity is something one can lose (even under the most extreme of situations). If being possessed of human dignity makes it impermissible for someone to humiliate you, you do not lose that dignity simply because you are impermissibly humiliated.

Awakening the Human Responses

There are moral resources that help restrain cruelty and help in restoring the sense of respect for the dignity of other people. One is through awakening our sense of disgust at cruelty, by erecting a barrier against the cold joke. One example of the cold joke is coercive public sexual humiliation while hurling at the same time contemptuous

---

10 Avishai Margalit, *The Decent Society* (Cambridge, M.A: Harvard University Press, 1996), p. 146

humor at the victims' expense. The humiliation is complete when other prisoners are forced to bear witness to the act. "A central part of a torturer's craft is to make his job easier by stripping the victim of protective dignity."[11] But a simple act of refusing to grant an audience, for example by turning one's back, destabilizes the abusive status quo from its very foundation. The cold joke is effective in proportion to the extent of the victims' total dunking into submission that it can project, and it is for that reason that any sign of insubordination is often met with harsh punitive measures. History proves time and again that it is precisely the display of pride and self-respect, and the refusal to acquiesce to one's debasement that eventually breaks the cycle of abuse and brings forth a breakthrough in the human response. A courageous stoic display of self-respect eventually breaks through the hardened shells of the torturers, or at the very least causes the game of cold joke to lose its unique appeal. An attempt at contemptuous humor at the expense of someone with a solid sense of self usually backfires, the absurdity of which only exposes the inadequacies and folly of the abuser himself. But proper psychological response to humiliation is only part of the story.

This certainly is not to suggest that victims of cruelty should seek salvation through the eventual breakdown of evil intention in the minds of their abusers. Nor is it an instance of blaming the victims for being vulnerable and powerless. It is only to remind and counsel that the victims themselves should not lose sight of their dignity and self-worth merely because their human dignity is impermissibly violated by others. It is a sobering thought to remind ourselves that our dignity is an absolute inner worth that exalts each of us above all price and bids us a normative authority to stand up for ourselves and exact respect from all other human beings; it is also something we should not forfeit by letting it be clubbed into dank submission. It is in that maverick disposition that the duty to treat ourselves with dignity can be recognized. "Be no man's lackey," Kant counsels. "Do not let others tread with impunity on your rights," for, despite the

---

11 Jonathan Glover, *Humanity*, 36

"widespread propensity to servility in men, one who makes himself a worm cannot complain afterwards if people step on him."[12]

The Limits of Evil and Morally Reactive Attitudes

Kant insisted that human beings have the capacity to be motivated by duty alone. But as anyone who has exhaustively studied history can attest, this is far from the truth. Human will and the motive to treat other people right do not necessarily arise from our capacity for rationality and intellectual rigor alone. Many find themselves in the old difficulty that even if judgments of right and wrong were self-evident, the will to act according to what one knows to be right is not given by that knowledge. In connection with this, P. F. Strawson once lamented it was "a pity that talk of the moral sentiments has fallen out of favour."

Earlier we emphasized the importance of cultivating a fitting psychological response to humiliation, which could serve as one protective shield against evil and malevolence. There is also what have come to be known as "morally reactive attitudes." Reactive attitudes are an integral part of the vast repertoire of moral resources available to individuals in order to hold others morally responsible. Strawson suggests that reactive attitudes (such as resentment, indignation, hurt feelings, anger, reciprocal love, and forgiveness) are central to our interpersonal relationships including our human fellowship as free and equal members of the moral community and are also the basis for holding persons morally responsible. He argues that the truth of determination, relating to the biological, social, and circumstantial factors strongly influencing our psychological state or given circumstances, will not affect our reactive attitudes as these sentiments are inherent to human nature.

Strawson's theory of moral responsibility however runs into trouble for it appears to suggest that great acts of evil and monstrosity evade the familiar ways of holding persons morally responsible. People who

---

12 Immanuel Kant, *Metaphysical First Principles of the Doctrine of Virtue* (6: 434-436)

carry out evil acts are considered to have, by their own act, removed themselves from membership in the moral community for they can no longer be seen as prospective interlocutors in the interpersonal moral sphere which serves as the basis of holding each other mutually responsible. There is a common reference to perpetrators of evil as monstrous and barbaric, as if the very idea of their existence defeats the conceptual space within which ideals of the moral community is to be found.

We cannot address evil people within the moral community, since by acting in despicable manner they prove to not share the moral framework of values. Gary Watson argues that Strawsonian theory of moral responsibility leads to a paradox. He takes it that if perpetrators of evil acts operate outside the moral framework of values and yet they are deemed to be morally responsible for their actions, then it must follow that moral responsibility does not require one to be a member of the moral community.[13] On the surface Watson seem to be right about the seeming incoherence of Strawson's account of moral responsibility. But his theory can be salvaged with a simple adjustment compatible with the general idea about the basis of moral responsibility. It may be argued that one can be held morally responsible for one's evil actions even if one has incidentally removed himself from being governed by the moral framework of values, as long as he has the capacity to be a member. The sheer fact that one has the ability to be a member is sufficient to establish moral responsibility. Incidentally this is the interpretation favored by some authoritative readers of Strawson.[14]

This is therefore to say that we can lay judgment that perpetrators

13 Gary Watson, "Responsibility and the Limits of Evil: Variations on a Strawsonian Theme," in Ferdinand Schoeman (edn.), *Responsibility, Character, and the Emotions: New Essays in Moral Psychology* (Cambridge: Cambridge University Press, 1987), pp. 256-286.

14 See Michael S. Mckenna, "The Limits of Evil and the Role of Moral Address: A Defense of Strawsonian Compatibilism," *The Journal of Ethics* 2:2 (1988), pp. 123-142; Stephen Darwall, *The Second-Person Standpoint: Morality, Respect and Accountability* (Cambridge, M.A.: Harvard University Press, 2006)

of radical evil are inhuman, barbaric, monstrous brutes while at the same time preserving the normative framework for holding them morally accountable.

A Sense of Moral Identity

Recently, we have witnessed a total collapse of the moral order and the established standards of human decency both in private and public life. It is certainly true of Syria, and also to a lesser extent of Iraq and Afghanistan. What seemed to have been considered unimaginable suddenly has become normal and acceptable. The negation of morality as such has become unsophisticated: It is not on the basis of a framework of values that good and evil are now defined, but by the simple measure of the identity of the actor. There seems to be a transference of goodness or evil to individual members in relationship to which predefined group they happen to belong. What we learn behind the news headlines of the beheadings, summary execution, and sexual enslavement of Yazidi women during the rise of ISIS in the Levant, is principally that the sense of moral identity of members of ISIS has been anaesthetized, as they seemed to be doing what they did as a matter of course, and it did not occur to them that there is something morally precarious about the state they sought to bring about.

In these similar predicaments, if we are to seek change from within the human spirit, our best hope is the moral awakening of the individual. Of crucial importance is one's sense of moral identity, which neither subjective psychological responses nor being motivated by duty alone can produce.

The trouble is that most moral philosophers are helplessly unable to articulate the inner mechanism in the person's psyche by which one cultivates an unshakable sense of moral identity. Many people who were a force for good during morally challenging situations happened to be ones who govern their lives with the mantra — "I wouldn't be able to live with myself if I (don't) do that." Similarly, Glover writes that "under extreme duress, a sense of moral identity can give courage and strength." What sort of person you want to be is central to a morality based on virtues, but the real question is this: What would be a general rule of thumb one should follow in order to be morally virtuous? One plausible answer to this question may be found in the most cherished Socratic proposition that "it is better to suffer wrong than to do wrong." It is safe to assume that most of us do care what sort of person we are, and overwhelmingly prefer the answer to be affirmative that we want to be good, fair and just. The Socratic dictum is however of interest only to those whose interest lies in being good, but would very likely lack persuasion for the ruthless amoralist.

The best antidote to evil perpetrated by amoralists is the moral awakening of the individual through constant prodding. It is not something new. Genuinely spiritual traditions have tried to offer this to humanity for thousands of years, which is the development of a truly integrated individual. They tried to remind us that it matters to the survival of humanity whether or not the individual gets his act together, that every time a person makes a pathological moral decision he moves the world one step closer to catastrophe. On the contrary, every time a person makes an exemplary moral decision and manifest moral courage in the face of one's vulnerability to evil and malevolence, one moves humanity one step onto the light. The core message is crystallised by the correct supposition one's capacity for evil is only matched by his capacity for displaying moral courage to move the world one step forward. The recognition that this poor little me is capable of participating in the most horrible act of evil imaginable can be truly humbling, in the sense that it matters. More than ever, it is imperative to create transformative communities that foster the cultivation of individuals with moral integrity and unshakable faith in their own humanity. For that reason, the contribution of organizations such as Human Dignity and Humiliation Studies in uplifting our common humanity is enormous and must be exalted beyond price.

Conclusion: on Taking Clowns Seriously

The Danish philosopher Søren Kierkegaard spoke of the allegory of the clown. He wrote: "A fire broke out backstage in a theatre. The clown came out to warn the public; they thought it was a joke and applauded. He repeated it; the acclaim was even greater. I think that is just how the world will come to an end: to general applause from wits who believe it's a joke."[15]

The parable has many faces and may be subject to multiple interpretations. One suggestive way is to relate it to what Shakespeare had to say; "All the world is a stage, and all the men and women merely players." Yet in this theatre of life the roles that a person plays may vary over time, with the exception that only a clown must always wear the same face and play the same goofy character. Unless society is framed in such a way that we are prepared to listen to the clown's warning, the general applause that Kirkegaard referred to will turn out to be the bad joke — only made at the expense of humanity as such.

The Trump phenomenon provides a telling example and also sets a dangerous precedent. In time of social crisis it becomes increasingly difficult to solely rely on our faith in humanity's capacity for rationality and intellectual rigor. Although it is terribly important to carefully analyze and articulate our moral resources, we must also be on the watch that what takes centuries to build can be undone in the blink of an eye. To install a sense of moral urgency, we must be willing to listen to the clown's warning whistles. Most of us did not take seriously the few dissenting voices, and declared as nonsense the clown's warnings; little did we know that the road to evil is paved with what only seems to be a joke about a fire in the backstage.

The disturbing truth is that ordinary persons' capacity for evil is much greater and infinite than meets the eye. There is an overwhelming probability that if you and I were in Nazi Germany in the 1930s we would have been perpetrators of evil. There's evidence throughout history that people take shelter in group identity and

---

15 Søren Kierkegaard, *Either/ Or*, Part I

cultural identification to help protect themselves from their inherent vulnerability; too much reliance on ideological purity may lead one to be willing to kill other people in defense of those beliefs, and, on the contrary, not having a solid moral foundation based on strong beliefs will leave individuals bereft. To reiterate, the way out is the development of the individual character

Evil results in the attempt to make the essential conditions of existence pathological, and it is motivated by conscious intent. There is therefore an increasing moral burden being placed in each of us to manifest enough moral courage in the face of human vulnerability. Our only hope and salvation lies in that, and it is perhaps the only thing closer to what we might mean by the spark of divinity dwelling in each one of us.

Chapter Thirteen

World Dignity University Initiative in the Amazon Rainforest: A Transformational Learning Experience

Mariana I. Vergara Esquivel

Abstract

This study explored the experience of cognitive transformation of participants over a four-week period following the implementation of MIA® (Mindfulness into Action). Psychological tools were used to evaluate the evolution before, during, and after the MIA® process. Implementation was made with students who took the course "Mindfulness into Action (MIA®) Research with Grounded Theory" at Columbia University. Once a week sessions were held during the semester. Each session lasted two hours. With the permission of the participants, the sessions were recorded and evaluations were done before and after the MIA® process. In addition, participants answered questions about their process before, during and after the MIA® intervention. This study was done with the research methodology called "Grounded Theory" in order to identify subconscious self-sabotage behaviors. Despite the fact that these students were under greater stress due to demanding academic work at Columbia University, the participants became clear-minded and grounded, capable of moving into action in complete mindfulness during and after the MIA® experience. This chapter includes the qualitative and quantitative analysis of this transformation, as well as comments from the MIA® conference about the student's presentations of the process, and reflections from students at the field research study in the Amazon rainforest in 2016.

Introduction

In June 2009, expanding on my work as a practitioner, I began to work with an indigenous community in the Amazon rainforest. At that time, this community was experiencing the intrusion of a mining company on their land (Vergara, 2016). After the MIA® intervention, by July 2010, this community had expelled four mining companies. I sought to build sustainability into the intervention in the Amazon rainforest by reaching out to universities to bring students to perform research. In December 2010, I met Dr. Evelin Lindner and Dr. Hroar Klempe at the "Workshop on Transforming Humiliation and Violent Conflict" at Columbia University Teachers College. My interactions with Evelin facilitated the development of a relationship with the World Dignity University (WDU) initiative, and, she ultimately founded a branch in the Amazon rainforest. My interactions with Hroar facilitated his becoming part of my dissertation committee and later on providing scholarships through Erasmus Plus to fund disser- tations developing the MIA® research studies in different contexts, including in the Amazon rainforest.

In 2011, as a result of a presentation at Washington & Jefferson College, two students displayed interest in supporting this effort. By October 2011, I began introducing my practice to these students via the Internet. In June 2012, after the Kichwa community completed the road into Rio Blanco, these participants came to the Amazon rainforest. Both students received grants from Washington & Jefferson College to perform their research. The grants included lodging and meal expenses that provided a financial income for the indigenous community. During one month, they performed research in sociology and environmental science. In July 2012, Evelin Linder arrived in the Amazon rainforest and funded the branch of the World Dignity University (WDU) initiative. A video was recorded with her camera documenting the experience of these students with MIA.* This video of participants confirmed that they did not only apply their knowledge about sociology and environmental science, but they also learned about human development regarding co-creation (doing research with people), rather than top-down approaches (doing research on people) (Vergara, 2016). In November 2012, Hroar invited me to present this video from the WDU branch in the Amazon rainforest as part of a presentation at a "Community Psychology Conference" at Norwegian University of Science and Technology, Trondheim, Norway.

In April 2013, I was a speaker at the Earth Summit, Columbia University, and at the TEDx at Teachers College, New York, New York (2013). After these presentations, students began to approach me and asked me to teach them about transformational learning. Soon after, with the support of Dr. Lyle Yorks, the Mindfulness into Action Initiative began when three students started meeting every week as part of the activities for the Organizational Leadership Association under the sponsorship of the Vice President's Grant for Diversity and Community Initiative at Teachers College (2013).

Furthering the efforts to understand and promote diversity, Teachers College sponsored the "Experiencing Diversity at TC study" (Carter et al., 2013). This multi-year and multi-phase study aimed to explore diversity in varying contexts. The study had three data-gathering phases and a fourth phase that integrated the findings from the prior three phases.

The first phase of this study sought to understand the existing context of Teachers College as it relates to diversity. The authors conducted mappings and visual inventories of images displayed across campus and analyzed Teachers College's historical documents relating to diversity. The second phase involved interviews with students, faculty, and staff. The third phase of data gathering consisted of focus groups that were divided by status and race, providing racial majority and minority groups in varying status positions. The final phase consisted of integrating the findings from the three previous phases and developing a survey instrument about the climate for diversity at Teachers College. In this fourth phase, the authors concluded that the "lack of institutional spaces and the absence of a collaborative dialogue about diversity and diversity work render the climate silo-ed, disaggregated, with well-intentioned but relatively short-lived efforts toward inclusivity" (p. 5). Furthermore, a finding from the second phase concluded that "White participants of the survey felt as though the campus climate for diversity was constantly improving and inclusive of difference" (p. 5). However, "People of Color at the institution who participated in our survey generally viewed the climate as hostile and unwelcoming, especially in terms of the lack of awareness of discrimination that occurs at the college and the dearth of spaces to grieve and cope with such discrimination" (p. 5). Concluding this study, the authors provided five recommendations that aimed to create a climate of inclusivity of diversity across the institution and academics (Vergara, 2016).

In line with the findings of this study, "Mindfulness into Action" began as an initiative to address these diversity issues that caused "humiliation" from a student perspective with the creation of a "space" for communal understanding of diversity work and shared meaning about what constitutes diversity work. This space is created at weekly meetings applying organizational learning techniques, such as Collaborative Developmental Action Inquiry (Rooke & Torbert, 1999) to facilitate inclusivity with a dialogue about diversity and diversity work to address this sense of separation and the silo-ed climate at Teachers College (Vergara, 2016).

Based on data from the interviews and focus groups from the "Experiencing Diversity Study at TC," our work addressed assumptions about diversity through organizational learning techniques. In the TC study, the authors described: a) the "lack of space" to discuss diversity that they found while doing their study, and b) assumptions about diversity (Carter et al., 2013, p. 5).

For the last two decades, the demographics at Teachers College have reflected a mainstream culture. Over the last decade, various neo-institutional scholars have discussed the relationship between institutions and humans. According to DiMaggio and Powell (1991), institutions do not merely constrain human agency; they are first and foremost the product of human agency. We have the tendency to believe that institutions and their policies have always been there and, as a result, many of us allow ourselves to be constrained by them (Vergara, 2016).

In November 2014, I went to the Norwegian University of Science and Technology (NTNU) as a visiting scholar. During my time at NTNU, I presented my research work in the WDU branch of Amazon rainforest to about 400 students. Sixty students signed up and 20 followed through the intervention. I created two groups that met weekly and we called it a science project. Many students wanted to go to the Amazon rainforest, and since I was developing a doctoral program for the Universidad Tecnica de Norte (UTN), NTNU students began an exchange program with UTN. This science project was called the "Mindfulness into Action Initiative." The goal of this project was to develop meaningful and effective interactions between Norwegian and Latin Americans participants, and the research goal was to detect factors that provide better interaction. Currently, stereotypical views of Latin American societies and cultures still exist due to news and information filtered through European and North American channels. These stereotypical views reflect our taken-for-granted assumptions (Fals Borda, 2006) that hinder meaningful and effective interaction between Norwegians and Latin Americans. From these NTNU participants, three students came to Ecuador to support the Mindfulness into Action Initiative on a volunteer basis. In July 2015, one participant came to Ecuador to visit the Amazon rainforest in order to return to Norway and recruit more students from NTNU. Later, in August 2015, two other participants came and we went to the Amazon rainforest to do research with the Kichwa community of Rio Blanco. In September 2015, one participant that was part of the exchange program began the implementation of the Mindfulness into Action methodology with ten Ecuadorian students at UTN. The other participant went back to Norway to continue with the implementation of the methodology at NTNU with ten Norwegian students and to recruit more students to go to Ecuador (to UTN or the Amazon rainforest) in the future. From this work we published a simultaneous study of the implementation of MIA® (Vergara, Tjernstad, Mac Quarrie, & Tamariz, 2017).

On December 17th, 2015, I was asked by Professor Barbara Wallace to teach in January 2016 the Mindfulness into Action methodology as an action research class using grounded theory at Teachers College, Columbia University. This chapter is about the transformational experience of the students using the MIA® process in this action research class. This transformation is explained in a qualitative and quantitative analysis. In May 2016, the MIA® conference was held, and in July 2016, a group of students from Columbia University, NTNU, and UTN arrived at the WDU branch in the Amazon rainforest. By 2017, the MIA® Institute was created.

Background

This project began in 2009 using organizational theory as a method to approach the task of determining how to build, nurture, manage, and sustain change at the NKRBNO (Nationality Kichwa of Rio Blanco Napo-Orellana) community. Currently, corporate America uses organizational theory to build effective corporations in making profit. Therefore, why not use the same techniques to build effective communities in preserving the Amazon rain forest?

This background section outlines some of the dynamic technology efforts involved with the implementation of the Amazon project as an initiative of the WDU. It describes the implementation of this project from an organizational theory lens as we use technology as a vehicle to achieve this implementation. A chapter was published about this effort using technology to move forward this effort to help the indigenous community in the Amazon rainforest (Vergara, Wallace, Du, Marsick, Yorks, Gordon, & Tamariz, 2017).

When we think about organizational theory, we think about global corporations, such as, mining companies. Mining companies are intruding (legally and illegally) into the Amazon rain forest. Mining companies use an organizational theory called the transaction-cost-economizing approach. Transaction cost economizing (TCE) has played a constructive role in pushing ahead the frontiers of organizational theory (Aldrich, 2001). However, its critics point out that TCE draws on an under-socialized conception of humans because individuals are presumed to behave individualistically, as isolated actors. Under-socialized people act without regard to the social damage they do, or the impressions they leave with others (Vergara, Wallace, Du, Marsick, Yorks, Gordon, & Tamariz, 2017). Thus, TCE theorists stress materialistic or self-serving motives, as Aldrich (2001) states about Loasby's description of TCE: TCE "follows the standard American practice in constructing self-interest as narrowly focused selfishness". Thus, this approach promotes humiliation and understates the importance of social exchange: reciprocity, cooperative, and trusts.

On other hand, the core philosophy of WDU is reciprocity, cooperation, and trust. WDU is a community of practice. Langer states that a community of practice is very much a social learning community as opposed to one that is based solely on the individual (Langer, 2005).

As Evelin Lindner (2012) stated, the WDU Amazon project has the aim of promoting "the Amazon as a university for the world". The indigenous population invites people from all over the world to learn everything about how sustainable livelihood has traditionally been achieved in the rain forest. Sustainable livelihood, rather than jobs, is what the world needs to learn more about in the future. The world population needs to learn and accept help from the indigenous population, rather than the other way round.

Core Philosophy

I am a member of the Global Core and Education Teams in the Human Dignity and Humiliation Studies (HumanDHS) network. This organization has evolved to create the WDU initiative. HumanDHS is:

> ...a global transdisciplinary network and fellowship of concerned academics and practitioners. We wish to stimu-

late systemic change, globally and locally, to open space for equality in dignity and mutual respect and esteem to take root and grow, thus ending humiliating practices and breaking cycles of humiliation throughout the world. We suggest that a frame of cooperation and shared humility is necessary — not a mindset of humiliation — if we wish to build a better world, a world of equal dignity for all. We are currently around 1,000 personally invited members, more than 7,000 more people support our work, and our website is being accessed by 40,000 people from more than 180 countries per year. (HumanDHS, 2011)

It is in the interest of a global society to not only protect the rainforest and its biodiversity, but also to learn from the cultural diversity of its indigenous population. In particular, the notion of sustainable livelihoods is important. To do this, the indigenous community has to be enabled to act as a resource community for global learning about social and ecological sustainability (Lindner, 2012).

Mindfulness into Action (MIA*) Approach

In January 2016, at Columbia University, Teachers College, the Mindfulness into Action (MIA*) with Grounded Theory course was created. This is a hybrid (online and in-person) qualitative and quantitative research course that uses the MIA* platform — which goes beyond traditional paradigms. MIA* uses Indigenous knowledge to take action, given that Indigenous people have a broad knowledge of how to live sustainably. This course teaches students how to use grounded theory, as well as the qualitative software program NVivo in data analysis, while focused on leadership skills development in the area of diversity issues within organizational settings.

Regarding individuals' context, students are from different cultural backgrounds and ethnicities, with different life experiences. With MIA,* we got together to reflect as part of a *conscientization process.* The concept of conscientization, which is at the heart of Paulo Freire's pedagogy of liberation (Freire, 1970), connotes both consciousness and conscience and thus captures the cognitive and normative processes that constitute this form of reflective knowledge. In our interactions, we emphasize the learning process, such as single-loop learning, double-loop learning, and deuteron learning (Argyris and Schon, 1996), with different focuses on behavioral and cognitive change. With the MIA° process, we are trying to address very difficult problems, problems related to *humiliation*. Therefore, we cannot stay on the single-loop learning, we must reflect and move to the double-loop and deutero-loop learning. The development of organizational learning is mediated through multiples levels. At the individual level, interpretation of the environment leads to the revision of individual knowledge structures (Walsh, 1995). At the group level, individual knowledge structures are synthesized to create shared beliefs. At the organization level, the routinization of shared beliefs leads to organizational knowledge and transforms individual experience into group knowledge. Transforming individual knowledge into organizational routines leads to complex and embodied knowledge. Organizational learning contributes to the strategy perspective by conceiving the organization as a dynamic, integrated system that constantly changes (Aldrich, 2001).

MIA° is co-inquiry, most concisely defined as doing research with people, rather than on them (Bray, Lee, Smith, & Yorks, 2000; Heron, 1996; Reason, 1988). This is a participatory action research initiative. Park (1999) states that "in participatory research people who share problems in common decide what problems to tackle and directly get involved in research and social change activities." In our work with Indigenous community Kichwa in the Amazon, using this approach of participatory action research has proven conducive to the outcomes we are working for, namely dignity for all. We want this community to go through emancipatory learning as a way to co-create a sustainable way to preserve the Amazon rainforest. The reason for this emphasis on popular participation is that participatory research is not just a convenient instrument for solving social problems through technically efficacious means, but it is also a social practice that helps marginalized people attain a degree of emancipation as autonomous and responsible members of society (Freire, 1982). It is allied to the ideals of democracy, and in that spirit it is proper to call it research of the people, by the people, and for the people (Park, 1997).

In this way, we have concrete tools to evaluate our social interaction because it is through social interactions between individuals that knowledge is synthesized. As Wiley states, "intersubjectivity is emergent upon the interchange and synthesis of two, or more, communicating selves" (1998:258). The interaction creates agreements in a communication process and thereby leads to shared beliefs. As David Teece (2001) states "knowledge is not primarily about facts and what we refer to as 'content'; rather, it is more about 'context.'"

The MIA® process does not include mindfulness techniques. It uses Indigenous practices with organizational learning techniques, which includes cycles of reflection (reflexivity). Data has suggested (Vergara, 2016) that after four weeks participants trained in this methodology develop a sense of being in a constant state of awareness (mindfulness) — as an attribute deemed vital for leaders being able to work in tune with those around them in diverse organizational settings.

Organization Learning

Essentially, the organizational learning theory has transported the idea of individual learning to the organizational level (Probst, Buchel, & Raub, 1998). However, Weick and Westley raised the issue of whether the literature on organizational learning is really about an organizational level phenomenon or simply about individuals learning within organizations. They argued that some theorists have ignored the issue by simply treating organizational learning as learning by individuals within an organization context, but what about the individuals' context? These individuals have mental models that shape the organization; they evaluate their work which is shaped by their ways of seeing and understanding themselves in context.

Organizational learning builds on the idea that individual learning is not sufficient for organizations to be successful. Organizational learning proposes that organizations need to be able to transform and distribute individual knowledge (Kim, 1993) and acquire new knowledge (MacDonald, 1995) in order to create a whole which is more than the sum of its parts.

Methodology

Phenomenology - Qualitative and Quantitative Analysis

Phenomenology (Husserl, 1964) is a study of phenomena that manifest themselves. The methods of analysis have the following objectives: 1) Pre-application of instruments to identify the initial situation, 2) Follow-up of the reflection processes to create effectiveness and sustainability about solving their problems, 3) Post-application of the instruments to evaluate the improved areas. Additionally, an interview was done with questions describing human behavior before, during, and after the implementation of MIA®.

Type of Research

This is participatory action research, which is a form of research that is often summarized as research with people and not with them as subjects (Bray, Lee, Smith, & Yorks, 2000; Heron, 1996; Reason, 1996). Such an approach requires recognition that academic researchers are not outside the system, but are an elemental part of the composition of the system involved in the study. Therefore, intentions, decisions, contributions to conversations, and actions are among the many factors that influence the results that arise from the activities and interventions in the study.

Techniques

The techniques used in this research are organizational tools and indigenous practices of the methodology Mindfulness into Action (MIA®) Research with Grounded Theory (Charmaz, 2006). MIA® was developed in the dissertation of Dr. Vergara (Vergara, 2016) at Columbia University (Department of Organization and Leadership). Later in 2016, it became a qualitative and quantitative research course (Department of Health and Human Behavior Studies) with transformative results (Vergara, 2017).

Instruments

The instruments used in this study are the Global Leadership Profile (GLP) and a vulnerability-to-stress test. The GLP is a leadership development framework developed by Torbert and Herman-Barker (2004) with the original factors arising from the University of Washington Prayer Terminator Test (WUSCT) instrument to assess personality development. GLP is an eight-stage model that identifies the logic of action or the mental complexity of individuals using vertical learning (of how an individual knows and tries to transform and of how an individual interprets, understands, and reacts to the world). GLP characterizes the problem-solving tendencies of an individual and their daily interactions with others using different styles of leadership (based on their psychological development). Another instrument is the assessment of stress vulnerability that includes anxiety, depression, and stress to determine the changes before and after the implementation of MIA® with respect to levels of stress, depression, and anxiety.

Findings

At the end of the four weeks, the interview protocol was provided to participants. The interview protocol has questions about how the participants felt before, during and after the implementation of MIA.® This chapter includes the answers to three questions from five participants:

Below are their responses before the implementation

Please describe how you felt about yourself before doing Mindfulness into Action?

Participant 1

I had been dealing with interpersonal and work-related stress, family issues, and addiction issues. When I began, I was in therapy for these issues (and still am), but I hadn't been able to fully implement my healthier behaviors regularly.

Participant 2

Prior to MIA, I often struggled with self-doubt about my ability to embody the dispositions of an effective leader. I felt I was lacking essential knowledge and skills set to facilitate professional growth in leadership. I did not embody the five agreements of Indigenous practices. I carried with me emotional baggage from the past that inhibited my growth.

Participant 3

I was considering not returning to school because of the stress with home factors. So I was quite stressed, feeling unsure of my ability to accomplish goals, confused.

Participant 4

I am naturally a very organized person and typically function in a very strict environment and can be very harsh on myself when things don't go as planned or when I make mistakes.

Participant 5

I was a practical person and most of the time I also always think on the basis of causality and the rational causes of particular things, but I can only think about "now." I normally push myself to be able to achieve things, thus I sometimes tried to do "beyond" my best/capability, nearly sometimes — I also demanded anyone who worked with me to be able to achieve almost everything we wanted to do. I perhaps also couldn't really focus on what I want to do.

Below are their responses during the implementation

Do you feel different from the time you began Mindfulness into Action and now?

Participant 1

I feel immensely different. I know how to take care of myself. I am more in tune with what my body needs in order to connect with others and be productive at work (I am in a direct service position so this is important).

Participant 2

I feel as though the cloud of unknowing has been lifted. My daily experience is more joyful and grounded in admiration of life. I have found that the willingness to be vulnerable with others is a source of strength and a position of mutual power. I am no longer fearful of being vulnerable (exposing my authentic self). I am content with who I am and the growth that I am in will continue to experience. I am pleased to be able to observe my feelings, actions, and those of others and respond in thoughtful and productive way that build relationship.

Participant 3

At first it seemed very self-indulgent to pay attention to myself every hour and give this time to me for practice. But MIA is not selfish, rather, this practice gave me more energy to give outward to others. Also, some things around me began to change without my making decisions…things started to "work out" more easily.

Participant 4

I think the puzzle really came together for me around the third week of the MIA exercise. I began to notice the change in my mood and social interactions, as well as my energy. I felt more and more positive as the days and weeks went on. I didn't necessarily notice the changes slowly as they were happening, but rather all at once. I think my first "aha moment" came on a day when I was walking to work and all of a sudden it was like a light switch came on for me mentally, and I was able to associated the change in my mood with the MIA exercises.

Participant 5

One small but meaningful thing is I found myself currently be a more open mind person and have an awareness that failure is not a big mistake that I have to blame myself (for not being able to do/ achieve/change something). I feel that if there is something that I cannot do as what I planned before is not a big deal, and that subsequently I have a belief that a much better achievement is waiting for me soon. Over the past four-and-a-half weeks, I feel that this practice helps me to achieve more and at the same time I learn what so-called "self-appreciation" on whatever I did, whether it worked or it didn't. In addition, the hourly reflection practice helps me to let go all the negative moods and feelings and "clean" my mind to stay focus on my goals at that time.

Below are their responses after the implementation

Do you look at your life differently? Have you accomplished a goal that you felt unreachable? If so, what changes or goals? Please describe.

Participant 1

I look at my life very differently than I did before I started MIA. I used to sacrifice my own health and happiness for work and for other people. Now, I know how to take care of myself first. This goal seemed unreachable to me before starting MIA. I didn't know if I would ever understand self-care, or ever be able to implement it. It has made me a better employee, a better mentor to students, and kinder to myself, and others. It has helped me become aware of all the ways I used to contribute to my own unhappiness and the unhappiness of others. Now I feel like I am in complete control of my reactions to everything that happens to me or around me. I am so much more equipped for what life brings, and completely at peace.

Participant 2

Through MIA I have developed a sense of belonging to a greater cause/energy. This is important to me because I have felt like an outcast in my family for many years. Now I am detached from this feeling/experience and feel as sense of belonging. I became more of an observer of various situations throughout the day. In essence I became more reflectively response and less reactive. I also became more fully present in my interactions with others as I sought to listen to hear the intent and message of what was being said.

Participant 3

Yes. It is the same life but with the edges smoothing out more... in process. My life is changing, I am ready for change, and I assist this transformation through action. With MIA, I can better observe myself to move forward and not go in circles.

Participant 4

I feel that my entire mentally has changed, including the way I approach my day to day and the way that I think forward. Before I was so intent on having a clear idea of what I needed to do, one week down the road, one month down the road, one year down the road (etc.), that I wasn't experiencing my life as it was happening, rather just planning for the next thing and the thing after that. After having a constant Mindfulness into Action practice, I feel that while at my core, I am still a planner, I have noticed a shift in my experiences, in summation, I feel that MIA has helped me to strike a balance between my life and my goals and has given me the tools to experience both fruitfully.

Participant 5

I think, yes I do. I appreciate my life more than before. I appreciate any achievements or changes that I and someone else made. I also feel an increased concentration, productivity, and my ability to respond mindfully to stressful or unexpected situations. The hourly reflection also helps me to decrease emotional reactivity.

Quantitative Analysis of MIA® (Vergara, 2018)

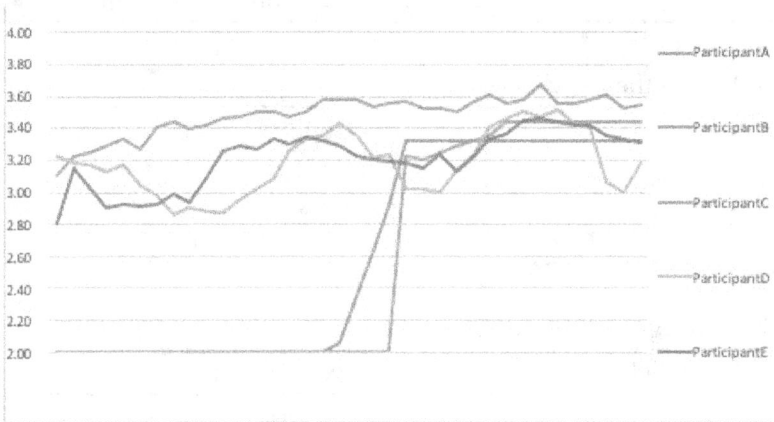

Observations:
*3 participants started in the neutral zone and 2 in the negative zone.
*4 participants completed the 4-week cycle in the positive zone, and 1 in the neutral zone.
*2 participants show an oscillatory behavior with 3 peaks and period of about 10 days.
*1 participant grows during the first half of the program and stays up with little variation for the second part.
*2 participants jump from negative into the positive zone and stay there.

Values in Table:
2.00 to 2.80 Negative emotions
2.80 to 3.20 Neutral emotions
3.20 to 3.80 Positive emotions

This table shows data from five participants, all of them achieved the "third head." Three students began their journey in the neutral zone. They did the methodology consistently and achieved the "third head." The other two students were resisting the methodology. These two students were African Americans. In the table, two of them begin in the negative emotions zone. But, as they observe the reflection from other students, they decide to do the MIA® practice and immediately achieved the third head, and stayed in the positive emotions zone.

Qualitative Analysis of MIA® (Vergara, 2016)

First-level Coding	Second-level Coding
Phase 1	
a) Before the Intervention	
1. Initial "Reactive" State	2. Conflict 3. Resistance 4. Stress 5. Victim Identity
Phase 2	
b) During the Intervention	
6. Identified Awareness	7. Exercises, Steps
8. To Be Present	9. Surprise 10. Connectedness
11. Observing Behavior	12. Cohesiveness
Phase 3	
c) After the Intervention	
13. "Ah ha" Moments	14. Control 15. Stepping Back
16. Identification of Third Person	17. Internal Reflection 18. Suspension 19. Reflection
20. Reflection of the Third Person	21. Writing (Journaling)
22. Coping Action – After Shift	23. Tolerance
24. Happiness	25. Being at Peace
26. Effectiveness	27. Personal Effectiveness 28. Academic Effectiveness 29. Professional Effectiveness

All students achieved what Vergara calls the "third head" (Vergara, 2016; 2017; 2018).

Definition of the "third head": The "third head" is a place of neutrality; when a person is in this place, it is without emotions. Participants in the "third head" are clear-minded and grounded, capable of moving into action in complete mindfulness. Data suggest (Vergara, 2016; 2017; 2018) that the achievement of the "third head" usually happens within four weeks of practicing MIA® consistently. Data suggest that when a participant stops doing MIA® for two days, the "third head" disappears. However, if the participant began to do MIA® again, it takes one and a half week to achieve the "third head".

MIA* Conference

The Mindfulness into Action for Cultural Humility and Awareness conference was held from 8:30 a.m. to 6 p.m. on Friday, May 13, 2016 at Teachers College, Columbia University. There were 69 attendees.

The event was sponsored by the Center for Health Equity and Urban Science Education (CHEUSE), Department of Health and Behavior Studies, with the support from The Office of the Provost, and The Office of the Vice President for Diversity and Community Affairs. Sixty-nine individuals attended the conference on May 13, 2016. Out of that number, twenty-three individuals (33%) filled the evaluation form.

The feedback from participants from the MIA® Conference, both via a formal survey and from anecdotal conversations on the day, indicated a very high level of satisfaction with the event. Please see below some of their comments:

- I enjoyed the opportunity to share more about the content of the conference and the benefits of the practice of MIA with attendees at the reception. Thank you!

- Having an open forum to share thoughts and experiences, without judgment really allowed for a deeper conversation to take place

- Excellent MIA presentation. Thank you.

- When Mariana spoke, it was clear. She was speaking from her heart and it touched my heart. This conference was excellent - informative and inspirational!

- It was an amazing experience! Thank you!

- This was a different type of conference! Thank you for the experience!

- This was truly an inspiring experience for me. It went beyond my expectations.

- This was a new experience for me and I loved it.

- How things are connected to us and at times we are not aware. Loved this conference. Needs more exposure.

- It is so impressive how MIA can change lives.

- Dr. Wallace and Mariana along with testimonials about the third head were inspirational.

- An excellent, informative, life-changing conference and experience that I was blessed to experience today. Thank you.

At the conference the keynote speakers were Dr. Emdin, Dr. Wallace, Dr. Vergara, and students, John-Martin Green and Susan Tirhi, with Dr. Yorks describing the subject-object perspective in transformational learning in the morning session. The afternoon session opened with Dr. Edmund W. Gordon, followed by a scholarly discourse regarding Mindfulness and how Mindfulness into Action (MIA®) does not include meditation or yoga to achieve "mindfulness". Mindfulness is achieved through indigenous practices with organizational learning techniques.

Then, the following presentations were from the implementation of MIA® in Norway by Carl Tjernstad from NTNU, in Ecuador by Adam Mac Quarrie from UTN, in India by Apeksha Mewani, and at a high school in New York by Adriana Reyes. At the end to the conference there was a panel discussion where Irma Hidayana joined the conversation about implementing MIA® in Indonesia, and Dr. Yorks summarized his observations of the MIA® presentations as the possibility to transfer this methodology. (Dr. Lyle Yorks https://youtu.be/GVud9KwSzWk)

TC, UTN, and NTNU students presented their MIA® process at the Conference. Please see below links of the videos from their description of the MIA® process. Students are from different race, gender, age, demographics, and location; and all of them achieved the "third head":

- Caucasian female online participant at Columbia University – Susan Tirhi (https://youtu.be/sxfYy11HcfQ).

- African American male participant at Columbia University – John-Martin Green (https://youtu.be/SErw9D8hnbI).

- Norwegian male participant in Ecuador – Adam Mac Quarrie (https://youtu.be/lsVEVjpCj38).

- International female student at Columbia University – Apeksha Mewani (https://youtu.be/63td4AQx6Rs).

- Norwegian male participant in Norway – Carl Tjernstad (https://youtu.be/UALnWNaYukU)

Field Research in the WDU Branch in the Amazon Rainforest

In July 2016, students went to the Amazon rainforest as part of a new summer cross-cultural fieldwork practicum. Their experience emphasized cultural exchange, humility, and ethics. Therefore, MIA® participants from three universities (NTNU, UTN, and TC) went to the Amazon rainforest.

Please see below some of student's reflections:

- The trip has helped me, not only to understand the power of a culture and the importance of preserving traditional practices and rights, it has given me a new sense of searching in order to help create a better future. I went on the trip wondering if I could finish my Master's program and came back a person who now wants to pursue my Ph.D. in this field.

- Going to the forest and staying at the village of Ruku Samay among the indigenous Kichwa people was an opportunity to expand my knowledge on multicultural populations. Living with members of this population taught me a lesson for life. Firstly, I felt privileged to observe every minute gesture, habit, and ritual and learn to "penetrate" their culture. I was able to observe closely the family dynamics and the manner in which mother and son, brothers and sisters interacted on a daily basis. They seemed bounded, remarkably genuine and proud to be a close-knit family. They were extremely warm people. They opened up their home to foreigners [that we were] and ensure that we were safe and well taken care of.

- After a five-hour bus ride from 12 a.m. to 5 a.m., from Quito to Tena in the Napo Valley, we were all very anxious to arrive in the jungle. We waited two-and-a-half hours for the van that would take our group to the drop off place to hike and forge a river that would lead us to our jungle habitat. I can hardly express my surprise at what would be my lodgings for the next four days.

  We walked up three flights of wooden slated stairs to our room. My roommate put her things down on the cot against the bare wood wall. Three feet across from her was my cot under the "window," a four-by-six-foot opening to the tree tops outside. I looked at the empty rope above our cots and felt chills pass through me. "Where is our netting for sleeping," I questioned. My roommate shrugged. I took off my backpack and began to pull out my bug spray and hat for our first hike into the jungle. As I prepared for our first hike into the jungle, I made a note to myself: Ask Mariana if the family has a net to put over our cots while we're hiking. I could feel my stomach tighten as I kept imagining trying to sleep in the jungle without a net. I sat down on my cot to lace up my hiking boots, when I looked out my "window." I caught my breath when I registered two spider webs that overlapped and covered the entire span of the window opening. Just off center, sat a black spider in each web. Each one was the size of my outstretched hand. It's body was the size of my palm and its eight legs were the size of my fingers. I can't sleep here, I panicked. I grabbed my daypack and raced down the stairs to find Mariana.

I could see Mariana from afar, talking under the thatched roof gathering area. I quickened my steps. I didn't notice the butterflies. I didn't notice the foliage. This is an emergency, I reasoned.

"Excuse me, Mariana, but I have a big problem." I interrupted.

Mariana turned to me.

"There are no nets above our beds and I have two behemoth spiders on my window opening." I shrilled.

Mariana smiled, "Don't worry. If you want netting, they have it and will put it up for you while we hike."

I opened my eyes wider. What could she possibly mean, If I want it? Of course I want a net over my bed. I thought. I continued. "OK, but I are you sure they will have it? I need it."

Mariana shook her head, "No problem."

I could feel myself breathe deeply as I pictured the netting tucked around my cot. "But what about the spiders? Are they outside spiders?" I blurted out.

Mariana smiled again, put her arms on my shoulders, and looked into my eyes, "You must manage your thoughts. The spiders won't come to you if you don't invite them with your energy."

I opened my mouth to protest.

"Remember, everything is perfect." Mariana said as she released me and walked over to discuss the details of our hike with our Shaman guide.

The hike was hot, humid, as we traversed three hours through many plants and herbs, learning from our guide about medicine and sustainable farming in the jungle. I listened to the talk and practiced MIA with each step I took. When we returned to our lodge, I went up to the room to see if the spiders had left and netting had arrived. There above my bed was beautiful purple hued netting dangling from the rope above my cot. I then looked out the window. My shoulders dropped. I would be sleeping with the two largest spiders that I had ever seen or imagined existed. The horn blew a second time for dinner, but I stood at the doorway. Everything is perfect, I thought.

I walked over to the spiders and looked closely at them. The webs were stunning intricate designs. Something other than fear was emerging. Something like awe and grace was pushing through. I looked up at the spiders and faced them the way Mariana had talked to me and I said, "Spiders, you are so capable and strong and have made beautiful web homes. I respect you and will honor your homes and not touch them or you. This is my home in the jungle." I pointed to my cot and netting. "Please respect my home and honor where I live and do not touch me."

I smiled as I walked down the stairs and on the path to join the others for dinner. I felt the grace of oneness with all living things. My well-being and the spiders' well-being were equal. We both had to be okay. The jungle is a great equalizer: size and titles don't matter. Respect and honor matter. I was filled with gratitude. I was filled with peace. I knew that everything was perfect."

These participants were from diverse background, culture and nationalities. Please see below a table describing their background.

Participant ID	Inst	Major	Degree	Gender	Ethnicity	Country	Age
Professor A	TC	Leadership	EdD	Female	Latina	Chile	50
Professor B	TC	Literacy	Masters	Female	Caucasian	USA	53
Student C	TC	Intern. Dev.	Masters	Female	Chinese	Malaysia	34
Student D	TC	Health Ed.	Masters	Female	Indian	India	34
Student E	TC	Health Ed.	Doctoral	Female	Black	Haiti	60
Student F	TC	Psychology	Masters	Female	Caucasian	USA	63
Student G	TC	English	Doctoral	Female	Latino	Mexico	26
Professor H	UTN	Architecture	Masters	Male	Latino	Ecuador	49
Student I	UTNU	Psychology	Bachelor	Male	Caucasian	Norway	24

Conclusion

In order to deal with the mental demands of modern life, adults' thinking needs to continue to evolve through higher level of consciousness. All of us (indigenous, scholars, practitioner, and students) are co-creating a sustainable way to preserve the Amazon rainforest. The task at these meetings is to bring together all relevant participants or stakeholders through inclusive processes of "organic or naturalistic recruitment" (Wadsworth, 2008). The MIA* meetings provide the opportunity to use ecological, hermeneutical, or 'big picture' systems thinking to assist us to see the challenges we are facing. Furthermore, through the action of reflective collaborative inquiry we were able to draw the best "theoretical maps" by which we could navigate until better ones were found.

This is an emergent process: What we are trying to do does not exist. We need to shift our paradigm before we go into action. Currently, Indigenous communities in the rainforest are experiencing the forces of globalization caused by the intrusion of mining, logging, and oil companies into their territories. Transnational companies go into the Amazon rainforest and take its resources, and it is destroying the livelihood of these indigenous communities. This process has happened before around the world. Now, we have to use this same system (globalization) regarding organizational theory to preserve the Amazon rainforest. In July of 2009, this intervention began with the Kichwa community. And, as a result, by July of 2010 the Kichwa Indigenous community has expelled 4 mining companies. As argued by Heron and Reason (1997), "having a critical consciousness about our knowing necessarily includes shared experience, dialogue, feedback, and exchange with others" (p. 283).

Ultimately, knowledge is socially constructed. Reflective knowledge has to do with critical engagement because it produces changes in participants that go beyond intellectual understanding. From the MIA° course, the anticipated result is a new generation of researchers with a different paradigm. Through participation in the MIA° leadership skills development methodology that incorporates indigenous knowledge and organizational learning techniques, students gradually become more aware of their own unconscious behaviors, in tune with the people surrounding them, and increasingly skillful in engaging in conscious and intentional action (Vergara, 2016).

This change of paradigm is an action that invariably entails modifying or going against existing social arrangements that actors perceive to be at the top of their problems. In the process of dealing with the social forces that stand in the way of change in such ways, new generations of researchers come to feel the power they can gain by engaging in actions as autonomous agents (without having self-sabotaging, unknown behaviors holding them back). Through MIA,° we, as researchers, learn how the world works. We learn what we can do and who we are, and this is how we become aware and emancipated. Through this proces, we become what Boyatzis and Mckee (2005) call, "resonant leaders." This means that we are capable of achieving a new awareness that is vital in cross-cultural interactions while overcoming self-limiting mindsets that promote humiliating behaviors against others.

References

Aldrich, H. (2001). *Organizations evolving.* London: Sage Publications.

Argyris, C., & Schon, D. (1996). *Organizational learning II: Theory, method, and practice.* Reading, MA: Addison-Wesley.

Boyatzis, R. and McKee, A. (2005). *Resonant leadership.* Boston: Harvard Business.

Bray, J. N., Lee J., Smith, L., & Yorks, L. (2000). *Collaborative inquiry in practice: Action, reflection, and making meaning.* Thousand Oaks, CA: Sage.

Carter, R. T., Oyler, C., & Goulding, C. (2013). Integrated report 2013: The research team's final observations and conclusions. Retrieved from Experiencing diversity, Three-year study on diversity at TC website: blogs.tc.columbia.edu/experiencing diversity/files/2013/05/Final-intefrated_Experiencing-Diversity-report.pdf

Charmaz, K. (2006). *Constructing grounded theory: A practical guide through qualitative analysis.* London, UK: Sage.

Diaggio, P., & Powell, W. (1991) Introduction. In W. Powell & P. DiMaggio (Eds.), *The institutionalism in organizational analysis* (pp. 1-38). Chicago, IL: Chicago University Press.

Fals Borda, O. (2006). Participatory (action) research in social theory: Origins and challenges. In *The handbook of action research* (pp. 27-37). Thousand Oaks, CA: Sage.

Freire, P. (1970). *Pedagogy of the oppressed.* New York: Plenum

Freire, P. (1982). Creating alternative research methods: Learning to do it by doing it. In B. Hall, A. Gillette and R. Tandon (Eds). *Creating knowledge: A monopoly?* New Delhi: Participatory Research in Asia, pp. 29-37.

Heron, J. (1996). *Co-operative inquiry: Research into the human condition.* Los Angeles, CA: Sage.

Heron, J., & Reason, P. (1997). A participatory inquiry paradigm. *Qualitative Inquiry,* 3, 274-294.

Husserl, E. (1964). *The phenomenology of internal time-consciousness.* Bloomington, IN: Indiana University Press.

HumanDHS, (2011). Human Dignity and Humiliation Studies Network. Retrieved on November 3, 2017 http://www.humiliationstudies.org/whoweare/index1.php

Kim, D. H. (1993). The link between individual and organizational learning. *Sloan Management Review,* 35: 37-50.

Langer, A. M. (2005). *IT and organizational learning*. New York, NY: Routledge.

Lindner, E. (2012). Visit to Ruku Kausay, conversation with Agustin Grefa. Retrieved on November 3, 2017. https://www.youtube.com/watch?v=ZZPw7lLHDg4

MacDonald, S. (1995). Learning to change: An information perspective on learning in the organization. *Organization Science*, 6: 557–68.

Park, P. (1997). Participatory research, democracy, and community. *Practicing Anthropology*, 19 (3):8–13.

Park, P. (1999). People knowledge, and change in participatory research. *Management learning*, 30 (2):140–57.

Probst, G., Buchel, B., and Raub, S. (1998). Knowledge as a strategic resource. In G. V. Krough, J. Roos, and D. Kleine (Eds.) *Knowing in firms: Understanding, managing and measuring knowledge*, 2140–252. London, UK: Sage Publications.

Reason, P. (1996). Cooperative inquiry. *Curriculum Inquiry*, 26(1), 81–87.

Rooke, D., & Torbert, W. R. (1999). The CEO's role in organizational transformation. *The Systems Thinkers*, 10(7), 1–5.

Mindfulness into Action (2013). TEDxTeachersCollege. Retrieved on November 3, 2017. https://www.youtube.com/watch?v=Gd-VjBww1w0&feature=youtu.be

Teece, D. J. (2001). Strategies for managing knowledge assets: The role of firm structure and industrial context. In I. Nonaka and D. Teece (Eds.) *Managing Industrial Knowledge: Creation, Transfer and Utilization*, 123–144. London, UK: Sage Publications.

Torbert, W., & Herdman-Barker, E. (2004). Global Leadership Profile. Retrieved from http://www.williamrtorbert.com/global-leadership-profile/the-global-leadership-profile-overview/

Vergara, M. I. (2018). Mindfulness into Action: Applying systemic thinking and exploring the potential for developing strategic leaders. In Victor C. X. Wang (Ed.). *Strategic Leadership* (pp. 77–96). Charlotte, NC: Information Age Publishing.

Vergara, M. I., (2017). Work stress, culture, and leadership:

Building a culture of health through mindfulness into action. In V.C. X. Wang (Ed.), *Encyclopedia of strategic leadership and management* (pp. 1205–1215). Hershey, PA: IGI Global.

Vergara, M. I., Tjernstad, C. D. B., Mac Quarrie, A., & Tamariz, M. I. (2017). Personal Growth and Leadership: Interpersonal communication with mindfulness into action. In V. C. X. Wang (Ed.) *Encyclopedia of strategic leadership and management* (pp. 507–525). Hershey, PA: IGI Global.

Vergara, M. I., Wallace, B., Du, X., Marsick, V., Yorks, L., Gordon, E. W., & Tamariz, M. I. (2017). Redressing situational leadership in the new world order through technology. In V.C. X. Wang (Ed) Encyclopedia of strategic leadership and management (pp. 553–566). Hershey, PA: IGI Global.

Vergara, M. I. (2016). Mindfulness into action: Transformational learning through collaborative inquiry. (Published dissertation). Teachers College, Columbia University, New York, NY.

Vice's President's Grant for Diversity and Community Initiatives Award (2013). Retrieved on November 3, 2017 from http://www.tc.columbia.edu/organization-and-leadership/ adult-learning-and-leadership/program-announcements/vice- presidents-grant-for-diversity-and-community-initiatives/

Wadsworth, Y. (2008). The mirror, the magnifying glass, the compass and the map: Facilitating Participatory action research. In P. Reason, & H. Bradbury,(Eds.), *Handbook of action research: The concise paperback edition* (pp. 322–334). Thousand Oaks, CA: Sage.

Walsh, J. P. (1995). Managerial and organizational cognition: Notes from a trip down memory lane. *Organization Science,* 6, 280–321.

Wiley, N. (1998). The micro-macro problem in social theory. *Sociological Theory,* 6:254–61.

Chapter Fourteen

Full Circle: With Gratitude to Our Dearest Evelin Lindner

Judit Révész

It all started about sixteen years ago when I was in a terribly chaotic and difficult situation both personally and professionally. While I had a pending green card application, I could not work, travel, or even enroll as a full-time graduate student for many years. I never knew how long I would be in this in-between situation (it took six years) but somehow I followed my intuition (for the first time in my life), managed to take non-credit graduate courses in conflict resolution and became a certified mediator in New York.

This was a period of my life when change was constant. As a result, I learned to get used to and thrive while being in an unknown and volatile situation. Not only did I fall in love with a new, indescribable, eclectic profession that I had never even heard of when I grew up in Budapest, Hungary, I also persistently pursued getting more work and experience in that new field with its many facets: conflict resolution, mediation, organization development, ombuds-ing, group facilitation, team building, applied behavioral science, and peacemaking.

It was during that first year of my studies that I met our dearest Evelin Lindner at the International Center for Cooperation and Conflict Resolution in 2001. I volunteered to assist her during the course on psychology of humiliation that she taught to graduate students for the first time at Teachers College, right across the street from Barnard College where I work now as their first Ombudsperson.

Learning about Evelin's research, and how she chose to change her methodology in Rwanda while conducting interviews for her second PhD study, was an eye-opener. It changed my thinking and how I have interacted with people at work and in my personal life ever since. Soon after we met, we started working on the first Human Dignity and Humiliation Studies (HumanDHS) conference at Teachers College, even though neither of us were employed at any of its institutes. If I think about that process, I truly believe that it was miraculous how it all came together. We found partners across Teachers College, Columbia University, received some in kind and some financial support, and most interestingly created a nontraditional conference design that is still the main structure for the annual December workshop after fourteen years.

The opportunity for Evelin and I to work together on the preparation of the first HumanDHS conference for almost a whole year was a wonderful experience. Although I knew that one needs some money to survive, the impact of Evelin's ability to foster loving kindness, nurturing support, and empowering relationships was profound, even when these relaltionships were established over the internet. With Evelin's encouragement, I had never felt more passionate and committed about work. I was, and I am, so happy to be part of such an interesting and meaningful project. As Evelin always reminds me, I was so happy that I completely forgot that working on the conference required working mostly at nights. We just went with the flow, and we really did not know how our network would continue to grow for years to come — one invitation at a time.

My journey started with Evelin and the psychology of humiliation and continued with the study of organizational development, with a social justice emphasis. At the American University and NTL Institute I continued to learn about group dynamics, oppression, power, privilege, gender and race relations, and about the use of self as the only instrument. On the way, many others touched my heart and influenced my thinking: Don Klein, Edie and Charlie Seashore, Cathy Royal, Lee Mun Wah, Leonard Riskin, Brenda Jones, Johnnie Smith, Karen Davis, Harrison Owen, Edgar Schein (not personally) and James Lee, just to mention a few of them.

When I think about the ten years of working at the United Nations Development Programme, I cannot count the number of times that Evelin's work on the HumanDHS project became the topic of our conversation no matter what task we worked on. It helped us understand our cross-cultural differences, and it enabled us to create effective working relationships.

What a privilege is to be close to Evelin for all these years, to learn from her and try to understand what dignity, humiliation, oppression and colonization mean. Even after being immersed in it for sixteen years, I may not have answers but I can certainly engage with my colleagues and visitors to discuss the undiscussable and create moments where we can sit together and create "humble inquiries" about very difficult issues (Edgar H. Schein, Humble Inquiry). I believe that these sensitive matters directly or indirectly influence the workplace and all these issues are present whenever we human beings interact with one another.

Lastly, as a result of my own experience, I wonder how learning about the psychology of dignity and humiliation can have a healing effect for those who are experiencing turmoil or trauma. Perhaps we could create a study program through the World Dignity University for those who have been impacted by trauma because it seems that what we all need — more than anything — is to feel connected and loved. The Dignity Now NYC gathering might illustrate this well.

Even though Dignity Now members have diverse interests and areas of study, creating a healing community is what seems to be the reoc-curring theme that holds their meetings together. I certainly felt saved and nurtured by being in contact and sharing a sense of community with Evelin since 2001. Evelin brought light into those dark years in my life and I am forever grateful for that.

Chapter Fifteen

Moving Beyond Humiliation: A Relational Conceptualization of Human Rights

Linda M. Hartling

Evelin Lindner is a trailblazing global researcher who has dedicated her entire life to realizing the promise of human rights ideals in the form of *equality in dignity*. Her singularly remarkable research has not only described the hopeful future that opens up to humanity through these ideals, she also cautions us that our transition to these ideals can spark profound and pervasive feelings of humiliation. On the one hand, subordinate or marginalized individuals or groups may become conscious of their undeserved devalued status and react with aggression. On the other hand, dominant groups may use aggressive methods to manage their fear of being humiliated by a loss of power or privilege. In our efforts to cultivate a world of equal dignity, Lindner's work challenges us to examine how we can realize the promise of human rights while reducing the risk that our efforts will trigger feelings of humiliation?

Revisiting a rarely told story of women's rights in the United States as an illustration, the paper proposes that we can strengthen our efforts to move toward human rights ideals and equal dignity by using a relational-cultural framework for understanding human experience, rather than the framework of individualism. This requires telling the truth about the impact of power that can elicit feelings of humiliation. It also requires identifying and applying a clear set of relational skills and practices to reduce the risk that humiliation will poison our efforts. Ultimately, this paper proposes that moving away from humiliation means *moving toward mutuality in relationships*, which opens the way to new possibilities for advancing the rights and dignity of all people.

Moving Beyond Humiliation: A Relational Reconceptualization of Human Rights

In 1840, Elizabeth Cady Stanton accompanied her husband, Henry, to the first World Anti-Slavery Convention in London, England (Stanton, Anthony, & Gage, 1889/1999).[1] Henry was among a number of respected American male delegates who, along with a half-dozen female delegates, made the difficult 3,000-mile journey across the Atlantic Ocean to participate in this historic event. Lucretia Mott, a Quaker abolitionist and peace activist from Philadelphia, was the most well known of the women delegates. The convention invited the participation of "all friends of slaves" from all parts of the world. At that time, women were esteemed leaders in the anti-slavery move-ment in the United States. Nevertheless, the convention organizers were shocked to discover that women were among the delegates. As a result, rather than discussing the abolition of slavery, the male delegates opened the convention with a heated, two-day debate to determine whether or not women should be allowed to participate.

Advocates for the women argued that the term "World Conven-tion" would be a misnomer without the inclusion of women. These allies asserted that the women delegates provided "essential aid" to the abolitionist cause in America and that "the most vigorous anti-slavery societies are those which were managed by ladies" (ibid., p. 57). Delegate Ashurst made a particularly poignant statement supporting the women:

> You are convened to influence society upon a subject connected with the kindliest feelings of our nature; and

being the first assembly met to shake hands with other nations, and employ your combined efforts to annihilate slavery throughout the world, are you to commence by saying, you will take away the rights of one-half of creation? (ibid., p. 58-59)

At one point some of the male delegates proposed that women might be allowed to participate if they willingly confessed their inferiority. Without such an acknowledgment, the men feared that the women's participation would place women on a "footing of equality." To strengthen opposition to women's inclusion, the convention organizers emphasized that women's involvement would be a violation of British customs — though it was noted that a woman ruled Britain at that time. In the end, an overwhelming majority of male delegates voted against women's participation in the convention. Lucretia Mott, Elizabeth Cady Stanton, and all the other women were dismissed to sit in the gallery at the back of the convention hall *behind a screen where they were ordered to remain silent.*

In this story, permitting women (a subordinate group) to participate in the convention — to have an "equal footing" — would have exposed the male delegates (the dominant group) to ridicule and derision by their male peers as well as the larger community. The male delegates found themselves in the position of inflicting humiliation (enforcing their power over a subordinate group) or risking humiliation (appearing to lose power to a subordinate group), in other words, humiliate or be humiliated.

This narrative is one illustration of a certain truth: that one cannot work for human rights without coming face-to-face with the pernicious dynamics of humiliation. In this case, the male delegates at the first World Anti-Slavery Convention ejected and silenced a small, but loyal group of activists and supporters who happened to be women. Since the subjugation and exclusion of women were norms for that time, we might be tempted to dismiss this example as an artifact of the nineteen century. However, in so doing we would miss valuable lessons about how humiliation can disrupt human rights efforts today.

Lindner (2001, 2006, 2009a, 2010, 2017) observes that humiliation is a fundamental mechanism that profoundly hinders the development of a global community that recognizes that all human beings deserve equal dignity.[2] According to Lindner (2001), the *equality-in-dignity* perspective has grown in the wake of major historical declarations of social reform, including the American Declaration of Independence, the French Declaration of the Rights of Man and Citizen, and the United Nations' Universal Declaration of Human Rights. These documents mark a shift from:

> …a condition where humiliation [in the form of human subjugation, exploitation, objectification] is normal and acceptable to a condition where it is regarded as an infringement of human right. (p. 10)

As support for human rights grows around the world, individuals and groups of people who were once led to believe that they deserved a devalued position in society will become conscious of the ways they have been treated as inferior and thus denied their rights. This consciousness may motivate those who have been subjugated or humiliated to seek to achieve a position of equal dignity through *constructive or destructive means*, including deadly forms of retaliation or aggression. Awakening to their humiliated status, subjugated groups may also become especially vulnerable to psychological hijacking and exploitation by dangerous, charismatic leaders who promise to restore their dignity.

Members of dominant groups, on the other hand, may utilize aggression to oppose or suppress the rights of subordinates because dominant groups may believe they will be forced to assume a humiliated position. Dominants may also feel that it is humiliating to relinquish power over others in order to reside in a position of equal dignity. These complex dynamics can derail and obstruct human rights efforts and foment disastrous acts of aggression and violence, as illustrated in the following examples:

- Within an emerging context of human rights, the humiliation of the German people following World War I may have made the Germans vulnerable to the persuasive rhetoric of Hitler who promised to help them transcend their humiliation, restore their dignity, and insure their rights (Scheff, 1994).

- Within an growing context of human rights, feelings of humiliation, deeply rooted in colonialism, may have fueled the 1994 conflict between the Hutus (the historically subjugated majority) and Tutsis (the historically dominant minority) that led to the slaughter of up to half a million people (Lindner, 2001).

- Within an political context that promotes feelings of humiliation, even minimum efforts to support human rights may trigger some to feel they are unjustly being threatened, left out, or displaced. This may explain the rise in extremist groups in the U.S. and else where, including white supremacists, religious extremists, or nationalists (Southern Poverty Law Center, 2019; Stack, 2019).

Today, we might like to think that we are more conscious of, and careful to avoid, the way humiliation can poison the advancement of human rights. However, Lindner's remarkable and extensive research provides strong evidence that this is generally not the case (2000a, b, c, d; 2001; 2002; 2006; 2007a, b; 2009a, b, c; 2010; 2016; 2017). She documents many examples of human rights efforts obstructed or derailed through the largely unacknowledged mechanisms of humiliation.

One tragic example of the collisions between human rights efforts and humiliation is the American occupation of Iraq. Beyond eliminating suspected weapons of mass destruction, the United States Government stressed that military action in Iraq was necessary to improve global security and gain human rights for the Iraqi people. Few would disagree that the Iraqi leader, Saddam Hussein, was a tyrant who brutally violated the human rights of many of his people. Nevertheless, advancing human rights through a process of forced "liberation" achieved by military intervention has also inflicted humiliation (Fontan, 2004, April). A survey of a randomly selected, representative sample of over 2,700 Iraqis polled on the first anniversary of the Iraqi war indicated that 41% of the Iraq people felt humiliated by the U.S. occupation (Langer, 2004, March). Recent revelations of sadistic humiliating abuse of Iraqi prisoners by U.S. soldiers has surely compounded and intensified these collective feelings of humiliation (Hersh, 2004).

Why should we be particularly concerned about humiliation contaminating human rights efforts? Based on her research, Lindner (2001) concluded that *humiliated people will strike back when they can.* This may be true even when humiliation is an unexpected outcome of well-intended interventions to advance human rights. Lindner notes that humiliation is at the root of many forms of interpersonal and international conflict, aggression, and terrorism. For example, following several successful terrorist attacks, Osama bin Laden, defiantly declared, "I'm proud of the great men who have lifted the humiliation that had befallen our nation" (CBS Worldwide, 2001). Perhaps bin Laden believed that terrorism is a justifiable and necessary way to protect the rights of his people? Or, perhaps like Hitler, bin Laden was simply a "humiliation entrepreneur" capitalizing on the vulnerabilities of people who feel degraded and alienated (Lindner, 2002a). We do not know, but these questions underscore the need to attend to the complex interactions between human rights efforts and humiliation.

Though aggression and violence are the most troubling reactions to humiliation, resistance to humiliation can follow a different course, which is revealed in the story of the women who attended the 1840 World Anti-Slavery Convention. These women were completely cast off despite their acknowledged status as prominent contributors to the abolitionist movement. They were forced into a humiliating position of "nobodiness," which Robert Fuller (2003) aptly characterizes as a toxic combination of "disconnection, invisibility, and powerlessness." Of these degrading characteristics, invisibility may be the most potent. As Jean Griffin (1991) observes:

> Invisibility is a form of humiliation that creates an espe-

cially intense rage over being in the position of having to submit to others defining you and your community as beneath their notice. (p. 157)

Yet despite being negated by invisibility, these women delegates did not consider using aggression or violence to challenge their degradation. Fighting, as Virginia Woolf (1938/1966) noted in her 1938 anti-war essay, seems to be the "habit" of men, not women. Women did not have the option of applying physical, military, or economic pressure in response to their experiences of injustice because they were in effect "civilly dead" (civilly invisible) due to their complete social, economic, and political dependence on men. They were denied the right to participate or represent themselves in society. As a result of these conditions, survival meant that most nineteenth century women had to accept and adapt to their devalued subordinate position and to their assigned social prison romantically known as the "sphere of domesticity" (Stanton et al., 1889).

Nevertheless, in a stunning defiance of social norms, Elizabeth Cady Stanton and Lucretia Mott dared to chart a revolutionary course of resistance to humiliation. Expelled from the convention, they found themselves sitting next to each other in the gallery. Publicly turned away, they privately turned to each other and commenced a conversation that would eventually change the entire social and cultural landscape of the United States. An historical account observed that:

The humiliation of this experience forged a life-long bond between Mott and Stanton. They vowed to expand the crusade for women's rights after they returned to America. (Dyer, 1994)

Mott and Stanton became determined to see that women attain civil, social, economic, and political rights. To achieve these extraordinary goals, they set out to educate all Americans about:

...the galling humiliation, the refinements of degradation to which women — the mothers, wives, sisters, and daughters of free men — are subject in this the last half of the 19th century. (Stanton, 1860/1973/1995)

Though it would take Mott, Stanton, and many, many others decades of nonviolent collaborative action, ultimately women in the U.S. acquired the right to own property, to vote, to participate in the political process, and to earn a living. Rather than becoming causalities of humiliating oppression, Stanton and Mott found courage and empowerment through their connection to each other and others. However, their collaborative pathway was seriously poisoned at a turning point along the way.

After working for the abolition of slavery and universal suffrage (in alliance with African-American collaborators such as Frederick Douglass), Stanton and other women's voting rights advocates must have felt betrayed when, in 1870, the 15th Amendment to the Constitution of the United States granted voting rights to black men and not to women of any color. From a modern perspective, it seems that the white partriarchal powers at that time applied a highly effective form of humiliation, pitting "women's suffrage against black male suffrage" while using "racist arguments that enfranchising white women, who, it was presumed...would vote like their white husbands, would negate the new power of black voters, and thus keep power in white hands" (Traister, 2018, p. 145).

In other words, white male politicians implemented a powerful form of humiliation that ruptured the broad movement for universal suffrage. They dropped a social-political bomb on the movement's leaders by not including women's right to vote in the 15th Amendment. In doing so, they very effectly divided the suffrage movement and damaged the alliances between the suffrage and the abolishionist movements, degrading the unified strength of these movements. Furthermore, feelings of humiliation surely contributed to Cady Stanton and others moving forward in a highly damaging direction:

> Some white suffragists, including Stanton and Susan B. Anthony, livid at having put aside their emphasis on women's enfranchisement to focus on abolition through the Civil War, and angry at their abolitionist allies for

what they understood as political abandonment — were so mad at having to stand back as their allies moved a step forward, that they struck out fiercely, revealing their own deep racism. (ibid., p. 145)

This sad turn of events should remind all human rights advocates that power holders will use humiliating "divide-and-conquer" strategies to sow deep divisions within their movements. Moreover, this should reminds us how even good intentions can be hijacked by humiliating attitudes or beliefs that can surface within a community. Therefore, *we must always strive to "walk the talk," to avoid inflicting humiliation while pursuing human rights causes.* But how? This chapter proposes that we can begin by:

1. Placing humiliation and human rights within a relational framework, rather than an individualistic frame,

2. Telling the truth about the dynamics of power that produce humiliation, and

3. Generating constructive and enduring relational-cultural change by identifying and applying the sophisticated *relational* skills necessary to prevent, eliminate, and overcome humiliation while advancing human rights.

This discussion reasserts a key principle of effective nonviolent action emphasized by Martin Luther King, Jr. (1965/1995): We must find ways to create "a clear program to relieve injustice that does not inflict injustice on others." We must promote human rights without inflicting humiliation.

A Relational Reframing of Humiliation and Human Rights

George Lakoff (Buzzflash, 2004, January; Lakoff & Johnson, 1980), professor of linguistics and cognitive science at the University of California Berkeley, notes that the words we use are attached to conceptual meanings that influence our thinking and behavior.

Thus, words "frame" our understanding of our experiences. Lindner (2000g) emphasizes this point in a paper describing an experiment by Ross (1993; Ross & Ward, 1995) in which two separate groups of individuals were directed to *play a game that was identical in every way* except that one group was told that they were playing "The Community Game" while the other group was told that they were playing "The Wall Street Game." Those who played the so-called "Community Game" tended to cooperate while those who played the "Wall Street Game" did not. Ross concluded that the name of the game — the frame — was the key predictor of how people expected others to play the game, which, in turn, influenced how they played the game. The words "Wall Street" trigger images of competing for one's self-interest and financial domination (D. T. Miller, 1999). The word "community" triggers images and accordingly actions of greater cooperation and mutual benefit. As this experiment suggests, a frame has a powerful influence on our understandings and expectations of human behavior.

Western psychology has too often framed human experience in highly individualistic terms (Cushman, 1995; Jordan & Hartling, 2002). Using the "self" as the primary unit of study, Western psychology historically over emphasized the values of independence and self-sufficiency, presupposing that separation from relationships is the ultimate outcome of healthy development. Enlarging our frame beyond a focus on the "self" opens the way to new understandings of human behavior and experience. A growing body of research provides evidence that a "relational" framework is a more constructive way of exploring human experience (Hartling, Ly, Nassery, & Califa, 2003). More and more researchers have found that a sense of connection, rather than separation from relationships, is essential to healthy psychological development (Jordan, 1997; Jordan, Kaplan, Miller, Stiver, & Surrey, 1991; J. B. Miller & Stiver, 1997); resilience (Hartling, 2003; Spencer, 2000; Spencer, Jordan, & Sazama, 2002; Werner & Smith, 1982); community engagement and responsibility (Putnam, 2000); physical health (Ornish, 1997), mediation and conflict resolution (Della Noce, 1999), as well as the prevention of psychological and substance abuse problems (Blum, McNeely, & Rinehart, 2002; Resnick et al. 1997). Hartling (1996; Hartling & Luchetta, 1999; Hartling, Rosen, Walker, & Jordan, 2000) and Lindner (2000b, c) have applied relational logic to examine the experience of humiliation.

Lindner (2000b) offered a map of the conceptual space in which the process of humiliation occurs at the personal and group level. Indeed, she suggests that humiliation "is the strongest force that creates rifts between people and breaks down relationships" (p. 2). Using a relational perspective, Hartling (1996) developed a scale, the *Humiliation Inventory* (HI), to assess the internal experience of cumulative humiliation and fear of humiliation triggered by interpersonal interactions.[3] In an exploratory study of narratives volunteered by a subset of respondents, Hartling found that those with high scores on the HI described their experiences of humiliation as if it had happened yesterday, even though the experience may have occurred many years in the past. The experience appeared to remain painfully vivid in the individual's mind. Research on the impact of social pain may account for this acute and enduring nature of humiliating experiences (Eisenberger, Lieberman, & Williams, 2003).

This paper proposes that we can enrich our understanding of humiliation and human rights by using a relational framework. While there may be a number of ways to apply a relational perspective (Spencer, 2000), this discussion will use the framework of Relational-Cultural Theory (RCT), which grew out of over twenty-five years of theory building and research conducted by scholars at the Stone Center's Jean Baker Miller Training Institute at Wellesley College (Jordan & Hartling, 2002). RCT posits that growth-fostering relationships are a central human necessity throughout people's lives and that acute or chronic disconnections — such as humiliation and human rights violations — are the source of psychological and social problems. RCT emphasizes that all relationships are defined and influenced by the cultural context in which they exist. Rather than self-development, *relational development* is the primary focus of study in RCT (See Figure 1). From this perspective, humiliation and human rights violations damage, disrupt, and block relational development and, consequently, obstruct and impede human development.

Figure 1: A Relational-Cultural Theory Framework

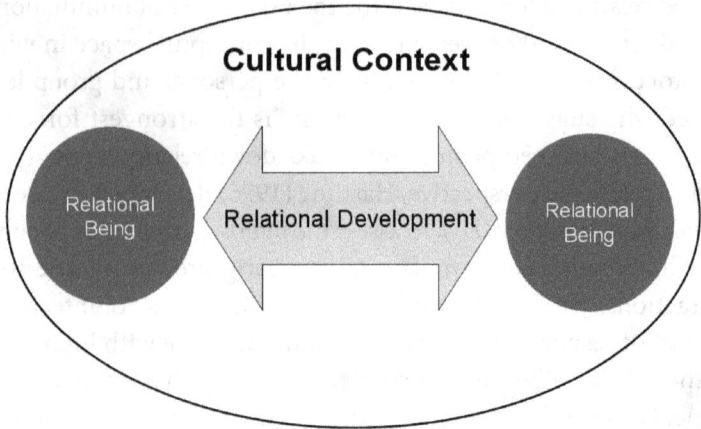

Humiliation has been relatively neglected in the literature; perhaps because it doesn't easily fit in the separate-self paradigm of Western psychology (Hartling, 1996; Hartling & Luchetta, 1999; Hartling et al., 2000). While there is an individual, internal experience associated with humiliation, the internal experience is triggered by events that occur in relationships. Klein (1991a, 1991b, 1992) describes the relational nature of humiliation as the *humiliation dynamic*, which involves the interaction of the: 1) humiliator; 2) victim; and 3) witness.[4] In a typical experience, a humiliator forces a victim to assume a degraded position that assaults that person's core sense of being in view of others. It is a *profound relational violation* (Hartling, 1996; Hartling & Luchetta, 1999; Hartling et al. 2000; J. B. Miller, 1988). Placing Klein's humiliation dynamic within a RCT framework helps us understand the complexities of the experience of humiliation (See Figure 2). For example, what is deemed humiliating and who has the power to humiliate depends on the cultural context. In a cultural context of race-based discrimination, certain individuals or groups will be individually and systematically humiliated through a variety of practices — implicit and explicit, physical and psychological, personal and political — that are presented as normal or necessary (Walker, 2004).

In the 1950s, African Americans in the U.S. were systematically humiliated when they were forced by members of the dominant white society to sit at the back of the bus, drink at "colored only" drinking fountains, and attend separate schools. Although overt forms of racial humiliation may be somewhat less prevalent today, covert forms of racism continue to thrive. This is exemplified by the practice of race-based profiling that results in African Americans being unjustly pulled over by police merely because they were "driving while black." Whether on an interpersonal, social, or even an international level, humiliation is clearly a profound relational violation in which one is made to feel unworthy of connection, often without hope of reconnection (Hartling et al. 2000). Margalit (1996) captures the relational magnitude of this experience when he states that humiliation is the "rejection of a person from the human commonwealth" (p. 3).

Figure 2: Klein's Humiliation Dynamic within a RCT Framework

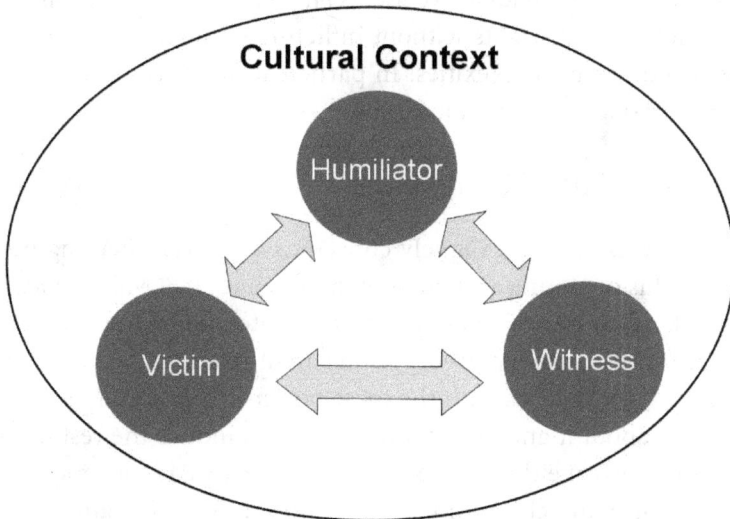

As with the experience of humiliation, a relational framework can

enlarge and enrich our understanding of human rights. A traditional self-based perspective would primarily focus on the right of each individual to social, cultural, economic, and educational opportunities provided by society, such as the right to work, the right to an education, or the right to vote. RCT extends our view to attend to the qualities of relating that support human rights ideals. In fact, if one believes that all people have a right to healthy development, human rights can be understood as the *essential qualities of relating necessary for human beings to grow toward healthy development* within a society. Relational conditions within a culture determine whether or not its individual members progress in the direction of psychological well-being, intellectual development, meaningful work, political participation, and equal dignity. It is also through relationships that people are protected from cruelty, abuse, and persecution. Relationships are central to human rights ideals.

Moving toward a relational framework helps us more accurately conceptualize the many complexities of humiliation experiences and human rights ideals, complexities that are often overlooked when the focus is solely on individual experience. If we are to succeed in efforts to promote human rights without inflicting humiliation, we must understand these complexities. In particular, we must understand how power operates in relationships.

Telling the Truth About Power[5]

Many of us are only vaguely conscious of power affecting our lives, yet it is operating around us all of the time (J. B. Miller, 2003). Our lack of awareness may be another outcome of the Western focus on individual experience rather than relational experience. Amazingly, those of us with the most power in our society almost never talk about it and even more amazingly, induce the rest of us not to recognize it either. For example, in the early days of American filmmaking many children enjoyed going to Saturday afternoon movies about the American West. For five cents children could see two full-length films, a cartoon, a newsreel, and an episode, or what was called a "chapter," of a long, ongoing adventure story, which was almost always a Western. Americans would see the "bad guys," the Native Americans, portrayed as strange-looking, uncivilized, savage murderers who were threatening the white cowboys. The theater rang with ear shattering cries, cheers, and whistles when the cowboys hurt or killed the Native Americans. It never occurred to the children that it was the white people who had taken power by force, robbing the Native Americans' land and destroying their cultures.

American children absorbed these humiliating untruths routinely every week. Thus, you can see how people were drawn into disparaging and even fearing these apparently powerful, violent people. History classes in elementary or high school did nothing to change these images. It was many years before Americans began to learn the truth that whites had brutally taken power over the Native Americans. Likewise, we never saw any other people of color portrayed with complete truth. This is an common example of how the "cultural materials" of a dominant group mystify its exercise of power. Instilling the degrading image of a group of people as savage and uncivilized allows the dominant group to justify denying the others human rights and suggests that they deserve humiliation. We can see this type of treatment happening to refugees and asylum-seekers around the world (e.g., Cobbe & Slattery, 2015).

A group that becomes dominant in a society tends to divide people with less power into groups based on differences. Dominance is built on a foundation that includes restriction of another group (Walker, 1999; Walker & Miller, 2001). These less powerful groups can include divisions by race, class, gender, sexual preference, cultural heritage, and the like. It isn't just the division by differences that are source of the dominant group's power, it is that these differences are "profoundly stratified" through miseducation that teaches subordinate and dominant groups who is superior and who is inferior.

A poignant example of this miseducation can be found in Lindner's (2001b) description of the events that led to the 1994 genocide of a half a million Tutsis in Rwanda. European colonizers taught Rwandans a "mythical early history," that the Tutsi were the superior group and the Hutus the inferior group. As Lindner states, "…European colonists simplified and intensified the system of structured inequality within Rwandan society" (p. 10). European colonists used their power to impose conditions that locked the Hutus and the Tutsi into decades of struggle that eventually led to the slaughter of thousands of Tutsis. Miseducation, disguised as education, is a powerful tool for institutionalizing humiliating practices and justifying the denial of human rights. Miseducation makes these practices seem normal and necessary (Walker, 2004, April). Thus, the dominant members of society gain tremendous power over the less powerful group in all realms, including economic, social, political, and cultural.

"Power" is by definition a relational concept — we experience power and powerlessness in relation to others. An individualistic frame obscures and mystifies the operation of power in people's lives. Power issues have a fundamental influence on our relational experience and therefore are central to our discussion of humiliation and human rights. Without reviewing all definitions, one definition of power is the "power to" produce change without the connotation of restricting or forcing anyone else. Another definition is "power-over." Power-over comes when one group has resources and privileges and, consequently, more ability to force or control others. Humiliation and human rights violations are more likely to occur in contexts where a dominant group inflicts power-over subordinate groups to keep them in their subordinate position (Hartling et al., 2000; Lindner, 2000d). Subordinate groups may respond with tactics to gain power-over a dominant group, perhaps through threats of violence or terrorism, and dominants will respond in kind. The power-over dynamics of dominant-subordinate relationships can trigger actions and reactions of escalating cycles of humiliation and counter-humiliation by both groups, defeating all efforts to improve the human rights of all people.

Defining power as "power to," rather than power over, transforms the way we think about creating change. "Power to" does not imply domination or force; it suggests shared power, the power of working with others to create change. This is what RCT refers to as mutual empowerment. Rather than exercising power-over others, Mott and

Stanton developed power to produce change by changing minds and empowering people through education, and by building a community of support for their efforts, that is, by building empowering relationships. Through this process, the efforts of Mott and Stanton eventually created a critical mass of like-minded people to ultimately influence those who resisted relinquishing their power-over practices that denied the rights of women. Mobilizing "power to" produce change, rather than exercising "power over," Mott and Stanton fostered the conditions that allowed people in America to consider new ways of being in relationship, new ways of relating between men and women. Though their efforts were far from perfect (to be discussed soon), they made progress. To effectively reduce humiliating practices and promote human rights ideals, we must find effective ways to promote "power to" create change — not power-over. This means creating new activity in relationships and new relational possibilities for all people.

Creating New Relational Possibilities, Creating Change

Eliminating humiliation and human rights violations cannot be accomplished through individual change, but through relational-cultural change. A relational lens not only offers a larger framework for understanding the complexities of humiliation and human rights, it leads us to explore the qualities of relating that promote movement and change in relationship that can prevent humiliation as well as promote human rights. RCT suggests that constructive movement or positive change in relationship (a.k.a., healthy psychological growth) depends on three essential, inseparable factors: *mutual empathy*, *mutual empowerment*, and *movement toward mutuality* (Jordan, 1986; J. B. Miller, 2002; Surrey, 1987).

Mutual empathy is a two-way dynamic process that involves openness and a joining in relationship that allows both (or all) people in the relationship to know and respond to the feelings and thoughts of the other person. Jordan (1986) describes mutual empathy as:

> ...the affective-cognitive experience of understanding another person...[It] carries with it some notion of moti-

vation to understand another's meaning system from his/
her frame of reference and ongoing and sustained interest
in the inner world of the other. (p. 2)

Mutual empathy *is not a relational courtesy*; it is a sophisticated skill that clears a critical pathway toward greater clarity and knowledge in relationships. It is an "empathic bridge" (Jordan, 1992) on which people from different perspectives can meet and engage in the dialogue necessary to create change without employing power-over tactics or inducing feelings of shame or humiliation. It requires the practice of "radical respect" (Walker, 2004), which presumes that all human beings deserve freedom from contempt and deserve to be treated with dignity. This is the type of respect that Miller and Savoie (S. M. Miller & Savoie, 2002) suggest leads to rights which lead to respect. Mutual empathy allows people to bring more and more of themselves into the relationship. It allows people to authentically represent their experience, that is, to "show up" in the relationship (Walker, 2004). This is what promotes greater clarity and knowledge about each person's experience, and this knowledge is essential for creating constructive, enduring change.

Mutual empowerment grows out of mutual empathy (J. B. Miller & Stiver, 1997; Surrey, 1987). When both (or all) people feel seen, known, heard, and respected in relationship, they begin to generate mutual empowerment. Like mutual empathy, mutual empowerment is a two-way dynamic process in relating, however, mutual empowerment involves the feeling that both (or all) people can have an impact on the relationship, can influence and shape the development of the relationship. Janet Surrey (1987) observes that:

The capacity to be "moved" and to respond and to "move"
the other represents the fundamental core of relational
empowerment. (p. 4)

J. B. Miller (1986) proposes that mutual empowerment is characterized by at least *five good things*: 1) a sense of energy or zest that comes from connecting with another person(s); 2) An increased ability and motivation to take action in the relationship as well as in other situations; 3) Increased knowledge of oneself and the other person(s) and of the relationship; 4) An increased sense of worth; 5) A desire for more connection beyond the particular one. Most of us who have suffered from disempowering, disconnecting, or humiliating relationships are keenly familiar with the opposite experiences of relating. Disempowering relationships lead people to feel drained, immobilized, confused, worthless, and increasingly disconnected or isolated. These types of relationships discourage and obstruct movement, change, and growth. In contrast, mutually empowering relationships open the way to new relational possibilities and new opportunities for growth.

Mutual empathy and mutual empowerment lead to a third key ingredient of positive change: *movement toward mutuality*. Jordan (1986) describes mutuality as the experience of:

> ...both [people] affecting the other and being affected by the other; one extends oneself out to the other and is also receptive to the impact of the other. There is openness to influence, emotional availability, and a constantly changing pattern of responding to and affecting the other's state. (p. 2)

Movement toward mutuality in relationship is movement toward emotional and cognitive action *that benefits both or all people* in a relationship (J. B. Miller & Stiver, 1997). Nonmutual relationships — e.g., dominant/subordinate, power-over relationships — are relationships in which emotional and cognitive actions primarily benefit the more powerful or dominant participant in the relationship. Nonmutual relationships obstruct the growth of all people, but particularly the growth and development of subordinate or marginalized groups. In nonmutual relationships, subordinate individuals or groups must exert massive amounts of energy to: 1) fend off exploitation; 2) gain access to necessary material resources (education, housing, transportation); and 3) to protect themselves from injuries intentionally or inadvertently inflicted by the dominant group. Nonmutual relationships also obstruct the growth of members of the dominant group because, among other things, dominants must exert massive amounts of energy to: 1) maintain their power-over subordinates; 2) they must constantly protect their access to material resources; and 3) distance and insulate themselves from real or imagined threats from subordinates. In nonmutual relationships the dominants tend to believe that subordinates should do all the changing, *e.g.*, women should be more like men, blacks should be more like whites, non-Western-European countries should be more like Western-European countries, "underdeveloped countries" should be more like developed countries, etc. Furthermore, in nonmutual relationships dominants can easily convince subordinates that they need to do all the changing because dominants set the standards by which subordinates are evaluated as deficient. This inflicts another form of humiliation on subordinates, the humiliation of unwarranted self-contempt.

J. B. Miller (2002) points out that positive "change requires mutuality in movement" (p. 4), i.e., all people in the relationship must be willing to change. Mutual empathy and mutual empowerment lead people to believe that it is possible to create mutuality in movement, that it is possible to take emotional and cognitive action that benefits all people in the relationship. Even when there are temporary inequalities in relationships (*e.g.*, teacher-student, parent-child) or functional hierarchies operating in relationships (*e.g.*, a pilot flying a plane, a conductor leading an orchestra, a president leading a country), movement toward mutuality, or the growth of all people in the relationship, can be promoted, though people are growing in different ways. Movement toward mutuality is achieved through building mutually empathic, mutually empowering relationships. Here are some examples of organizations creating constructive change through building mutual empathy, mutual empowerment, and movement toward mutuality in relationships.

Tostan: Dramatic Relational-Cultural Transformation[6]

Tostan (2002, 2003), a nongovernmental organization based in Senegal, has been highly successful in eliminating what some might consider one of the most physically hurtful forms of human rights violations, the practice of *female genital cutting* (FGC). Since 1997, Tostan's efforts led 1,271 communities, representing 600,000 people in Senegal, to abandon this practice. Tostan uses a teaching model of creative participation and respectful consultation, which begins with engaging village women in discussions of what they want for their communities. This process of listening and understanding the experience of the Senegal women creates the conditions for mutual empathy to develop among the women and their Tostan allies.

Tostan found that Senegalese women, like many other women around the world, want to improve the health and education of their families, especially their children. Starting with this in mind, the Tostan program works with women to provide them with the education, skills, and support needed to move toward their goals. Through education conducted in local languages, the village women examine the obstacles to creating better health. According to Molly Melching, Tostan Executive Director:

> It was through learning about women's human rights and responsibilities concerning health that discussions of FGC first arose. (Wellesley Centers for Women, 2004, p. 16)

Kerthio Diarra, a Sengalese village woman who has become a human rights activist after participating in the Tostan program, explained:

> Before, we thought that the tradition [FCG] was a religious obligation. But when we began to learn about the dangers and consequences of the tradition, we understood that we needed to change. It was learning about human rights that changed everything for us. (p. 17)

These Senegalese women strengthened their determination to create change through building mutual empathy for each other. This empathy grew out of sharing their firsthand experiences of infections, hemorrhaging, and family deaths associated with FCG. Empowered by their shared experience and their participation in the Tostan

program, the women successfully made public declarations calling
for their communities to unite in abandoning the practice of FGC.
Although the initial response to these public declarations was often
ridicule and contempt, these women endured by doing "everything
together as a group," exemplifying *courage through connection.* They
also learned to build alliances with religious and community leaders
who could support and contribute to their efforts. Ultimately, their
collective courage helped them maintain a patient, empathic dialog
with the most resistant members of their communities who eventually supported their efforts.

The Tostan program epitomizes relational-cultural change fueled
by mutual empathy, mutual empowerment, and movement toward
mutually. It created new relational possibilities for individuals and
communities by practicing an ethic of radical respect and nonhumili-
ation. It advanced human rights ideals by creating new conditions
of relating that promoted the health and well being of Senegalese
women and their families.

The Piedmont Peace Project

Even within a country that touts human rights ideals around the
world, much more can be done to eliminate humiliation and to ensure
the rights and dignity of all people. Linda Stout (1996), in her book,
Bridging the Class Divide, describes the formation of a social justice
organization that was highly effective in engaging the participation
of diverse communities of poor and marginalized Americans, people
whose interests were often neglected or overlooked by the dominant
society. Stout founded the Piedmont Peace Project (PPP) in a region
of North Carolina where many people struggled to survive severe
hardships, such as abject poverty, minimal health care, and limited
education. Up to 80% of the citizens in this area lived in substandard
housing.

Noting that most social justice groups were comprised of and
managed by members of the middle class or a more privileged class,
Stout worked to establish a grass-roots organization in which low-
income and working-class individuals could fully participate and

develop their leadership skills. Based on her own experience of poverty, Stout observed:

> Usually without intending it or seeing it, middle-class people behave in ways that disempower low-income or working-class folks. (p. 89)

For example, without thinking, middle-class or other privileged groups may use words and language that is unfamiliar to low-income and working-class people. This is a particularly insidious way of inflicting feelings of humiliation. Using an extensive vocabulary, professional jargon, or academic language is often an admired way of presenting oneself and establishing one's credibility in middle-class circles. People unfamiliar with this language, which might include members of working-class and low-income groups, will feel excluded and alienated as result of this practice. In particular, because vocabulary is equated with intelligence in our society, not being able to understand the vocabulary of a middle class or privileged person may lead a low-income or workin-class person to believe she or he is too stupid to participate in a conversation or, on a larger scale, in efforts to change unjust social practices or policies. In addition, a middle-class person may assume that a working-class person is not smart enough to engage in social justice efforts just because she or he is unfamiliar with words or concepts used by the middle class. What's more, educationally advantaged individuals may feel they have the right to correct the language and vocabulary of others in public, inflicting further humiliation on a humiliated group. In response to this and other ways the middle class can inadvertently disempower working class or low-income groups, Stout formed an inclusive social justice organization designed to engage and empower low-income and working-class individuals to participate in the political process at local and national levels. Stout's organization paid particular attention to removing the barriers of language and educational differentials that shame and humiliate members of PPP.

The story of the PPP illustrates the practice of creating effective change by building relationships characterized by mutual empathy, mutual empowerment, and mutuality, relationships uninhibited by shame or humiliation. One way the PPP began developing mutual empathy was by going door-to-door and asking members of the community about the issues that most concerned them. This effort led to the formation of a small nucleus of low-income and working-class individuals to work together on shared concerns.

Members of the PPP supported each other in developing the skills and knowledge necessary to become leaders empowered to take action in their own lives and in their communities. For example, in 1985 the PPP organized four different groups (a group of peace activists, a low-income group, an African American group, and a disabled group) to meet with their state legislator at different times on the same day to lobby against military funding growing at the expense of cuts to social security, health care, and support for the disabled. Each group explained its specific concerns and criticized spending on the MX missile program. Two weeks later the congressman voted against the MX missile program. Over the years, in response to additional efforts by the PPP, this same legislator began voting more and more in support of peace and justice issues (ibid., p. 55).

The PPP became nationally recognized as one of most successful grass roots social justice organizations of working-class and low-income individuals in the United States. Linda Stout's book describes how the PPP empowered its members by offering them the opportunity to participate in a nonhumiliating, inclusive, empathic, supportive, and responsive community — regardless of race, gender, sexual orientation, or economic status. The PPP had to face many individual and political opponents as well as other challenges throughout its history of working for social justice. It developed the organizational resilience to keep creating change. Perhaps this is because:

> We shaped the PPP to be an organization that celebrates the connections between people's lives." (p. 180)…"Personal connections have made us strong — strong enough to be able to stay together and move forward even during times of internal conflict and tremendous opposition. (p. 184–185)

More Work to Be Done

Evelin Lindner's global research, which inspired this chapter, will continue to challenge us to examine how we can realize the potential of human rights while reducing the risk that our efforts will trigger feelings of humiliation. Much needs to be done. The Tostan, the Piedmont Peace Project, and the women's rights efforts of Lucretia Mott and Elizabeth Cady Stanton are encouraging stories of collaborative action that have allowed people to move beyond feelings of humiliation toward human rights and hope. These examples illustrate that there are promising ways to promote effective social change while transforming feelings of humiliation and upholding the dignity of all the people involved. As we become more skilled at detecting and preventing practices that trigger feelings of humiliation, these stories suggest that our efforts will be more productive and enduring. Furthermore, though human rights interventions may never be completely "humiliation-free," these examples provide evidence that we can do much to eliminate practices that lead people to feel devalued, degraded, or invisibilized while we move toward a world that respects human rights.

An important part of this process is for each of us to regularly assess the individual and cultural biases that blind us to some forms of humiliation. Even the most honorable activists engaged in heroic efforts to improve the rights of one group may fail to attend to the obvious degradation of another group. For example, in a quote noted earlier, Elizabeth Cady Stanton (1860/1973/1993) stated that she was striving to educate Americans about the humiliations experienced by "the mothers, wives, sisters, and daughters of *free men*." Though Stanton and her husband were staunch advocates of the abolitionist movement in the mid-1800s, this quote indicates that Stanton was shortsighted about exposing the humiliations experienced by *all* women. In a similar vein, the Women's Rights Movement has likely induced feelings of humiliation in African American and other marginalized groups of women by not fully understanding and attending to the unique experiences of degradation and human rights violations experienced by these women. As these examples illustrate, whenever we work for human rights we must be conscious of our limited perspectives that obstruct or distort our view of many insidious forms of humiliation that poison human relationships. Perhaps, as epitomized in the efforts of Nelson Mandela and Mahatma Gandhi, the most effective human rights movements — movements that simultaneously prevent and heal feelings of humiliation — are wisely informed by an *ethic of humility.*

This paper suggests that a relational-cultural framework provides us with a broader view of the dynamics of humiliation associated with human rights efforts. Through this framework we can begin to develop a more complex and sophisticated understanding of the intersections between human rights interventions and humiliation. In particular, a relational approach brings power issues to the forefront of our thinking about humiliation and human rights. Moreover, a relational-cultural framework can help us understand how initiatives like Tostan, the Piedmont Peace Project, and the Women's Rights Movement have been successful without employing the tools of domination to create change. Understanding these and other successful efforts opens the way to new possibilities for enhancing the human rights of all people.

Sadly, most people have never heard of Tostan or the Piedmont Peace Project. Most Americans do not know the names of Lucretia Mott or Elizabeth Cady Stanton, despite the fact that their nonviolent, collective efforts preceded the work of Mahatma Gandhi and Martin Luther King, Jr. As stated earlier, invisibility is a powerful form of humiliation. Educated members of the dominant group have often been the principle scribes of history; thus, it is not surprising that their records may neglect the lives and collective efforts of subordinate groups. Moreover, invisibility may operate on many levels. Though Mott and Stanton were made invisible at the 1840 World Anti-Slavery Convention and then "invisiblized" in U.S. history books, it is critical to note that there was a more invisiblized, subjugated group in this story: the many, many victims of slavery.

In addition, historical accounts tend to reduce social change into stories of heroic individuals, rather than capturing the complexities of courageous collective efforts that support heroic acts. When Rosa Parks (Parks & Haskins, 1992) refused to give up her seat on the bus, she was not alone; she was actively involved with the NAACP. Scholars, researchers, leaders, and the media can do more to account for the effectiveness of collective, nonviolent action to end humiliation, advance human rights, and create constructive relational-cultural change.

On an important note of caution about change, the most powerful countries cannot afford to view themselves as paragons of virtue or models of moral superiority. Powerful countries, the U.S. for example, cannot insist that other countries change their practices without themselves being open to change. As J. B. Miller (2002) asserts, if positive change or "growth is to occur in any relationship, both — or all — of the people involved have to change" (p. 4). For example, U.S. policies that encourage equal rights for women around the world could be construed as hypocritical since America has failed to change the U.S. Constitution and ratify the Equal Rights Amendment (ERA), which simply states:

> Section 1. Equality of rights under the law shall not be denied or abridged by the United States or by any state on account of sex. (Alice Paul Institute & ERA Task Force of the National Council of Women's Organization, 2004, May)[7]

In other words, *the U.S. has failed to ensure the equal rights of over half of its citizens in one of its most important governing documents.* Given that American women are contributing to and participating in all aspects of civil society, women could view this irony as profoundly humiliating.

This paper emphasizes that humiliating experiences and human rights efforts can reflect the *quality of our participation in relationships* on many levels — personal, social, or international. It proposes that a relational-cultural framework helps us understand the complex dynamics of humiliation that can obstruct and derail interventions designed to advance human rights.

For example, the humiliating psychological, sexual, and physical abuse of Iraq prisoners by U.S. soldiers in 2003 offers us one shocking example of the "radioactive" impact of humiliation that no individual or nation can afford to ignore. Shortly following the release of these photos, Sultan Somjee, a Kenyan ethnographer honored by the United Nations for his efforts to preserve indigenous people's peace traditions, offered this important warning to the world:[8]

> Humiliation does not have nationality. Humiliation of one human being humiliates humanity and our dignity of being. Humiliation has no nationality, religion, colour or gender. (May 10, 2004)

To move beyond humiliation, as Evelin Lindner teaches through her life's work, this chapter proposes that we can more effectively advance human rights by promoting methods that foster mutually empathic, mutually beneficial relationships, moving away from dominant/subordinate, power-over relating and *moving toward mutuality*. Movement toward mutuality is a profoundly radical notion. Mutuality leads us toward new relational possibilities, that is, new ways of participating in relationships that ultimately enhances the rights, well-being, and growth of all people.

Evelin Lindner challenges us to join with her in a global movement toward mutuality, toward universal human rights, toward equality in dignity. She calls us to hold hands with all who "walk the talk" of this lifelong journey, and she reminds us that this path requires us to courageously live up to a new definition of heroism:

> The new definition is respect for equality in dignity for all, dignity for all people, and for the nature we are part of and depend on. Nature speaks to us now, and its message is a warning to us all. The old world was one of higher beings presiding over lesser beings and nature...In the new interconnected world in which we live now, we all need to gather in the middle, leaving behind the old world of higher

and lesser beings. In the new world we need all beings to hold hands in mutual respect for equality in dignity...

I would therefore like to ask you, on behalf of humanity, to acknowledge that you have a responsibility not just for yourself and your immediate family. You have a responsibility for humanity at large!

Please know that I would like to invite you, on behalf of humankind, to assume ever more significant roles or positions of responsibility for humankind as a whole in the future![9]

Notes

1. *The History of Woman's Suffrage* is not in print despite being described as "perhaps the most magnificently written set of books produced" in the 19th Century. However, it is available on CD-ROM from Emmett F. Fields, Bank of Wisdom, P.O. Box 926, Louisville, KY 40201.

2. Evelin Gerda Lindner is an international scholar and researcher who is the founder and principle leader of Human Dignity and Humiliation Studies (HumanDHS), a global network of scholars and activists dedicated to "reducing — and ultimately eliminating — destructive disrespect and humiliation around the world" through disseminating information, generating research, and promoting action. More information about this organization can be found at: http://www.humiliationstudies.org/index.shtm

3. The Humiliation Inventory is a 32-item self-report scale evaluating the internal experience of humiliation. An exploratory study of the item-trial sample (n=253) indicated that women scored significantly higher than men on cumulative humiliation and fear of humiliation. The complete scale is published in: Hartling, L. M., & Luchetta, T. (1999). Humiliation: Assessing the impact of derision, degradation, and debasement. *The Journal of Primary Prevention,* 19(4), 259-278.

4. Donald Klein's seminal efforts to describe the experience of humiliation led to the publication of a collection of papers discussing the pervasive and varied nature of humiliation that impacts race relations, gender relations, intergenerational relations, homelessness, the criminal justice system, and relations with the disabled. These papers can be found in two special editions of the *Journal of Primary Prevention,* volume 12, number 2 (1991) and number 3 (1992).

5. The title and content of this section was derived from a paper presented by Jean Baker Miller, M.D., at the 2003 Summer Advanced Training Institute sponsored by the Jean Baker Miller Training Institute at Wellesley College,

Wellesley, MA. This paper was later published as: Miller, J. B. (2003). Telling the truth about power. *Work in Progress,* No. 100. Wellesley, MA: Stone Center Working Paper Series.
6. For more information about Tostan, please visit their web site: http://www. tostan.org
7. For current information about the status of the Equal Rights Amendment, visit the web site: http://www.equalrightsamendment.org
8. For more information about Sultan Somjee, visit the web site: http://www. humiliationstudies.org
9. From an "Invitation to a Future that Dignifies People and the Planet: New Definitions of Heroism" by Evelin Lindner, on Behalf of Humankind, August 12, 2017.

References

Alice Paul Institute & ERA Task Force of the National Council of Women's Organizations (2004, May). The ERA: A brief introduction. Retrieved May 23, 2004, from http://www.equalrightsamendment.org/overview.htm

Blum, R. W., McNeely, C. A., & Rinehart, P. M. (2002). Improving the odds: the untapped power of schools to improve the health of teens [Monograph]. Minneapolis, MN: University of Minnesota Center for Adolescent Health and Development.

Buzzflash (2004, January). Inside the frame. *Alternet.org* [online magazine]. Retrieved May 16, 2004, from http://www.alternet.org/story.html?StoryID=17574

CBS Worldwide Inc. (2001). In his own words [Television segment]. In J. Fager, (Executive Producer), *60 Minutes II.* New York: CBS News. Print version retrieved May 25, 2004, from http://www.cbsnews.com/stories/2001/09/26/60II/main312660.shtml

Cobbe, E., & Slatery, D. (2015). Syrians fleeing to Europe get 'treated worse than dogs.' *The New York Daily News.* Retrieved from http://www.nydailynews.com/news/world/syrians-fleeing-europe-treated-worse-dogs-article-1.2350552

Cushman, P. (1995). *Constructing the self, constructing America: A cultural history of psychotherapy.* Reading, MA: Addison-Wesley/Addison Wesley Longman.

Della Noce, D. J. (1999). Seeing theory in practice: An analysis of empathy in mediation. *Negotiation Journal, 15*(3), 271-301.

Dyer, G. (Writer), & A. Mondell & C. S. Mondell (Producers & Directors). (1994). *Dreams of Equality* [Film]. (Available from the Eastern National Park & Monument Association, 466 North Lante, Conshohocken, PA 19428).

Eisenberger, N. I., Lieberman, M. D., and Williams, K. D. (2003). Does rejection hurt? An fMRI study of social exclusion, *Science, 302*: 290-92.

Fontan, V. F. (2004, April). *The dialectics of humiliation: Polarization between occupier and occupied in post-Saddam Iraq.* Paper presented at the Jean Baker Miller Training Institute Members Meeting, Wellesley, MA.

Fuller, R. W. (2003). *Somebodies and nobodies: Overcoming the abuse of rank.* Grabriola, British Columbia, CA: New Society Publishers.

Griffin, J. T. (1991). Racism and humiliation in the African-American community. *Journal of Primary Prevention, 12*(2), 149-167.

Hartling, L. M. (1996). Humiliation: Assessing the specter of derision, degradation, and debasement. Unpublished doctoral dissertation, Union Institute, Cincinnati.

Hartling, L. M. (2003). Strengthening resilience in a risky world: It's all about relationships. *Working in Progress, No. 101.* Wellesley, MA: Stone Center Working Paper Series.

Hartling, L. M., & Luchetta, T. (1999). Humiliation: Assessing the impact of derision, degradation, and debasement. *The Journal of Primary Prevention, 19*(4), 259-278.

Hartling, L. M., Ly, J. K., Nassery, N., & Califa, K. (2003). Relational References: A selected bibliography of research, theory, and applications. *Project Report, No. 7* (2nd ed.). Wellesley, MA: Stone Center Working Paper Series.

Hartling, L. M., Rosen, W., Walker, M., & Jordan, J. V. (2000). Shame and humiliation: From isolation to relational transformation. *Work in Progress, No. 88.* Wellesley, MA: Stone Center Working Paper Series.

Hersh, S. M. (2004). Torture at Abu Ghraib. *The New Yorker,* May 10, 2004, p. 42.

Jordan, J. V. (1986). The meaning of mutuality. *Work in Progress, No. 23.* Wellesley, MA: Stone Center Working Paper Series.

Jordan, J. V. (1992). Relational resilience. *Work in Progress, No. 57.* Wellesley, MA: Stone Center Working Paper Series.

Jordan, J. V. (Ed.). (1997). *Women's growth in diversity: More writings from the Stone Center.* New York: The Guilford Press.

Jordan, J. V., & Hartling, L. M. (2002). New developments in Relational-Cultural Theory. In M. Ballou & L. Brown (Ed.), *Rethinking mental health and disorders: Feminist perspectives* (pp. 48-70). New York: Guilford Publications.

Jordan, J. V., Kaplan, A. G., Miller, J. B., Stiver, I. P., & Surrey, J. L. (1991). *Women's growth in connection: Writings from the Stone Center.* New York: Guilford Press.

King, M. L. (1965/1995). Address to the American Jewish community. On *The Reverend Martin Luther King, Jr.: In search of freedom* [CD]. New York: PolyGram Records.

Klein, D. C. (1991a). Introduction to special issue. *Journal of Primary Prevention, 12*(2), 87-91.

Klein, D. C. (1991b). The humiliation dynamic: An overview. *Journal of Primary Prevention, 12*(2), 93-121.

Klein, D. C. (1992). Managing humiliation. *Journal of Primary Prevention, 12*(3), 255-268.

Lakoff, G. (2003, March). Framing the dems. *American Prospect, 14*(8), 32-35.

Lakoff, G., & Johnson, M. (1980). *Metaphors we live by.* Chicago: University of Chicago Press.

Langer, G. (2004). A better life poll: Most Iraqis ambivalent about the war, but not its results. *ABCNews/BBC/Time Magazine.* Retrieved May 25, 2004, from http://abcnews.go.com/sections/world/GoodMorningAmerica/Iraq_anniversary_poll_040314.html

Lindner, E. G. (2000a). The "framing power" of international organizations, and the cost of humiliation. Human Dignity and Humiliation Studies: http://humiliationstudies.org/documents/evelin/FramingPowerInternationalOrganization.pdf.

Lindner, E. G. (2000b). The anatomy of humiliation and its relational character: The case of victim. Human Dignity and
Humiliation Studies: http://humiliationstudies.org/docu-
ments/evelin/RelationalAnatomyHumiliationVictim.pdf.

Lindner, E. G. (2000c). The relational anatomy of humiliation:
Perpetrator, victim, and third party. Human Dignity and
Humiliation Studies: http://humiliationstudies.org/docu-
ments/evelin/RelationalAnatomyHumiliation.pdf

Lindner, E. G. (2000d). Humiliation and how to respond to it:
Spatial metaphor in action. Human Dignity and Humilia-
tion Studies: http://humiliationstudies.org/documents/evelin/
SpatialMetaphor.pdf

Lindner, E. G. (2001). Humiliation and the human condition:
Mapping a minefield. *Human Rights Review, 2*(2), 45-63.

Lindner, E. G. (2002). Healing the cycles of humiliation: How to
attend to the emotional aspects of "unsolvable" conflicts and
the use of "humiliation entrepreneurship," *Peace and Conflict:
Journal of Peace Psychology,* 8 (2): 125–138.

Lindner, E. G. (2006) *Making Enemies: Humiliation and International Conflict, Contemporary Psychology*, Westport, CT:
Praeger Security International.

Lindner, E. G. (2007a). The Concept of Human Dignity," Human
Dignity and Humiliation Studies: http://humiliationstudies.
org/documents/evelin/TheConceptofHumanDignityfor-
NoelleQuenivets.pdf.

Lindner, E. G. (2007b). In times of globalization and human rights:
Does humiliation become the most disruptive force? *Journal of
Human Dignity and Humiliation Studies,* 1 (1): http://humili-
ationstudies.org/documents/evelin/HumiliationandFearinGlo-
balizingWorldHumanDHSJournal.pdf

Lindner, E. G. (2009a). *Emotion and conflict: How human rights
can dignify emotion and help us wage good conflict*, Westport,
CT, London: Praeger.

Lindner, E. G. (2009b). Humiliation and global terrorism: How to
overcome it nonviolently. In *Nonviolent Alternatives for Social
Change*, edited by Ralph Summy, 227–248. Oxford: Nonviolent
Alternatives for Social Change.

Lindner, E. G. (2009c). Why there can be no conflict resolution as long as people are being humiliated. *International Review of Education*, 55 (May 2–3): 157–181. doi: DOI 10.1007/s11159-008-9125-9.

Lindner, E. G. (2010). *Gender, humiliation, and global Security: Dignifying relationships from love, sex, and parenthood to world affairs, contemporary psychology*, Santa Barbara, CA: Praeger.

Lindner, E. G. (2016). The journey of humiliation and dignity, and the significance of the year 1757. Human Dignity and Humiliation Studies: http://humiliationstudies.org/documents/evelin/Significanceof1757.pdf.

Lindner, E. G. (2017). *Honor, humiliation, and terror: An explosive mix—And how we can defuse it with dignity*, Lake Oswego, OR: World Dignity University Press.

Margalit, A. (1996). *The decent society*. Cambridge, MA: Harvard University Press.

Miller, D. T. (1999). The norm of self-interest. *American Psychologist, 54*(12), 1053-1060.

Miller, J. B. (1988). Connections, disconnections, and violations. *Work in Progress, No. 33*. Wellesley, MA: Stone Center Working Paper Series.

Miller, J. B. (2002). How change happens: Controlling images, mutuality and power. *Work in Progress, No. 96*. Wellesley, MA: Stone Center Working Paper Series.

Miller, J. B. (2003). Telling the truth about power. *Work in Progress, No. 100*. Wellesley, MA: Stone Center Working Paper Series.

Miller, J. B., & Stiver, I. P. (1997). *The healing connection: How women form relationships in therapy and in life*. Boston: Beacon Press.

Miller, S. M., & Savoie, A. J. (2002). *Respect and rights: Class, race, and gender today*. Lanham, MD: Rowman & Littlefield.

Ornish, D. (1997). *Love and survival: The scientific basis of the healing power of intimacy*. New York: HarperCollins.

Parks, R., & Haskins, J. (1992). *Rosa Parks: My story*. New York: Puffin.

Putnam, R. (2000). *Bowling alone: The collapse and revival of American community*. New York: Simon & Schuster.

Resnick, M. D., Bearman, P. S., Blum, R. W., Bauman, K. E., Harris, K. M., Jones, J., et al. (1997). Protecting adolescents from harm: Findings from the national longitudinal study on adolescent health. *Journal of the American Medical Association, 278*(10), 823-832.

Ross, L. D., & Samuels (1993). *The predictive power of personal reputation versus labels and construal in the Prisoners' Dilemma Game.* Stanford, CA: Stanford University.

Ross, L. D., & Ward, A. (1995). Naive realism in everyday life: Implications for social conflict and misunderstanding. In T. Brown, E. Reed, & E. Turiel (eds.), *Values and Knowledge.* Mahwah NJ: Lawrence Erlbaum Associates.

Scheff, T. J. (1994). *Bloody revenge: Emotions, nationalism, and war.* Boulder: Westview Press.

Somjee, S. (2004, May 10). Images of humiliation. *Human Dignity and Humiliation Studies.* Retrieved May 10, 2004, from http://www.humiliationstudies.org/news/

Southern Poverty Law Center. (2019). Hate Map. Retrieved from https://www.splcenter.org/hate-map

Spencer, R. (2000). A comparison of relational psychologies. *Work in Progress, No. 5.* Wellesley, MA: Stone Center Working Paper Series.

Spencer, R., Jordan, J. V., & Sazama, J. (2002). Empowering children for life: A preliminary report from the Robert S. and Grace W. Stone primary prevention initiatives, *Project Report, No. 9.* Wellesley, MA: Stone Center Working Paper Series.

Stack, L. (2019). Over 1,000 hate groups are now active in United States, civil rights group Says. *New York Times.* Retrieved from https://www.nytimes.com/2019/02/20/us/hate-groups-rise.html

Stanton, E. C. (1860/1973/1993). Address to the NY State legislator. On *Great American women's speeches* [audio recording]. New York: Harper Collins, Caedmon Audio.

Stanton, E. C., Anthony, S. B., & Gage, M. J. (1889/1999). *History of woman suffrage* (Second Edition, Vol. I) [CD-ROM]. Rochester, NY: Bank of Wisdom.

Stout, L. (1996). *Bridging the class divide and other lessons for grass-roots organizing.* Boston: Beacon Press.

Surrey, J. L. (1987). Relationship and empowerment. *Work in Progress, No. 30.* Wellesley, MA: Stone Center Working Paper Series.

Tostan (2002). Tostan Annual Report [Report]. Dakar, Senegal: Author.

Tostan (2003). Tostan: Putting African communities at the center of development [Brochure]. Dakar, Senegal: Author.

Traister, R. (2018). Good and mad: The revolutionary power of women's anger [electronic book]. New York, Simon & Schuster.

Walker, M. (1999). Race, self, and society: Relational challenges in a culture of disconnection. *Work in Progress, No. 85.* Wellesley, MA: Stone Center Working Paper Series.

Walker, M. (2004). *Releasing the power of relational intelligence in the workplace.* Paper presented at annual Spring Institute sponsored by the Jean Baker Miller Training Institute, Wellesley College, Wellesley, MA.

Walker, M., & Miller, J. B. (2001). Racial images and relational possibilities. *Talking Paper, No. 2.* Wellesley, MA: Stone Center Working Paper Series.

Wellesley Centers for Women (2004). Human rights activists from West Africa visit WCW. *Research & Action Report, 25*(2), 16-17.

Werner, E. E., & Smith, R. S. (1982). *Vulnerable but invisible: Study of resilient children.* New York: McGraw-Hill.

Woolf, V. (1938/1966). *Three guineas.* Orlando, Fl: Harcourt Brace.

About the Authors

Michael Britton, Ed.D., is a psychologist and retired therapist who has done research on parental influences that help children grow up to do well in love; interview research with retired high level military on the complex issues of moral responsibility involved in the planning and command of the nuclear weapons build-up in the Cold War; and the ways in which traditional, modern, and post-modern architecture express changing cultural feelings for the era we live in, the era we're leaving behind, and the era we hope to be creating. He co-established the New York Human Dignity and Humiliation Studies (HumanDHS) group, Dignity Now NYC, with Janet Gerson, Judit Révész, Gaby Saab, and Chipamong Chowdhury. He is on the Board of Directors for the HumanDHS network and is a member of its Global Core Team.

Philip M. Brown, Ph.D., is a Senior Consultant for the National School Climate Center and a Fellow, Center for Applied Psychology at Rutgers University. Following twenty-five years managing student support services in the Pennsylvania Department of Health and the New Jersey Department of Education, he created and directed the Center for Social and Character Development at Rutgers University through two federal U.S. Department of Education grants that conducted research on social, emotional, and character development programs. He is the author of numerous government publications and articles, and edited the two volumes, *Handbook of Prosocial Education* (2012) and *School Discipline: A Prosocial Perspective* (2016). Phil serves on several boards and advisory groups, and is currently president of the Buddhist Sangha of Bucks County, Pennsylvania.

Chipamong Chowdhury is a 2017–2018 Beyond the Bars Fellow at Columbia University's Center for Justice. He is a member of the HumanDHS Global Core Team and co-coordinator of the HumanDHS World Gender Relations for Equal Dignity (WGenderRED) project. He is a Theravada Buddhist monk, an independent researcher, inter-

preter, and mobile teacher of relational mindfulness. He is a dharma
teacher at the Chautauqua Institute in New York, and spiritual leader
at the Rainforest Foundation in the U.S. His research primarily focuses
on Theravada/contemporary Buddhism–Buddhist Cinema, Buddhism
and politics/nationalism, sacred biography, monastic migration,
and Buddhist diaspora. His essays and reviews have appeared in the
Harvard Divinity Bulletin, the *Journal of Contemporary Buddhism,*
Buddhist Studies Reviews, Studies in Religion, the *Journal of Religion
and Popular Culture,* and the *Fair Observer,* among other publications.
He was a visiting scholar at Tallinn University and University of Tartu
Estonia. He holds two master's degrees in Religious/Buddhist Studies
and South Asian Studies/Anthropology from Naropa University and
the University of Toronto. Defining himself as a digital/global citizen,
he travels extensively in North America, Europe, and Asia, teaching
"active love" and "social meditation." Currently, he is working on a
children's book, a Buddhist graphic novel.

Claudia E. Cohen, Ph.D., is an Adjunct Faculty member in the
Social-Organizational Psychology Program at Teachers College,
Columbia University in New York. Between 2008 and 2015 she was
the Associate Director of the Morton Deutsch International Center
for Cooperation and Conflict Resolution (MD-ICCCR.) She is also
the founder and President of The Third Alternative, LLC consulting
group. Her areas of expertise include dialogue and facilitation, leadership, organizational justice, mediation, and conflict management
systems in organizations. Her career has combined research, teaching
and consulting in a range of settings. Dr. Cohen has consulted about
leadership, organizational climate and justice, conflict management
systems, and employee development to many organizations, including
AT&T, Lucent Technologies, Princeton University, The NJ-ACLU, the
United Nations, Thomson Reuters and St. Barnabas Hospital. As an
Ombuds at AT&T, she provided individual coaching to executives,
managers, and employees, facilitated 360 Degree Feedback sessions,
and consulted about employee well-being. Dr. Cohen was part of the
Social Psychology faculty at Rutgers University and has taught in the

Stevens Institute of Technology Project Management Program. At Teachers College, Dr. Cohen teaches Managing Conflict in Organizations (MCIO), a required course for Social-Organizational Psychology MA students. In MCIO, foundational theories about organizations as systems and constructive conflict resolution provide a scaffold for experiential learning and reflective practice, encouraging students to connect course learning with past and future professional experiences. Her current interests focus on interpersonal, group, and organizational practices that promote individual dignity. She has written and spoken about "Everyday Dignity" as an important component of civil society. Dr. Cohen serves on the Anti-Racism Committee of the Interfaith Council in Summit in New Jersey. She facilitates Dialogue Circles on Race, bringing together citizens for conversation about race and racism in a process that balances honesty with empathy and respect. Dr. Cohen has mediated for the municipal and civil court systems in New Jersey and the Philadelphia-area EEOC since 2005. She specializes in employment cases.

Zaynab El Bernoussi, Ph.D., is a visiting scholar at the Department of Government and the Lewis Global Studies Center at Smith College and Assistant Professor of International Studies at the School of Humanities and Social Sciences at Al Akhawayn University. Dr. El Bernoussi switched from a career in public finance after graduating from IE Business School and Columbia University to study postcolonial development at the University of Hong Kong. She received her Ph.D. in political and social sciences from the Université Catholique de Louvain. Her research interest in postcolonial development focuses on the politics of dignity, particularly in the Arab world. She was a Fulbright Visiting Scholar at the Weatherhead Center for International Affairs, Harvard University. She received the Carnegie Fellowship in Support of Arab Social Sciences in 2014 and the Arab Prize for the Social Sciences and Humanities in 2015.

Tony Gaskew, Ph.D., is Associate Professor of Criminal Justice, Director of Criminal Justice, and Founding Director of the *Prison*

Education Program at the University of Pittsburgh (Bradford). He is a Fulbright Hays Scholar, a University of Pittsburgh Faculty Diversity Fellow, and the 2015 recipient of the Human Dignity and Humiliation Studies (HumanDHS) Beacon of Dignity Award. He is the book series editor of *Critical Perspectives on Race, Crime, and Justice* (Lexington-Rowman & Littlefield). He is the author of numerous publications focusing on race, crime, and justice including his latest book, *Rethinking Prison Reentry: Transforming Humiliation into Humility*. Dr. Gaskew is a former police-detective at M.P.D., where he was assigned as a member of the Department of Justices, Organized Crime Drug Enforcement Task Force.

Kebadu M. Gerbremanrian, Ph.D., is a moral and political philosopher who is just appointed as Assistant Professor of Philosophy at Addis Ababa University in Ethiopia. Kebadu received his DPhil (Ph.D.) from the University of Zurich in Switzerland in 2016. His forthcoming book, *Human Dignity and Moral Rights,* is an extension of his dissertation; it explores the normative relation between having rights and being possessed of human dignity. He has recently worked as a visiting scholar at the Department of Aging and Life Course of the World Health Organization (WHO), where his work relates to developing an ethical framework for the global strategy of aging and health.

Janet Gerson, Ed.D., is Education Director, International Institute on Peace Education (IIPE) and former Co-Director, Peace Education Center, Teachers College, Columbia University. She has collaborated with the Morton Deutsch International Center on Cooperation and Conflict Resolution (MD-ICCCR) since 1996, including Morton Deutsch's last project on Global Community and Evelin Lindner's first conference held there. As a Board Member of HumanDHS, she co-hosts Dignity Now Circles initiated by Michael Britton with Judit Révész, Gaby Saab and Chipamong Chowdhury. A political theorist and peace educator, her research focuses are democratizing justice, public deliberation, creativity, and conflict processes, and peace pedagogy. She received the 2014 Peace and Justice Studies Association (PJSA) Award for her dissertation Public Deliberation on Global Justice: The World Tribunal on Iraq. Her publications include contributions to In *Factis Pax: Journal of Peace Education and Social Justice*, *The Handbook of Conflict Resolution* (Eds., Coleman, Deutsch, & Marcus, First & Second Editions), GCPE *Newsletter, Learning to Abolish War: Teaching toward a Culture of Peace* (Reardon & Cabezudo), *Theory into Practice, Analysis of Social Issues and Public Policy, and Holistic Education*. She is on the Editorial Board of In *Factis Pax: Journal of Peace Education and Social Justice*. As a painter, former choreographer, and dancer, she used the arts for community building, primarily in the immigrant community of Washington Heights/ Inwood, in New York City, where she lives. She also co-produced shared choreographers' concerts and was active on the Board of Arts Interaction, the Arts Council of Upper Manhattan.

Linda M. Hartling, Ph.D., is the Director of Human Dignity and Humiliation Studies (HumanDHS) and is part of a global leadership team facilitating affiliated projects, including the World Dignity University initiative and Dignity Press. Dr. Hartling is the past Associate Director of the Jean Baker Miller Training Institute (JBMTI), part of the Wellesley Centers for Women (WCW) at Wellesley College in Massachusetts. She holds a doctoral degree in clinical/community psychology and has published papers on Relational-Cultural Theory, workplace practices, resilience, substance abuse prevention, humiliation, and is the co-editor of *The Complexity of Connection: Writings from the Jean Baker Miller Training Institute* at the Stone Center. Dr. Hartling is the author of the Humiliation Inventory, the first scale to assess the internal experience of humiliation. The scale has been translated into Italian, French, Japanese, Korean, Portuguese, Russian, and Norwegian (in progress) and continues to be used for research around the world. In addition, Dr. Hartling is the recipient of the 2010 Research Award presented by the Association for Creativity in Counseling, American Counseling Association, and the 2015 HumanDHS Lifetime Achievement Award.

Michelle Jones is a first-year doctoral student in the American Studies program New York University, and a Research Fellow at the Charles Warren Center for Studies in American History at Harvard University. After being granted a bachelor's degree from Ball State University, Michelle completed a four-year seminary ministerial diploma from the University of the South. Her interest in history, women, race, and prisons led her to participate in a scholarly project challenging the narratives of the history of women's prison with a group of incarcerated scholars. Even while incarcerated, Michelle published and presented her research findings to dispel notions of about the reach and intellectual capacity of justice-involved women. Michelle's advocacy extends beyond the classroom. While incarcerated, she presented legislative testimony on a re-entry alterative she created for long-term incarcerated people that was approved by the Indiana State Interim Committee on the Criminal Code. She is currently on the board of Constructing Our Future, a re-entry alterative for women created by incarcerated women in Indiana, which provides women leaving prison with access to rehabilitative programming, carpentry job skills and the means to earn their own home, and she serves as Entrepreneurship Development Director for The Ladies of Hope Ministries, as well as a 2017 Beyond the Bars fellow. Michelle is currently under contract with The New Press to publish the history of Indiana's carceral institutions for women. As an artist, Michelle is interested in finding ways to funnel her research pursuits into theater and dance. Her original play, "The Duchess of Stringtown," was produced in December 2017 in Indianapolis and New York City.

Maggie O'Neill, Ph.D., is Professor in Sociology/Criminology at the University of York. Her research activity has been instrumental in moving forward debates, dialogue, and scholarship in three substantive areas: sex work and the commercial sex industry; forced migration and the asylum-migration nexus; innovative participatory, biographical, performative, and visual methodologies. Maggie has a long history of conducting research in participatory ways and has been a member of the Board of HumanDHS global network since 2005.

Her latest book, coauthored with Brian Roberts, will be published by Routledge in 2018 and explores walking as a mobile and relational method for doing research.

Michael L. Perlin is Professor of Law Emeritus at New York Law School (NYLS), founding director of NYLS's Online Mental Disability Law Program, and founding director of NYLS's International Mental Disability Law Reform Project in its Justice Action Center. He is also the co-founder of Mental Disability Law and Policy Associates. He has written thirty-one books and nearly 300 articles on all aspects of mental disability law, including a treatise, *Mental Disability Law: Civil and Criminal* (Lexis-Nexis Press), universally seen as the standard text in the area (co-authored with Professor Heather Ellis Cucolo). An earlier book, *The Jurisprudence of the Insanity Defense* (Carolina Academic Press, 1995) won the Manfred Guttmacher award of the American Psychiatric Association and the American Academy of Psychiatry and Law as the best book published that year. Before becoming a professor, Perlin was the Deputy Public Defender in charge of the Mercer County Trial Region in New Jersey, and, for eight years, was the director of the Division of Mental Health Advocacy in the NJ Department of the Public Advocate. His hobbies include playing the clarinet, birding, fishing, the opera, and the music of Bob Dylan. He is a member of the Board of Directors of the Washington Crossing Audubon Society, the Board of Trustees of the International Society for Therapeutic Jurisprudence, and the Lawrence Township (NJ) Community Band.

Judit Révéz, JD, MSOD, became the first Ombudsperson of Barnard College in August 2016. She is a member of the Global Core Team of the Human Dignity and Humiliation Studies Network. Judit worked as a Consultant Case Officer at the United Nations Office of the Ombudsman for Funds and Programmes (UNDP, UNFPA, UNICEF, UNOPS and UN Women), providing services for those whose want to resolve their workplace related conflict within the informal conflict resolution system, from 2011 to 2016. She worked for the United

Nations Development Program as a consultant on various assignments related to internal communication, change, compliance, and procurement from 2006 to 2010. In 2007, Judit received her Master of Science in Organizational Development from the American University and the National Training Lab Institute's joint program. Prior to that, she graduated from ELTE School of Law Budapest, Hungary in 1998, and practiced litigation and corporate law for a year in Hungary. She then studied conflict resolution and mediation at Columbia University, Teachers College in New York in 2001. Judit subsequently worked as a mediator in New York on cases referred by the Small Claims Court. In this capacity she experienced how mediation actually fulfills the deepest meaning of conflict resolution for all parties as opposed to litigation. She also worked as a facilitator on numerous conflict resolution courses and trainings at Teachers College and at the United Nations. Judit has been the recipient of Morley Segal and Edith Whitfield Seashore Fellowship and the Beacon of Dignity Award by Human Dignity and Humiliation Studies. She has been involved with Human Dignity and Humiliation Studies since its inception, as its NY resident, and has kindly taking upon herself the important role of the HumanDHS website contact person.

Mariana I. Vergara Esquivel, Ed.D., has been building the MIA® model of transformational learning for the past eighteen years and continues to investigate it through her courses at the Universidad Tecnica del Norte, in Ecuador, and her course at Teachers College of the Columbia University (New York) where in 2016 she taught Mindfulness into Action (MIA®) Research with Grounded Theory and had the MIA Conference. In 2017, she began to teach at the Universidad Tecnica del Norte where she applied the MIA® model of transformational learning with blind participants. She published seven chapters on the implementation of MIA® in different contexts in the *Encyclopedia of Strategic Leadership and Management,* IGI. In 2018, she also published in the book *Strategic Leadership,* with the editor Victor Wang, through Information Age Publishing. She is also part of the Editorial Review Board of the International Journal of

Responsible Management Education, and the International Journal of Vocational Education for Adults and Technology.

David C. Yamada is a Professor of Law and Director of the New Workplace Institute at Suffolk University Law School in Boston. David is an internationally recognized authority on workplace bullying. He wrote the first comprehensive analysis of workplace bullying and American employment law (*Georgetown Law Journal*, 2000), and his model anti-bullying legislation (named the "Healthy Workplace Bill") is the template for law reform efforts in this realm. David is frequently interviewed by the media on employment law and policy topics. His current non-profit leadership work includes Human Dignity and Humiliation Studies (board member), the International Society for Therapeutic Jurisprudence (founding board chair), and the Western Institute for Social Research (WISR) (board member). David has earned degrees from New York University School of Law, WISR, SUNY-Empire State College, and Valparaiso University.

HUMAN DIGNITY

Practices, Discourses, and Transformations

Essays on Dignity Studies in Honor of Evelin G. Lindner
Editors: Chipamong Chowdhury, Michael Britton,
and Linda Hartling

～

Books by Evelin Lindner

- *Making Enemies: Humiliation and International Conflict*

- *Emotion and Conflict: How Human Rights Can Dignify Emotion and Help Us Wage Good Conflict*

- *A Dignity Economy: Creating an Economy that Serves Human Dignity and Preserves Our Planet*

- *Gender, Humiliation and Global Security: Dignifying Relationships from Love, Sex, and Parenthood to World Affairs*

- *Honor, Humiliation, and Terror: An Explosive Mix — and How We Can Defuse It with Dignity*

- *From Humiliation to Dignity: For a Future of Global Solidarity*

Other Resources

For articles and papers by Evelin Lindner, or by other authors affiliated with Human Dignity and Humiliation Studies, please visit our website: www.humiliationstudies.org

Please also visit Dignity Press for books by authors dedicated to advancing the dignity of all people and the planet: www.dignitypress.org

www.ingramcontent.com/pod-product-compliance
Lightning Source LLC
Chambersburg PA
CBHW061001280326
41935CB00009B/784